PENGUIN BOOKS

THE FEMINIST KILLJOY HANDBOOK

'A celebration . . . Ahmed, one of the world's leading feminist
and queer theorists, is both clever and generous, and has a talent
for bringing her readers with her, without ever dumbing down or
sugar-coating her politics, love of theory, or lived experience
as a queer woman of colour . . . Ahmed addresses the
challenges of the present and her ongoing project of
platforming and protecting the feminist killjoy
remains vital and refreshing' Zora Simic, *Inside Story*

'The iconic feminist Killjoy Sara Ahmed rides her horse,
stands her ground, speaks her truth in this mighty little book . . .
Armed with the gift of her wisdom, a new generation of Black and
brown Killjoys will have the weapons to outwit the tyranny of
white supremacist heteropatriarchy – subverting its machinations
to define our minds and bodies with our collective Killjoy voice'
Heidi Safia Mirza, author of *Young, Female and Black*

'The feminist killjoy reclaims an ugly stereotype and gives it voice.
In maxims, equations, truths and commitments, this brilliant
survival manual retells feminism, spanning a pantheon of queer,
black, awkward, eye-rolling, angry, laughing killjoys. Sara Ahmed
tells feminist stories that we know in our bodies, and encounter in
our daily lives. Her work literally changes how we
inhabit our worlds' Lucy Delap

'An incredible queer theorist . . . The compelling way in
which Ahmed uses metaphors to describe structural inequalities
evidently strikes a chord with people, from the "vandal", to, most
famously, the "feminist killjoy". The figure of the "feminist killjoy"
takes a fundamental role in everything Ahmed does; wilful in
her disruption of problematic narratives and taking up space
unapologetically' Sana Ali, *Varsity*

'Odd and exciting to let out a shout as one reads a book of
theory, theory written for and about the ordinary outrages that
demand a feminist response . . . Ahmed moves from scene to
scene with clarity, rage, and joy, building through each refrain to
mark the brutal violence of everyday encounters and to show us
what a life-affirming response can be . . . throughout, the humility of
this brilliant feminist thinker shines through. This book is a great
. . . . vercoming this vicious trans/feminist
. . . . -racism and the struggle for
. . . . ral to feminist and queer
. . . . itics' Judith Butler

'Sara Ahmed's profound reflection on the feminist killjoy is in fact a joyous experience for folks who understand the impact of the trivializing, displacement, and erasure of our anti-racist feminist commitments . . . A moving and brilliant book that belongs in our libraries, homes, classrooms, and social movements' Chandra Talpade Mohanty, author of *Feminism Without Borders*

'Feminist books often encourage us to make the world a more just place, but without offering us the tools to navigate the inevitable pushback that we will likely encounter. Thankfully, Sara Ahmed's *The Feminist Killjoy Handbook* provides the latter. Simultaneously inspiring and practical – a wonderful guide for becoming a more powerful and thoughtful social justice activist in everyday situations' Julia Serano, author of *Whipping Girl*

'This book arms readers with a sense of vital energy, often lost due to burnout, compassion fatigue, and microaggressions. Audiences curious about navigating the intersection between feminism and daily life, intellectualism, poetry, and activism will love this title' *Library Journal*

'In this fervent manifesto, Ahmed brings impressive clarity to a field of study often opaque in the hands of others' *Publishers Weekly*

'In her characteristic style, Ahmed offers yet another distilled and revealing account of what institutions are and how they function to protect and reproduce themselves by denying difference, deflecting criticism, and displacing their problems onto the usual suspects: the unhappy feminist, the angry woman of colour, the transgender bully, and so on. This book is for them, for us: for the killjoys whose voices and bodies trouble institutions and their scripts of inclusion and justice, who shatter the images institutions project of themselves' Eden Kinkaid, *AAG Review of Books*

'A deliberate intervention written in direct and accessible prose, building and nurturing the community it addresses . . . sharp and usable tools for readers who have been made to feel isolated, insignificant and difficult. It is a generous offering from an important theorist, and highly recommended' Carol Ballantine, *Irish Times*

ABOUT THE AUTHOR

Sara Ahmed is an independent feminist scholar of colour. She worked as a feminist academic for over twenty years before she resigned in protest at the failure of her university to deal with the problem of sexual harassment. She has published ten books, including *Living a Feminist Life*, described by *Bitch* as 'not just an instant classic but an essential read for intersectional feminists'.

The Feminist Killjoy Handbook

SARA AHMED

PENGUIN BOOKS

PENGUIN BOOKS

UK | USA | Canada | Ireland | Australia
India | New Zealand | South Africa

Penguin Books is part of the Penguin Random House group of companies
whose addresses can be found at global.penguinrandomhouse.com

Penguin
Random House
UK

First published by Allen Lane 2023
Published in Penguin Books 2024
006

The publisher and author are grateful to the following for permission
to reproduce material: lines from 'The Phenomenology of Anger', from *Diving
into the Wreck: Poems 1971–1972* by Adrienne Rich, copyright © W. W. Norton &
Company, Inc., 1973, are used by permission of W. W. Norton & Company, Inc.;
'scream', from *When You Ask Me Where I am Going* by Jasmin Kaur, copyright
© Jasmin Kaur, 2019, is used by permission of Folio Literary Management, LLC.

Typeset by Jouve (UK), Milton Keynes
Printed and bound in Great Britain by Clays Ltd, Elcograf S.p.A.

The authorized representative in the EEA is Penguin Random House Ireland,
Morrison Chambers, 32 Nassau Street, Dublin D02 YH68

A CIP catalogue record for this book is available from the British Library

ISBN: 978–1–802–06189–5

To Nila, Gulzar and bell
And for all the feminist killjoys out there
still doing your thing

Contents

1/ Introducing the Feminist Killjoy   1

2/ Surviving as a Feminist Killjoy   43

3/ The Feminist Killjoy as Cultural Critic   87

4/ The Feminist Killjoy as Philosopher   131

5/ The Feminist Killjoy as Poet   175

6/ The Feminist Killjoy as Activist   217

Killjoy Truths, Killjoy Maxims, Killjoy Commitments
and Killjoy Equations   261

Recommended Reading for Feminist Killjoys   273

Feminist Killjoy Reading Group: Discussion Questions   289

Notes   293

Acknowledgements   321

1/ Introducing the Feminist Killjoy

Let me begin with a story, my story, of becoming a feminist killjoy.

We are seated at the dinner table. We always take up the same seats, as if we are securing more than our place. We are having polite conversations. My father would ask about school, then this, then that. And then he would come out with it, say something offensive, often sexist, looking at me as if making a challenge. I would try not to respond, sit there quietly, hoping to disappear. But sometimes, I couldn't not. I might have spoken quietly. I might have become wound up, recognizing with frustration that I was being wound up by somebody who was winding me up. Whatever I said, however I spoke, if there was an argument, if the discussion became heated, I would be treated as the cause of it. I would hear the accusation, 'Sara, another dinner ruined.'

You become a feminist killjoy when you get in the way of the happiness of others, or when you just get in the way, ruining that dinner, also the atmosphere. You become a feminist killjoy when you are not willing to go along with something, to get along with someone, sitting there quietly, taking it all in. You become a feminist killjoy when you react, speak back, to those with authority, using words like *sexism* because that is what you hear. There is so much you are supposed to avoid saying or doing in order not to ruin an occasion. Another dinner ruined, so many dinners ruined!

I became a feminist killjoy. And I write this handbook *as* one. Are you one? How do you know? Ask yourself these questions: Do you refuse to laugh at jokes you find offensive? Have you been called divisive when you point out a division? Have you been told 'Smile, love, it could be worse,' or 'Cheer up, love, it might not happen'? Do you just have to open your mouth for eyes to start rolling? Does the atmosphere become tense when you turn up or because of what you bring up? If you answered yes to any or all of these questions, you too might be a feminist killjoy. And I have written this handbook for you.

The story of the feminist killjoy does not begin when we speak up or speak back around that table. Her story starts before we get there. The feminist killjoy begins her political life as a stereotype of feminists, a negative judgement, a way of dismissing feminism as causing and caused by misery. In reclaiming the feminist killjoy for ourselves, we turn the judgement into a project, because if feminism causes misery, that is what we might need to cause. So often the terms used to dismiss feminism provide evidence of its necessity. By naming ourselves as feminist killjoys, we not only commit ourselves to the task of killing joy, we recover a feminist history. The feminist killjoy *is* a history. The feminist killjoy *has* a history. A history can be a handle. It can help to know

2

that where we are, others have been. In this handbook, we travel with feminist killjoys, going where they have been. Through these travels, the feminist killjoy becomes our companion. We need her companionship.

The feminist killjoy has been my companion for some time, a life companion as well as a writing companion. Although I have written about feminist killjoys before, I wanted her to have a book of her own. Why is her book a handbook? The term *handbook* originally applied to a small or portable book that 'gives information such as facts on a particular subject, guidance in some art or occupation, instructions for operating a machine, or information for tourists'. *The Feminist Killjoy Handbook* does not give you a set of instructions, information or guidance on how to be a feminist killjoy. Rather, it shows how being a feminist killjoy gives you a set of instructions, information and guidance about living in this world. Whilst being a feminist killjoy can sometimes be messy and confusing, it can also bring us moments of clarity and illumination. I thus throw in some **killjoy truths**, **killjoy maxims**, **killjoy equations** and **killjoy commitments** that come up when they turn up, in the middle of killjoy experiences, and which I have collected together at the end of the book. Some of these truths, maxims, equations and commitments first appeared as ordinary sentences in earlier books of mine. I sharpen them by using them again in a different way, emphasizing them, making them bolder.

This handbook is intended as a resource for feminist killjoys, a helping hand. You might have come out to your parents only to be met with grief about the happiness you are giving up. *The feminist killjoy can help with that.* You might have tried to make a complaint about sexual harassment or bullying in your workplace only to have ended up under interrogation. *The feminist killjoy can help with that.* You might have offered careful and nuanced critiques of racism or transphobia only to have them dismissed as 'wokeism' or evidence of 'cancel culture'. *The feminist killjoy can help with that.* You might be enraged by how so many media sources represented the MeToo movement as going too far before it got very far. *The feminist killjoy can help with that.* It is my hope this handbook will be a helping hand for those of us who are fighting against inequalities and injustices of many kinds. We need helping hands, also handbooks, because the costs of that fight are made so high. I begin this introductory chapter with a discussion of what we can learn from the history of the word *killjoy*, before turning to how the figure of the feminist killjoy is used to dismiss feminism as motivated by misery, and finally to a consideration of how and why we reclaim the feminist killjoy for ourselves, in part by telling our own stories of becoming one.

It is time to introduce you to our travelling companion. She might not need an introduction. You might know her already. You might be her already. Even for those of us who think of ourselves as feminist killjoys, we have more to learn about them. To learn about feminist killjoys is not to start with them. Not all killjoys are feminist. The word *killjoy* has, in fact, been around longer than the word *feminist*. To give you a sense of how the killjoy has come up,

I include direct quotes from historical and contemporary sources. The *Oxford English Dictionary* gives as its first recorded use of the term *killjoy* a note in Charles Burney's *General History of Music* from 1776, 'The Gods were not then, says M. Rousseau, regarded as kill-joys, and shut out of convivial meetings.'[1]

This rather curious reference suggests that to be regarded as a *killjoy*, human or God, would mean to be shut out of meetings to keep them convivial. The second reference listed under *killjoy* is to George Eliot's novel *Romola*, first published in 1863. One character, Savonarola, is described as 'the killjoy of Florence', and is detested by 'licentious young men'. The killjoy is set apart from a city, a party, a meeting, restraining those who find, in joy, their freedom. A picture of something is often created by depicting what it is not. Historically, through minor references, the killjoy helped to create a picture of conviviality, by embodying those who would bring an end to it. The killjoys kill the joy of others, not their own joy, perhaps because they do not have their own joy to kill. Synonyms for killjoy are buzzkill, miserabilist, party pooper, wet blanket, dampener and spoilsport.

We can find more substantial references to killjoys in the early and mid-twentieth century. Alice Lowther, most often described as the wife of a British diplomat but who was herself a writer, published a short story 'The Kill-Joys' in 1929 about three sisters, two of whom kill the joy of the other. When the youngest, Adela, gets married after the death of their father, her older sisters, Jane and Susan, come to work for her new family, an improvement of their status; 'fired with hope and grateful', they 'worked with a will'.[2] But later, when their request to be paid for their work is denied, they are led to labour 'under a sense of injustice'.[3] The sisters became 'a nuisance to the family they served', no longer 'useful', even their devotion a source of aggravation. 'Can't anything be done,' one of Adela's children laments, 'those old kill-joys give me the creeps.'[4] This tragic tale, which ends with the suicide of the sisters, in obedience to the wish of the family that they remove themselves, although obscure, is familiar given its reuse of old tropes of sad spinsters and ugly stepsisters. Even though the story is not told from the killjoys' point of view (a killjoy is usually somebody's else view), it does sympathize with them by giving an account of the cruelty that follows being judged as one, creating the impression that the killjoys might be right to labour 'under a sense of injustice'.

The psychoanalyst Edmund Bergler published two essays, 'The Psychology of the Killjoy' and 'The Type: "Mr Stuffed Shirt"'[5] in 1949 and 1960 respectively, which offered far less sympathetic portrayals of killjoys. For Bergler, the killjoy names both a pathology and a type of person. For Bergler the killjoy is 'popularly regarded as a person who gloats over the fact that he spoils other people's pleasure'.[6] In other words, 'his revenge is the killjoy attitude'.[7] In this account, the killjoy is in self-denial; he does not recognize himself as a killjoy but is judged to be so by others. Bergler refers to the 'wife of one killjoy', who described her husband's 'ability to freeze people . . . by maintaining a stony silence in a gay gathering or by greeting every proposed plan of amusement with derogatory and biting remarks'.[8] The killjoy is presented as a type of person who is removed from the warmth of human sociability, who is powerful and punishing, who, having invented their own misfortune to justify their cruelty, employs a range of methods to spread misery from 'stony silence' to 'biting remarks'. Who would want to be such a person? The *point* of this picture of the killjoy might be to evoke a person no one else would want to be.

Even to give a brief history of the term *killjoy* teaches us how it was used to create a picture of those who are 'not us' and who have the power to take from us what we want for ourselves. If the killjoy once functioned to picture a type of person, it is now more often used for a style of politics. We might call this style of politics *mean-spirited*. We hear, for instance, about *politically correct killjoys*, whose concern with correcting what other people do or say is framed as imposing an agenda upon them as well as stealing their enjoyment. One columnist writes, 'politically correct killjoys have pulled festive fun off the menu by trying to ban crackers'.[9] Another summarizes, 'PC killjoys have banned offensive flags.'[10] We also hear about *health and safety killjoys*, whose concern with public safety, however well-meaning, is framed as paternalistic and symptomatic of an ever-widening will to restrict previously enjoyed freedoms. One author gives his book on the problem of paternalism the pithy title *Killjoys*.[11] We have been told that 'health and safety killjoys' have banned mums from tea making, model steam boats, get well cards, trampolines, ice-cream vans, Punch and Judy shows, hanging baskets and cheese-rolling races. In case you have never heard of the latter, they are 'one of Britain's oldest most trad-itional events'.[12] The headline: 'Cheese Rolling axed after 200 years: thanks to Health and Safety Killjoys'. Because of killjoys, the story goes, we are not allowed to keep our trad-itions, to do what we had previously enjoyed doing in a relaxed and uncontroversial manner. So much enjoyment has become predicated on distancing ourselves from *them*, those others who are either mean and menacing, or weak and simpering, who are stopping us not only from enjoying ourselves but from being ourselves. Pointing out spoilsports has become quite the sport.

You read the headlines and killjoys keep popping up. But behind the sensational headlines are usually more compli-cated stories. Take the example of cheese rolling. The story is framed as the cancellation of an age-old tradition. Read the fine print and you learn that an event was cancelled by the organizers because the previous year's attendance was three times more than expected and they wanted to avoid another logistical nightmare. The object is changed (the cancellation of an event becomes the cancellation of a tradition) to mag-nify the story, so that it becomes something it was not.

The problem with these stories is not just that they are false. Many are ideologically motivated. One journal-ist described stories of Christmas being cancelled as 'almost as traditional as the wreath on your door'.[13] Telling the story of cancelled Christmases has, in other words, become a Christmas tradition. These stories typically use as their evidence relatively minor decisions made by councils about language. Much seems to have been made of the use of the

8

word *Winterval* by Birmingham council in 1998.[14] The *Daily Mail* issued a correction to one of its many stories about Winterval: 'We are happy to make clear that Winterval did not rename or replace Christmas.'[15] You can happily correct the story but keep telling it. Many put the blame not only on politically correct councils but upon those they are assumed to be acting on behalf of – the offended. One headline from 2 November 2005 made it clear who they think are the offended: 'CHRISTMAS IS BANNED: IT OFFENDS MUSLIMS'.[16] I return to explore what this figure of the too-easily-offended-Muslim is doing in due course. None of the stories include quotes from British Muslims about being offended. If some people can be killjoys without saying or doing anything, perhaps it is their very existence that is experienced as the end of tradition.

Since the coronavirus pandemic, new 'Christmas killjoys' have been ushered in, those arguing for, or enforcing, restrictions on social gatherings during the holiday season.[17] One minister said, 'People are sick and tired of this level of micromanagement of their lives. They want to be free and joyful, and they want to be free and joyful at Christmas – without the Christmas killjoys.' Yes: freedom and joyfulness can be asserted as indifference to the potentially harmful consequences of actions upon others. Some of these stories of Christmas killjoys during the pandemic still manage to blame the minorities: 'Civil servants have blocked the word "Christmas" as it may offend minority religions.'[18] Note the use of the word *blocked*. The story also uses the word *banned*. The explanation for not using the word *Christmas* in the leaked email does not mention causing offence but rather 'the need to be inclusive'. Any change to the wording of communications so that they address more or different communities can be, will be, turned into a story of cancellation.

When the killjoy is used to picture a style of politics, it still brings with it a picture of a person and a pathology, perhaps the kind of person who participates in what is now called *cancel culture*. If *cancel culture* is a new term, it is an old story. Another news story: 'Off with their shrunken heads! A leading UK museum decides the display of South American human remains is racist. Killjoys at an Oxford Museum have decided to remove from view its popular exhibit of shrunken human heads. The woke arbiters of British culture have decided that this exhibit reinforces "racist and stereotypical thinking".'[19] Stealing enjoyment is often framed as stealing history. It is not just joy that killjoys kill. It is the killjoys who would deprive us of history by using words like *racist* to describe that history. The killjoys steal the past, our history, our heritage, sometimes by removing objects from the present we might otherwise be able to view, to consume and enjoy.

The killjoy and the 'woke arbiter' are close kin, those who are deemed to be depriving us of something we assume as ours. Feminism is often deemed to be about *deprivation*. If the term *killjoy* has been around longer than *feminist*, to place feminists within a history of killjoys throws new light on old feminist histories. A 1972 article in *The New York Times* describes a group of cheerleaders by evoking the feminist killjoy as who they are not: 'At Madison Square Garden yesterday, it didn't take long to see that rah-rah world of cheerlead-ing had no room in the squad for Gloria Steinem, Germaine Greer and Other Women's Lib Killjoys.'[20] The moral contrast between cheerful cheerleaders and killjoy feminists does a great deal of work. The article begins by quoting from some of the cheerleaders themselves: 'Sexist exploitation?' asked Mary Scarborough of Western Kentucky University, twirl-ing her vinyl pompon. 'What in the world are they talking about?' 'Burn our bras?' said Rooney Frailey of Notre Dame. 'Oh my goodness. No way. You'd never last through the game.' The implication here is that feminists would object to cheer-leading as 'sexist exploitation' and that this very language is foreign to how women themselves experience such practices. The feminist killjoy is used to create the impression that to be a feminist is to be against so much, everything, even, to be for being against.

Feminist killjoys appear in a similar fashion in a later article, which claims, 'A group of militant feminists want to ban all men from wolf-whistling and calling women "darling". According to the band of bony-fingered killjoys, this is a form of sexual harassment on par with groping and flashing.'[21] Killjoys are treated not only as a collective made up of those of a similar physical type (a bony-fingered band no less) but as being indifferent to scale. Feminist kill-joys turn small things into big things or treat small things, little acts of harmless fun, *darling*, it's a compliment, *darling*, those terms of endearment, as if they are the same as big things. In the case of the MeToo movement, many denun-ciations took this exact form: that feminists have become a

11

mob of bony-fingered killjoys, wielding power over others. Calling something sexual harassment is to killjoy, to stop something that is nice; such as not being allowed to do nice things like calling women 'darling'. The figure of the feminist killjoy teaches us how the *minimization of harm* and the *inflation of power* often work together. Even to identify something as harmful is treated as an attempt to exercise or to hold power over someone, as if feminists make slights bigger than they are to make themselves bigger. This is how the terms and concepts introduced by feminists to explain how power works, such as sexual harassment, also become killjoys, carriers of bad feeling, impositions made by outsiders.

It is worth adding that this article was partly about former British prime minister David Cameron's pledge to sign a treaty from the Council of Europe to mark International Women's Day, which included a clause that would outlaw 'unwanted verbal, non-verbal or physical conduct of a sexual nature with the purpose or effect of violating the dignity of a person, in particular when creating an intimidating, hostile, degrading, humiliating or offensive environment'. This clause is in fact a standard definition of sexual harassment and had already been adopted in the UK as part of its equality framework. But it was reported as new and foreign, and as a European imposition: 'It's no surprise that the bureaucrats in Brussels and the dictators in Berlin were long-ago given sense of humour bypasses.' As an aside, post-Brexit, one can immediately see how Europe itself came to be identified with the figure of the killjoy, as imposing moral restrictions and humour bypasses. If equality is treated as a humour bypass, inequality, we are being told, is humorous. It was not surprising that Brexit was framed as a promise of happiness. Arguments for leaving took the form of a promissory version of *nostalgic nationalism*, to borrow terms from the anthropologist Sarah Franklin; to 'take back control' as to go back to the past, to 'take back control' as taking the nation back.[22] Given nostalgia is a fantasy of a past, that fantasy can be preserved whether or not promises are realized. One politician quipped that the 'fish are better and happier now that they are British.'[23] Wherever you find the figure of the killjoy, you will find a fantasy of happiness. To be a killjoy is to threaten not just happiness but *a fantasy of happiness*, an idea of where (and in whom) happiness can be found.

Feminism has created new words to suggest there are problems with the old ways of doing things. Make no mistake: we do want to change some of the old ways. When you become a feminist you learn just how much some are invested in them. To call for change in how people speak or act can be sufficient to be judged as a killjoy, which implies that killjoys tend to come up *more* in periods of *more* intense social transformation. If you have to insist on being addressed by the right pronouns for yourself or your partner – and those who have to insist on the right pronouns are often those who are addressed by the wrong pronouns – you can be judged as a killjoy, as imposing yourself upon others, stopping them from being free to do what they have always done. The killjoy comes up to demarcate a boundary; to say something is *compelled* is to say it does not originate with us. Once something has become a habit, a norm, a routine, it is not deemed an imposition. So, for example, feminists introduced Ms to avoid Miss or Mrs, to challenge the assumption that a woman's status should be about whether she is married or not. In a newspaper article from 2012, Jasmine M. Gardner notes, 'Everybody knows that if you call yourself Ms, it's because you have a point to make.'[24] So many of these words we introduce have *killjoy histories*; when we use them we are heard as making a point, a sore point, although in time some of them become less pointed, more habitual. I return to this question of habit when I consider the feminist killjoy as a philosopher.

If not all killjoys are feminists, all feminists are killjoys. By this I mean: to be identified as a feminist or to identify yourself as a feminist is to be judged as a killjoy, whether or not you understand yourself in these terms. This is not to say that all feminists are *really* killjoys by nature or inclination. The point of the figure is to create this impression, as if to be a feminist is to deprive yourself of enjoyment or to be intent on depriving others of enjoyment. An article on the post-feminist generation published in *The New York Times* in 1982 quotes a student, 'Look around and you'll see some happy women, and then you'll see these bitter, bitter women. The unhappy women are all feminists.'[25] Behind the perception that 'the unhappy women are all feminists' are two competing claims: the first that unhappiness leads women to become feminists because they can't get what they want, perhaps a husband or baby; the second that feminism

14

makes women unhappy. Author Fay Weldon argues that 'the fight for gender equality is bad for the looks. It makes no one happy unless you find some reward in struggling for a justice that evolution failed to deliver.'[26] The implication is that fighting for gender equality makes you unhappy as you are fighting against nature; becoming feminists lessens our femininity, our attractiveness.

The extremity of the *kill* in *feminist killjoy* is telling us something. We learn about the nature of feminist demands by the fact that they have been judged to be deadly as well as depressing. You might have noticed how the term *feminist killjoy* is used to refer to a person, to a movement, to a word or concept introduced by that movement. The term *feminist killjoy* slides. As a stereotype, the feminist killjoy creates a sticky association between feminism and unhappiness. So, if the feminist killjoy slides, *she sticks*, rather like Velcro, fastening on to a 'me' or a 'we' as an explanation of all that we do. That is why once you are designated a feminist killjoy you tend to be stuck with her.

A stereotype is a repeated utterance, a characterization that in being simplistic as well as flattening is also, in a profound sense, false. I say profound because what makes something a stereotype is about *what it fails to capture*. We can understand why some responses to stereotypes of unhappy feminism and feminist killjoys might be to counter or to contradict that stereotype, to say feminism is not *that* or feminists are not *her*. It might be tempting to try and appear happy and positive in order to counter the myth of feminist misery, to make feminism less frightening, more appealing. It might be tempting to try to rescue feminism from the feminist killjoy, to create picture books of shiny happy feminists. There are such picture books.

I have a different strategy. My aim is not to rescue us from the feminist killjoy but to give her a voice. If we try not to be feminist killjoys, to claim distance from them, we would miss what they can tell us, about ourselves, the kind of work we do, and why we do it. To reclaim this figure is to recognize a truth in her. Feminists are judged as threatening (of happiness) because we threaten what is deemed by some to be necessary (for happiness): a belief, a practice, a way of life, a social arrangement. As cultural critic Lauren Berlant describes so eloquently, 'There is nothing more alienating than having your pleasures disputed by someone with a theory.'[27] Perhaps the feminist killjoy both has a theory and is one. The feminist killjoy helps us to explain why feminism is perceived as threatening, alienating people from their pleasures.

I write this handbook for those who are quite willing to be feminist killjoys, which is *not* the same thing as being miserable, willing or not. To reclaim the feminist killjoy is not to agree with the negative judgement behind it (that such and such person *is* an unhappy and threatening person) but to channel the negativity, pushing it in another direction. When you reclaim the term *feminist killjoy* you end up in conversation with other people who, like you, find a potential in that term, in how its negativity can be redirected. There is a long tradition in activism of reclaiming the terms that have been used against us, insults as well

16

as stereotypes – terms like queer, for instance – to say something about who we are as well as what we are against. I explore the *queerness* of the project of killing joy in my chapter on the feminist killjoy as activist.

I have been collecting feminist killjoy stories. *This* handbook is *that* collection. Alongside my own experiences of being a feminist killjoy, I include stories shared with me by others. When I talked to feminist students and academics about their experience of making complaints, I noticed how often the feminist killjoy came up. This is not surprising: to be a killjoy is to be heard as a complainer, as saying something negative, as being negative. I include some of these stories of complaint in this handbook.[28] I also share instances of how feminist killjoys are evoked in feminist writing, focusing especially on writings by Black feminists and feminists of colour, as well as in wider culture, including literature and film. To share feminist killjoy stories is to move from lived experiences to representations, and back again. We can recognize a killjoy character in a story because of our own experiences of being assigned her; and then, having recognized her, we return to our experiences with a fresh lens.

Let me return to my story of becoming a feminist killjoy. It was familiar, that scenario around the table. Anything can become familiar if it keeps happening. Why would my father keep making the same points knowing how I would react? Perhaps I was being given a lesson in patriarchal authority, being taught that he could say whatever he wished to say, and that I should learn to take it. Perhaps he kept making those points because he wanted me to react in the way I sometimes did, to reveal myself to be as he judged me, a problem child, a wilful child, immature, impulsive, insubordinate. Feminism is often dismissed as a personal failing, not just a tendency but a flaw, as if a person disagrees with something *because* she is being disagreeable; as if she opposes something *because* she is being oppositional. Your reaction to what is said can be used to justify a judgement that has already been made: *she would say that*. She would say that; I did say that.

KILLJOY TRUTH:
TO EXPOSE A PROBLEM IS TO POSE A PROBLEM

I think of this **killjoy truth** as a *core truth*, a truth from which so much else follows. If you expose a problem, you pose a problem; if you pose a problem, you become the problem. The management of a problem becomes the management of a person. In other words, one way of dealing with a problem is to stop people from talking about it or to make the people who talk about it go away. If people stop talking about a problem, or the people who talk about it go away, it can then be assumed that the problem has gone away. I hear an instruction here. We are being told to stop talking about problems or to go away. We don't always do what we are told. But, then, the more we talk about a problem, the more we encounter it. Reclaiming the feminist killjoy is about more than taking her name for ourselves. It is also about what we are willing to keep encountering. If questioning an existing arrangement makes people unhappy, we are willing to make people unhappy. We make a commitment, which I think of as *the core killjoy commitment.*

KILLJOY COMMITMENT:
I AM WILLING TO CAUSE UNHAPPINESS

The feminist killjoy becomes an assignment not only in the sense of how we are given meaning or value, but also as a task. If taking on the feminist killjoy assignment means being willing to cause unhappiness, we can now say what it does not mean. The point of the figure, what makes her so sharp, is the exercising of a judgement that she *intends* what she causes as if the point of what she is doing or saying is to get in the way of other people's happiness or just get in the way. We are not *intending* to cause unhappiness; we are *willing* to cause unhappiness. A distinction can be obscured by a judgement. So, we don't talk about sexism or racism because we want to make people unhappy; we are willing to talk about sexism or racism even when it makes people unhappy.

We learn so much from taking on the feminist killjoy as our assignment. If you say you are a feminist you are more likely to hear the kinds of comments that led you to become a feminist in the first place. Here is a collection of some memorable comments shared with me, or directed at me, by family, friends and acquaintances over dinner tables: 'Women can't be equal because babies need breastmilk',

'Enoch Powell had it right', 'It is selfish for gay people to have children', 'This is what happens when you marry a Muslim', 'Sara, I didn't know you were Oriental', 'Divorce discriminates against men'. You will hear about the context for each of these comments in this handbook. Some of the comments were directed towards me personally. Others could be newspaper headlines. If they were newspaper headlines, it would be easier to know whether or how to respond. Sometimes we enter a debate because, let's face it, we have heard it before and we have out of necessity fine-tuned our skills of argumentation. Sometimes we refuse to enter a debate because entering it would elevate a position as worthy of being debated. However hard it is to respond to sexism, homophobia, transphobia or racism in the public domain, it is even harder to know how to respond in more intimate spaces. Becoming a feminist killjoy is about learning how to handle it when friends or family members make such comments. There are no right ways, just different handles.

To handle something is to learn from it. This means we can think of dinner tables alongside other kinds of meeting tables, as political sites, where we are doing our feminist work. In her book *Just Us*, poet and critic Claudia Rankine takes her readers on a journey between sites: the airport, the theatre, the dinner party and the photo booth. What connects these sites is the uncomfortable conversations she has with white people about whiteness. Rankine stresses that to have a conversation about whiteness is not to bring something into the room that is not already there. But it can feel like that, because you are not supposed to point to some things, and if you do, a conversation becomes turbulent, like wind, 'the mutual anxieties and angers blow invisible in the room'.[29]

Discomfort can be a connection. We can turn here to Ama Ata Aidoo's novel *Our Sister Killjoy*. Sissie, our sister killjoy, is the narrator. Her story is written like a travel diary; she travels from Africa to Europe, from Ghana to Germany and England. Her killjoy story begins before she even gets to Europe. On a plane, a white hostess invites her to sit at the back with 'her friends', two Black people she does not know. She is about to say that she does not know them, and hesitates. 'But to have refused to join them would have created an awkward situation, wouldn't it? Considering too that apart from the air hostess's obviously civilized upbringing, she had been trained to see to the comfort of all her passengers.'[30] Sissie's hesitation speaks volumes. Not to go to the back of the plane or to say she does not know the other Black people would be to refuse the place she had been assigned. If the air hostess is trained 'to see to the comfort of all', not to follow her instruction would be to cause the discomfort 'of all'.

At this point, Sissie goes along with it. But she can see what is wrong with it. And because she can, we can. Over the course of the novel, Sissie becomes more herself, a sister killjoy, in what she says and does. I am deeply indebted to Ama Ata Aidoo's repurposing of the figure of the sister killjoy, and I will return to Sissie's catalogue of killjoy encounters throughout this handbook. Aidoo's is the *first* text to give the killjoy her own voice. Aidoo (and also Sissie) show us how being a sister killjoy or feminist killjoy is to be conscious of what we create, 'an awkward situation'. So often to create an awkward situation is to be judged as being awkward. When we take on the feminist killjoy assignment, turning a judgement into a project, it is important that the project is shared.

Once we become a feminist killjoy, we become more attuned to feminist killjoys, noticing when and how they turn up. I think of one scene in Rachel Cusk's novel *Arlington Park*. There is a dinner, there is a table, around which friends gather. One character, Matthew, is speaking. He 'talked on and on. He talked about politics and taxes and the people who got in his way.'[31] He 'talked on and on' about women who take maternity leave. He relays a story of a woman he is going to sack unless she comes straight back to work after having a baby. One woman, Juliet, is silent at first. But eventually she can't stand any more to let the silence imply she is in agreement. She says, 'That's illegal.' She says, 'She could take you to court.' Illegal: that word cuts through an atmosphere like a knife, challenging his assumed right to do what he is doing. It is Juliet who is heard as sharp. Matthew responds: 'You want to be careful.' And then, 'she saw how close she was to his hatred: it was like a nerve she was within a millimetre of touching. "You want to take care. You can start to sound strident at your age."' It is because she speaks up, speaking up as not taking care, that she comes close to his hatred. That hatred was already there, in the background, like a nerve. To be a feminist killjoy is *to live in proximity to a nerve*.

Note the reference to age. Perhaps the feminist killjoy is an ageing assignment, you become a hag as well as a nag.

Radical feminist Mary Daly defines the hag as 'an intractable person, especially: a woman reluctant to yield to wooing'.[32] You become a hag by not yielding, whether to a sexual advance or another kind of advance; sexism can be an advance, how women are told to make themselves available to others. When you don't yield, you don't smile, you don't stay silent, you are perceived as being forceful. I think of that word *strident*. To sound strident is to be heard as loud, harsh or grating. Other people can be saying the same thing over and over again, even saying those things loudly, and not be heard as strident. But you become a problem if you even dare to say what they say is a problem. Oh, the frustration of being found frustrating! Oh, the difficulty of being assumed to be difficult! It is enough to make you difficult.

You might even begin to *sound like* what they hear you as *being like*: you talk louder and faster as you can tell you are not getting through. You end up sounding furious because you are assumed to be furious. We might even become what we are judged as being. I talked to a lesbian academic about being the kind of person who ends up locked in that dynamic: 'And then of course you get witch-hunted, you get scapegoated, you become the troublesome uppity woman; you become the woman who does not fit; you become everything the bully accuses you of, because nobody is listening to you. And you hear yourself starting to take that, not petulant tone [bangs table with hand], come on. You can hear them saying, oh there you go.' A diversity practitioner had said something very similar to me: that she only had to open her mouth in meetings to witness eyes rolling as if to say, 'Oh, here she goes.' Both times we laughed, recognizing that we both recognized that scene. You don't even have to say anything before eyes start rolling.

KILLJOY EQUATION:
ROLLING EYES = FEMINIST PEDAGOGY

When I share this equation, people often laugh. Sometimes we do laugh. We need each to laugh so we can laugh. In that laughter can also be a groan. To be followed by rolling eyes is to be followed by eyes. The more we laugh, the more we are seen. We laugh under the weight of that scrutiny. If we laugh, we don't laugh it off. We know there is so much we are supposed to laugh off; remember, inequality is routinely presented as humorous. So many feminist killjoy stories begin with an experience of *not* finding something funny.

KILLJOY MAXIM:
WHEN IT IS NOT FUNNY, DO NOT LAUGH!

I talked to a lecturer whose head of department kept making antisemitic and homophobic comments: 'I think she thought she was being funny,' she told me. 'I have a very obviously Jewish last name, and my family is Jewish, and I am not religious but anyway it is my background, I am Jewish, she made a lot of comments, Jewish jokes and stuff about Jews being stingy and that kind of thing. And I am openly gay and she thought that was something she could tease me about and she was always saying about other people, do you think he's gay, do you think she's gay, so there was a lot of things.'

'I think she thought' means she has an idea of why this person is speaking like this; so much verbal abuse seems to be intended as 'being funny', which gives us an idea of the utility of intentions. A sense of 'being funny' can enable some to keep saying things that are demeaning and derogatory to others. These forms of verbal harassment 'had been going on for years'.

If you keep having the same problem, it can be hard not to feel that the problem is you. She describes: 'I have been told I have a chip on my shoulder, that I've got a chip on my shoulder because I am Jewish, that I have a chip on my shoulder because I am foreign, living in this country and you're upset about Brexit, or because you're gay and you are just looking for problems. And you start thinking, am I looking for these problems? I just turn it inwards, is it me, is it my fault? I lie awake at night thinking, is it actually a problem with me here?' When you are heard as having a chip on your shoulder, a grievance can be dismissed as a grudge, as if you are only making a complaint because you are sore. The very fact of being different (*because* I am gay, *because* I am Jewish, and so on) is used to explain (and dismiss) what you are saying.

To become a feminist killjoy is to hear how we are dismissed. In hearing it, the lecturer also hears herself doubting herself: 'Maybe I am being over-sensitive. You can see I am starting to take the blame on myself, over-sensitive, I can't take a joke, blah, blah, blah, the kind of thing you tell yourself when you are just trying to get over it.' She can see what she is doing as she is doing it, taking the blame on herself. You can end up warning yourself not to become a feminist killjoy, telling yourself not to make something bigger than it needs to be. Getting over it can be an injunction you impose on yourself. She uses the word *over-sensitive* twice. Feminist killjoys are often deemed *over-sensitive*.

KILLJOY EQUATION:
OVER-SENSITIVE = SENSITIVE TO WHAT IS NOT OVER

Even self-identifying feminist killjoys can 'turn it inwards', hearing those external voices inside our own heads; saying that we are being too sensitive, making problems bigger than they are. Those external voices are loud: we hear them everywhere. Consider the widespread use of the image of the 'snowflake generation', a generation who are 'coddled', who won't tolerate disagreement, who can't take jokes because they can't take reality. A typical example of this kind of rhetoric: 'No one can rebut feelings, and so the only thing left to do is shut down the things that cause distress – no argument, no discussion, just hit the mute button and pretend eliminating discomfort is the same as effecting actual change.'[33] For some commentators, the use of trigger warnings is evidence of an over-sensitive generation who shuts down whatever causes distress. In fact, trigger warnings are better understood as techniques that can enable some people to remain in the room in order to have difficult conversations about distressing material. Trigger warnings are about providing more information, not less. They are not about putting an end to difficult conversations but enabling those with a history of trauma to participate in them.

The idea that the younger generation have become a problem because they are too sensitive relates to a wider public discourse that renders *offendability* as a form of moral weakness that then restricts our freedom of speech. We are back to those woke arbiters who are depriving us of our right to say and do as we wish. Some people *assert their right to occupy space* by being more and more offensive towards others. Racism and transphobia both function like this. The positioning of racial or religious minorities, especially Muslims, and trans people as too easily offended leads to an *increase* in racist and transphobic speech. There is an 'incitement to discourse' in a story of its suppression: so many people continue to make racist and transphobic statements by saying they are not allowed to make them.[34] One comedian at the end of a set that included much transphobic content claimed, 'I think that's what comedy is for, really – to get us through stuff, and I deal in taboo subjects because I want to take the audience to a place it hasn't been before, even for a split second.'[35] This so-called 'taboo subject' is in fact a well-travelled path, where we are used to going rather than where we haven't been; a confirmation of, rather than challenge to, the transphobia of mainstream culture. But then, if you call it out, give the problem its name, that person will most likely represent themselves as 'cancelled', quickly embarking on a cancellation tour. And so, we end up with some people speaking endlessly about being silenced, given more platforms to claim they are no-platformed. Being positioned as a feminist killjoy teaches us how power often works through reversal: those who are *more* represented in the public domain tend to represent themselves as *more* censored. Whenever people keep being given a platform to say they have no platform, or whenever people speak endlessly about being silenced, you not only have a performative contradiction, you are witnessing a mechanism of power.[36]

Sometimes even saying you find something distressing is sufficient to be positioned as a killjoy who is trying to shut someone up or shut something down. One time a student doing an undergraduate degree in English Literature and Women's Studies came to my room in tears. She said that a lecturer had shown a film that involved a graphic depiction of rape. When she told him afterwards that she found the film and the discussion upsetting, he had said to her that she was only upset because she was reading the film wrong by 'taking it literally'. He said rape was 'just a metaphor'. Hurt is dismissed as literalism. His aestheticization of rape allowed him to show, and to keep showing, the film. The insistence on one's right to use certain kinds of materials can become a scathing indifference to how these materials affect others.

You become a killjoy, a threat to someone's right to express themselves in a certain way, by being affected too much or in the wrong way. I talked to another student about her experience of verbal harassment by a student at a conference:

'The atmosphere of the two days was really oppressive. It was the cultural shift I recognized as I came through the doors. There was a lot of touching going on; shoulder rubs and knee pats. It was the dialogue. They were making jokes, jokes that were horrific, they were doing it in a very small space in front of staff, and nobody was saying anything. And it felt like my reaction to it was out of kilter with everyone else. It felt really disconnected, the way I felt about the way they were behaving and the way everybody else was laughing. They were talking about "milking bitches". I still can't quite get to the bottom of where the jokes were coming from. Nobody was saying anything about it: people were just laughing along. You start to stand out in that way; you are just not playing along.'

You can open the door and be hit by it: a change in atmosphere, intrusions into personal space. The sexist expression 'milking bitches' seemed to have a history. History can be thrown out like a line you are supposed to follow. You don't quite know where the jokes are coming from. But everyone else seems to be laughing. When laughter fills the room, it can feel like there is no room left. To experience such jokes as offensive is to become alienated not only from the jokes but the laughter that surrounds them, propping them up, giving them somewhere to go.

29

When other people are going along with it, you are being told there is nothing wrong with it. You can kill-joy without intending to do so because of how your body expresses something. This is why I describe feminist killjoys as *affect aliens*. We are alienated by not being affected in the same way as those around us.

KILLJOY EQUATION:
AFFECT ALIEN = ALIENATED BY HOW YOU ARE AFFECTED

If you do not participate in something, if you do not laugh when others laugh, you stand out. Perhaps some people laugh in order not to stand out. To stand out can mean to be targeted. If those who do not participate in harassment are targeted, one method for avoiding being harassed is to participate in it. The student describes what happened next: 'He specifically went for me, verbally, at a table where every-one was eating lunch. It was a large table with numerous amounts of people around it, including staff . . . I was having quite a personal conversation [about her research] with someone and he literally leant across the table or physically came forward, he was slightly to one side of me, he was really close, and he said, "Oh my god, I can see you ovulating."'

Because she does not find the jokes funny, because she expresses in her reaction that she is not condoning the behaviour, that she is not happy, he comes after her. Her personal space invaded, she is reduced to body; she is stopped from doing her own thing, from having a conversation about her

30

own work. She leaves the room. And when she walks out of the room, she is followed out by a staff member who says, 'Oh you know what he's like, he's got a really strange sense of humour, he didn't mean anything by it.' Perhaps language is assumed not to mean anything at the moment we identify it as problematic: it's a metaphor; it's a parody; it's irony; it's a style; it's art.

Violence is repeated by being emptied of meaning and force. If you object or complain, you are then judged as forcing your viewpoint upon others. She does complain. When other students find out that a complaint has been made, the situation worsens: 'There was a real physical aggressive threat that these men were starting to build up, and things had been said like, we might get a brick through our window or we might get our hand pounded in iron.' You complain because you are harassed; you are harassed because you complain. Even threats of violence can be made light of. Another student I spoke to describes this: 'When threats of violence were made, it was implied it was just talk and it didn't mean anything.' He didn't mean anything; it didn't mean anything. She told me how the head of department refused to intervene, saying, 'I can't be seen to side with either student, so we can't formally take a line on this.' Not wanting to be seen as taking sides is taking sides because there is no attempt to stop the harassment. Treating harassment as a side, perhaps in an argument or of a debate, is how harassment is not seen.

What you try to stop, others don't see. And so, you have to keep saying *no*. And the more you say *no*, the more you show or indicate in some way that you don't agree with something, the more you are pressed upon not to say no, *not* to say anything, *not* to do anything. We might end up snapping because of that pressure. I think of a scene depicted in Andrea Levy's novel *Fruit of the Lemon*. The novel tells the story of Faith Jackson, a Black British girl whose parents migrated to England from Jamaica. She is getting along with her life, doing her own thing. She does not think of herself as any different to those around her; her white friends are just her friends. They share a house; they share a life.

Then there is an event. She and her flatmate Simon witness a violent attack on a Black woman. We witness the event through Faith's eyes:

> *A black woman was standing in the doorway of a bookshop. She looked composed, although she had a startled stare – like she's just won the pools and couldn't quite believe it. But sliding slowly down one side of her face were several strings of blood – thick, bright, red blood. I stood in front of her and asked, 'Are you all right?' and felt stupid when she collapsed down onto the ground.[37]*

They return home to tell the story of the event. The telling creates a certain kind of drama, in which Simon becomes the centre of attention. They gather around him as if what happened, happened to him, as if what made the event an event was how it affected him:

'Simon's hands shook as he lifted his cigarette to his mouth – he couldn't hold it steady. Marion put her hand over his hand to support it. "I think you're in shock. Sweet tea is what you need," she said looking closely into Simon's face. "Mick, put the kettle on"'[38] Faith watches the Black woman disappear as they gather kindly around him; concerned. She tries to bring her back into the story: 'I interrupted the story twice. "She was a black woman," I said. Simon had just called her the woman who worked there. Twice I had to tell them that the woman that was struck on the head was black like me. And both times Simon and Mick had looked at me and nodded.' The word *interrupt* comes from rupture, or break. To bring the Black woman back into the story, Faith has to stop them from telling it. But they don't stop; they keep going, nodding as keeping going; as if her Blackness is just a detail that can be passed over. They all fuss over him: laughing, giggling, excited, full of the drama of an event.

But then Faith can't bear it any more. She can't bear the violence of the event, a violence that was directed against a Black woman, to be passed over. She snaps: 'But then I tipped my cup of tea slowly over the table. "Will you all just shut up. Just fucking shut up. It's not funny!" And there was complete silence as they stopped and stared at me. I left the house.'[39] A raised voice, a spilt cup of tea: it might seem like the start of something. For Faith, she is right in the middle of something. She brings to the surface a violence that is already there, that has travelled with them into the room; the violence directed towards a Black woman, the violence of how that violence goes unnamed; the violence of attention, how whiteness becomes the centre of attention; the concern, the drama; all about him.

I think of what Andrea Levy was able to show through

Faith's snap. A snap is often understood as a sudden break or a quick movement. Snap can be used to refer to a sharp sound. You might hear the sound of a twig snapping. You might not have noticed the twig before, not noticed the pressure on the twig, how it was bent. When it snaps, it catches your attention. You might hear the snap as the start of something. A snap is only the start of something because of what you did not notice, the pressure on the twig. You might hear someone when she shouts, because she shouts; at that moment a voice is raised it is heard over everything else. It does not mean she starts off by shouting.

KILLJOY TRUTH: IF YOU HAVE TO SHOUT TO BE HEARD, YOU ARE HEARD AS SHOUTING

A snap is a moment with a history. To hear a snap, to give that moment a history, we need to slow down, listen to the slower times of wearing and tearing, of making do. We learn to hear exhaustion, the gradual sapping of energy when you have to struggle to exist in a world that negates your existence. A breaking point is a point you have to reach. It might seem, at first, that the feminist killjoy is reacting to something in the present time. But from listening to stories of the killjoy, snappy stories, we learn about the importance of timing; how the killjoy comes up because of what is said or not said, what did or did not happen, *before.* Think of that feeling of being wound up by someone who is winding you up; you become tighter, and tighter, the more you are

34

provoked. Tighter, tighter, tighter still, gasp, there is no air left: until, snap. A group coheres by witnessing her snap: look at her, look, look, see how she spins!

See how she spins. Earlier I shared comments made in the middle of conversations I have had with friends and family. Each comment was made in the heat of a moment, and in hearing each of them I go back to that moment. One of these sentences, 'Women aren't equal because babies need breast-milk', was said to me by my father. It was said to me not when I was a child, seated at that family table, but when I was an adult, a lecturer teaching students about feminism. It was said to me before I began writing about feminist killjoys but after I had come to recognize myself as one, in a hotel foyer in Lancaster. My father had come to see me; he was there with his second wife. It was said to me quite late in an argument. It was a point we had reached, because I refused to agree with what he had been saying. I knew what I was being told. I was being told inequality is natural. That it is because of biology that such-and-such situation exists. This is how it is; what babies need; what women provide, who we are, what we are for. And when you are told, in one way or another, that you oppose what is natural, you are made unnatural.

KILLJOY EQUATION:
FEMINISM = A HISTORY OF UNNATURAL WOMEN

Feminism is treated as a flight from nature. Ideology is history turned into nature. To fight against inequalities is to hear how they are justified. Justifications become tired. And so we become tired, too. This time, I snapped. I didn't come out with a fine-tuned argument. I didn't even come out with words. I could hear in that sentence a history, a history of being wound up by someone who was winding me up, a history of provocation, of being, becoming, the problem child. I saw her appear. I saw myself disappear. I left the room.

When Faith snaps, she has to leave. She has to leave not just because she snapped at her friends but because of how her bond with her friends was broken; she realizes what that bond required of her: to overlook at whom violence was directed, to overlook racism, to overlook sexism, to overlook, even, herself. To have to keep making that point, that she was a Black woman, makes Faith aware of what she cannot share with her white friends. They don't see it, they won't see it, *they won't see her.* If pointing out sexism or racism means being judged as snapping a bond, as cutting yourself off from friends or family, it does not mean that was the aim. Rather, your experience of snapping teaches you about that bond; how it comes with conditions. We often learn conditions by failing to meet them. You realize that sustaining a bond might mean not saying certain things, not doing certain things, not noticing them, even. So even if you did not aim to snap a bond, when a bond snaps as a consequence of what you say or do, snapping can teach you why you needed to snap; you snap, you get out of the room, you can breathe.

When a bond requires overlooking violence, overlooking

racism, overlooking ourselves, even, we might need to snap the bond. Perhaps that is what a killjoy is doing or saying: she is showing that she is unwilling to meet the conditions for being with others. It is important for me to note here that not all bonds are destructive. To sustain a life, we need to sustain the bonds that sustain us. Some bonds, family or friendship, give us strength and shelter, others we need to be sheltered from. When someone you love expresses viewpoints that you find problematic, painfully so, you don't always want to hear it, because to hear it, *really* to hear it, would be to hear the glass shattering, the sound of something breaking.

Being a killjoy can sometimes be a crisis because it is not always clear which bonds are sustaining and which are not. A bond we had thought of as sustaining can end up not being so. That was Faith's killjoy lesson. That's our lesson. When so much violence is passed over, you become a killjoy because of what you do not pass over. You can just try to make something visible, the violence directed towards a Black woman, say, and you will be heard as getting in the way. This is also why feminist killjoys do not disappear when we create feminist spaces. Audre Lorde, bell hooks, Sunera Thobani and Aileen Moreton-Robinson, among others, have taught me to think that the figures of the angry Black woman, the angry brown woman or woman of colour, as well as the angry Indigenous woman, are feminist killjoys in the sense of killers of feminist joy.[40] To talk about racism within feminism is to get in the way of feminist happiness.

37

KILLJOY COMMITMENT: I AM WILLING
TO GET IN THE WAY OF FEMINIST HAPPINESS

Audre Lorde's work gives us so many instances of how, when women of colour speak about the problem of racism within feminism, we are made into the problem. One instance: 'When women of Color speak out of the anger that laces so many of our contacts with white women, we are often told that we are "creating a mood of helplessness", "preventing white women from getting past guilt", or "standing in the way of trusting communication and action".'[41] Women of colour are asked to let go of our anger so white women can move on. These quotes are from letters sent by white women to Lorde. I think of all the letters, how they add up. I think of Lorde's letter she sent to Mary Daly. Her letter was a response to Mary Daly's use of Lorde's work in her book *Gyn/Ecology*, to Daly's failure to cite Black women, to how she mentions Black women only as victims and not as sources of wisdom and power.

Lorde writes:

We first met at the MLA panel, 'The Transformation of Silence into Language and Action.' This letter attempts to break a silence which I had imposed on myself shortly before that date. I had decided never again to speak to white women about racism. I felt it was wasted energy, because of destructive guilt and defensiveness, and because whatever I had to say might better be said by white women to one another, at far less emotional cost to one another, and probably with a better hearing.[42]

Recall Daly's description of the hag. At the end of her letter, Lorde makes a request, 'I would like not to destroy you in my consciousness, not to have to. So as a sister Hag, I ask you to speak to my perceptions.' In writing the letter, Lorde broke her own silence. She wrote the letter knowing that the problems she was trying to address would most likely mean she would not be heard. But still, she wrote it 'as a sister Hag' because unless those problems were addressed, sisterhood, consciousness of a shared struggle, would not be possible. Sometimes we become killjoys even when we doubt we will get through because that is what we must do. More recently, Reni Eddo-Lodge, Ruby Hamad and Rafia Zakaria have also talked about the difficulty of speaking about racism to white people.[43] When we speak about whiteness we come up against whiteness, as defensive feeling, sometimes as tears.

Feminism is *occupied* by whiteness. I do not use that word *occupied* lightly. I was brought up in Australia, a settler colonial country. I have learnt from Indigenous feminists how whiteness occupies not just the land but feminism. In the second edition of her landmark book *Talkin' Up to the White Woman*, Aileen Moreton-Robinson reflects on a panel, A *World of Difference: Decolonizing Feminism*. Moreton-Robinson quotes from the promotional blurb for the panel: 'Nearly twenty years ago, Moreton-Robinson's pioneering work *Talkin' Up to the White Woman* took a sledgehammer to the idea of a unified sisterhood serving the common good of all women.' A sledgehammer: we need to let ourselves be hit by the violence of this description of her contribution.

Moreton-Robinson shows how this use of the metaphor of the sledgehammer positioned her as 'the angry black woman', who is being 'bad tempered, hostile, and overly aggressive'.[44] To point out racism within feminism is to be treated as violent, as smashing up what held women together. We re-encounter that stereotype, the angry Black woman, the Black feminist killjoy, that history, in the spaces set up to challenge it. I think of Lorde's letter. I think of Moreton-Robinson's afterword as another kind of letter, a public letter, about how whiteness remains occupying even in spaces set up to 'decolonize feminism'.

KILLJOY TRUTH: WE HAVE TO KEEP SAYING IT BECAUSE THEY KEEP DOING IT

Even if we keep saying it because of what they keep doing, we are heard as the ones repeating ourselves. To be a feminist killjoy, especially a Black, Indigenous or brown feminist killjoy, is to be heard as too insistent. Being insistent is a reflection of how the same things keep coming up. We have behind us many such killjoy letters, sent and unsent, telling us the same things keep happening. These letters are shared resources. As feminist killjoys, we create our own resources.

As feminist killjoys, we could all write our own handbooks. Even when we make the same points, because the same things keep coming up, our handbooks would be quite different. We are not just telling killjoy stories; we tell them because we are *in* them. This handbook is shaped by my

40

own queer trajectory as a person of colour of mixed heritage, with family connections to Pakistan and Australia as well as the UK, a lesbian, a middle-class person, a cis gender woman, and as a scholar who was based in universities for over twenty years and who now works independently. (I leave the snappy story of why I left my post and profession for later.) *The personal is institutional.* Our biographies, however quirky or idiosyncratic we feel them to be, are how we are inserted into bigger histories.

I have learnt so much in writing this handbook, from reflecting back on my own killjoy trajectory, on when and how the feminist killjoy came up, sometimes explicitly, sometimes not, in my own writing and research. I share with you this learning process throughout the handbook, which means I sometimes refer back to my earlier work. Whether you already identity as a feminist killjoy or are a *killjoy-to-be*,[45] I want to show you, I want you to know, that we *always* have more to learn not just about feminist killjoys but from them. From what might seem like a difficult but relatively minor situation, such as an argument with a parent or a friend around a table, we end up on a path that leads us to a different consciousness of the world and of our place in it. We can be surprised each step of the way. In the next chapter, I address how we survive as feminist killjoys (there can also be surprises in that story), before turning in the remaining chapters to how the feminist killjoy gives us the skills we need to navigate an unjust world.

2/ Surviving as a Feminist Killjoy

Even when you have claimed the feminist killjoy for your-self, it can feel like you have made your life harder than it needs to be, making problems bigger by attending to them. I have heard this sentiment expressed as advice, sometimes meant kindly, sometimes not; let it go, just *go with the flow*. And there is no doubt about it, going with the flow can make progression easier. You can be carried forward by a momentum.

KILLJOY TRUTH: THINGS ARE FLUID IF YOU ARE GOING THE WAY THINGS ARE FLOWING

If you don't go with the flow, you become an obstacle, get-ting in the way of the progression of others. You might even begin to experience yourself as an obstacle, as getting in the way of your own progression as well as that of others. As I suggested in my introduction, if you keep having a problem it can be hard not to feel that the problem is you. Still, you can feel otherwise. I remember when I first began giving talks about feminist killjoys how the atmosphere would change. People would sit up, pay attention. I could almost hear a sizzle, another kind of snap, the sound of electricity: snap, snap, sizzle. Even though she brings up a difficult history, a painful history, the feminist killjoy seems to pick us up. How can this be so?

This chapter is an answer to that question of how what seems to slow us down is what picks us up. My answer takes the form of **killjoy survival tips**. You might need to survive *as* a feminist killjoy – to find ways of holding on by holding onto her. Or the feminist killjoy might be how we survive *as* feminists by reclaiming the very terms that have been intended to punish us for being so. In the chapter, I reflect back on what I have learnt about feminist survival and also draw on experiences shared with me by readers. Survival is a shared project.

Why use the word *survival*? Audre Lorde shows us that for some, those who were 'never meant to survive',[1] survival is ambitious. Black feminist poet and critic Alexis Pauline Gumbs quotes Lorde's words from an edition of her essay, 'Eye to Eye', that did not make it to the final version. Lorde wrote: 'I love the word survival; it always sounds to me like a promise. It makes me wonder sometimes though, how do I define the shape of my impact upon this earth?'[2] Gumbs then repeats those words, *I love the word survival*, at the beginning and end of her own essay. Gumbs does not use quote marks around the words, *I love the word survival*, and I follow her by not using the marks. Those words, *I love the word survival*, are shared between Lorde and Gumbs, passing from one to the other. Survival can be about words that survive, words that have lives of their own. The word *survival* survives. Sometimes to survive is to pass the words on. I will return to the importance of these words in considering the feminist killjoy as poet in chapter 5. Survival here refers not only to living on, but to keeping going in the more profound sense of keeping going with one's commitments. *Feminism needs feminists to survive.* We might still need to be able to *take it*, the pressure we are put under to give up those commitments.

Feminists need feminism to survive. Feminism needs those of us who live our lives as feminists to survive; feminism survives through us. Surviving as a feminist killjoy might be how we learn to take care of ourselves, given what we keep coming up against. The word *self-care* is probably familiar; perhaps self-care conjures up images of relaxation, scented candles and bubble baths. I have nothing against scented candles or bubble baths, but that is not what I mean by self-care. The idea of self-care – or perhaps more accurately caring for oneself – has a militant Black feminist history. In *A Burst of Light*, Lorde wrote: 'Caring for myself is not self-indulgence, it is self-preservation, and that is an act of political warfare.'[3] When the world does not care for you, because of who you are, or what you do, you have to care for yourself to have any chance of survival. For some, survival is ambitious. For some, survival is protest. Lorde wrote *A Burst of Light* after she learned that her cancer had spread to her liver. The expression 'a burst of light' is used for when she came to feel the fragility of her body's situation: 'that inescapable knowledge, in the bone, of my own physical limitation'.[4] Throughout *A Burst of Light* Audre Lorde compares her experience of battling with cancer (she is willing to describe this situation *as war*) to her experience of battling against anti-Black racism. The comparison is effective, showing us how racism can be an attack on the cells of the body, on the body's immune system.

This is why, for Lorde, caring for one's self is *not* self-indulgence but self-preservation. In an article in a special issue of *Southern Atlantic Quarterly* on 'crip time', Jina B. Kim and Sami Schalk offer a nuanced interpretation of Lorde's call to care and attend to its implication for disability justice as well as racial justice. They show how Lorde herself stresses the importance not only of looking after one's body, accepting its limits, but of *learning* from the situation, being purposeful and reflective, using time 'in service of what must be done'.[5] As Kim and Schalk show, Lorde's idea of using one's time is a critique of the capitalist requirement to be more productive and a call to give one's time to the project of crafting a community; care work as *crip care*.

Why use the word *crip*? That word has a killjoy history. Feminist scholar Alison Kafer explores how the word 'crip' is a charged word. Drawing on Nancy Mairs's essay on wanting people to wince at the word, she suggests that 'this desire to make people wince suggests an urge to shake things up, to jolt people out of their everyday understandings of bodies and minds, of normalcy and deviance.'[6] To reclaim the word *crip* is to refuse to aspire to be normal, a close proxy for becoming worthy of care, or to hide disability as a source of shame and stigma, or to tell stories of disability as a weakness to be overcome through acts of individual heroism and resilience. By thinking of Lorde's legacy in terms of disability justice, Kim and Schalk enable us to 'see the connection' between self-care and 'the emergence of care collectives and online communities of sick, ill, and disabled people who share knowledge, support, and resources in order to help another survive, physically, mentally, and emotionally'.[7] Disability justice emerges out of the ordinary and practical task of navigating systems that make it harder for some people to get what they need. Disability justice is precisely what we need in these times of austerity, these pandemic times, because to think creatively about access is to build different and more liveable spaces.

Care can also be the ordinary and practical ways we look out for each other because the costs of refusing violence or protesting violence are made so high. We create 'care collectives' or communities of care. We reassemble ourselves through the painstaking work of looking after ourselves; looking after each other. I think also of LGBTQI+, that assembly of letters pointing to our assembly, how we turned up for each other. There can be survival in those letters. We might have hung out in the same bars, laughing and living, surviving the worlds that decided that our lives were lifestyles, our choices whims, our ideas false; that we were selfish or dangerous because of what or who we refused to give up. We might have marched in the same marches, recognizing something of ourselves in each other, as we fought for a world that could reflect our own images of ourselves back to ourselves; however tired, however worn, we loved what we could catch in each other's reflections. We became family because we were there for each other when we were cast out from our homes, our communities. A survival tip can also be to learn from our history. We learn each other's survival tips.

Survival can be a feminist project, a queer project, a trans project, a crip project. For some of us, to survive a world we need to transform it. But we still have to survive the world we are trying to transform. I think of my friendship with Nila Gupta, brown, Bengali, crip, chronically ill, queer, trans. Nila, like Lorde, took the risk of naming themself, of being themself. Nila took their own life on 10 June 2021 at the age of forty-six. I was writing these words on survival when Nila died. They did not survive the world; they did not get the support they needed to live their life. Nila and I would snap together, rolling our eyes at the same time, recognizing what each other recognized, what we were up against, how often it was assumed that unhappy brown queer and trans folk would be rescued from our families by happy white LBGTQI+ communities. Another queer event with all-white keynotes? Really, I mean, really? We would roll our eyes at whiteness, how it managed to keep its place, despite all our efforts.

When I shared my equation **rolling eyes = feminist pedagogy** in the previous chapter, it was not our own eyes I was referring to. But perhaps that's how survival is going to happen. The gestures directed at us acquire a different meaning for us. We take them on, turn them out. I have learnt so much from how other feminist killjoys have made use of this equation. In 2019, I gave a talk that was introduced by Christina Hajjar, a queer woman of colour. She described my equation as 'a killjoy's resistance'. She explained, 'We roll our eyes in disbelief, in pleasure, in transcendence and euphoria – our eye sockets as portals for escape.'[8] I love this description. Rolling our eyes at each other can be how we claim freedom, sharing our survival.

Still, sometimes Nila had to roll their eyes at me, a cis lesbian, for what I didn't get, for what they had to keep pointing out, like the time I organized a panel on the film *Paris is Burning*, an all-trans person of colour panel, but without any trans women. Really, Sara, I mean, really? They worked with me so I could learn to do better. I still have much to learn. We all have much to learn from each other. I dedicate these thoughts on survival to Nila.

KILLJOY SURVIVAL TIP 1: BECOME A FEMINIST KILLJOY

My first tip to surviving as a feminist killjoy is to become one. By using the word *become*, I want to stress the dynamic and social nature of that process. To become a feminist killjoy is not a private, individual affair. When you name yourself a feminist killjoy, you are relating yourself to others, hearing in a term that comes from elsewhere, that has its own history, something of yourself. In other words, the *exteriority* of the feminist killjoy matters; to become her, you take her on by taking her in. Sometimes, it can help us to keep doing what we are doing when we have a name for it. Even when we become her, the feminist killjoy remains exterior to us. That is why I sometimes describe myself as a feminist killjoy and at other times describe her as my companion.

I noted in my introduction that I have been writing about the feminist killjoys for some time. I have been a feminist killjoy for much longer. But the writing helped me to become a feminist killjoy in *another way*. How? Because by picking up the figure of the feminist killjoy, and putting her to work, I created a feedback loop. The feminist killjoy first appeared in my 2010 book, *The Promise of Happiness*. It was not until *Living a Feminist Life*, published seven years later, that I made her a central character in how I approached feminism. Since then, I have been profoundly touched by how readers picked up the figure of the feminist killjoy. One reader ended her letter by thanking me from the bottom of her 'feminist killjoy heart!' Another described how when she first read about feminist killjoys, she said to herself, 'Yep, that's me.' Another wrote, 'I am a Feminist Killjoy, and I didn't know these two words described everything I've ever been all my life.' Yet another called finding the feminist killjoy a 'rebirth'. The feminist killjoy can travel between tenses, present, past, future; giving us the words to describe who we are, who we were, who we can be.

The feminist killjoy, in providing another way of describing yourself can be another way of being yourself. There is creativity in description. And I have been struck by the creativity of feminist killjoys; readers have told me how they made use of this figure in songs and music, performance and poetry, in memoirs and notebooks. One reader wrote to me about doing a killjoy performance, in which she would kill the girl that was happy to please to create room for a 'truly killjoy girl'. Although being positioned as a feminist killjoy is difficult and painful, we make something from her or through her. Perhaps there is a link between creativity and confidence. When judgements made about us chip away at our confidence, the feminist killjoy can give us the confidence to face these judgements, to face even her as a judgement. We can find our confidence by finding her.

Becoming a feminist killjoy gives you a set of tools. When we become a problem because of what we name, we can give problems their names. I talked to a lecturer about her experience of making a complaint about sexual harassment. I was struck by how the feminist killjoy came up in her testimony. She was talking about how, in making a complaint, you become a complainer: 'In getting to that point, the complainer, you never shed it, it is like the problem child: having done it, you cannot go back.' A complaint becomes part of you, who you become, that problem child, you can't shed it; you can't shed her, having done it, made it, 'you cannot go back'. She described how becoming a complainer allows you to see more: 'It's a bit like if you complain you get extra vision. It is suddenly like you can see in ultra violet. And you can't go back.' Being able to see more, to see what is going on, is also to see what you did not see before. She added: 'The feeling of being able to name what is happening to you is very powerful.' Being able to name what is happening means you are better equipped to explain what is happening.

Being able to name what is happening brought her to the feminist killjoy. Why? Because the feminist killjoy is also about how we are changed by what we can name. She said, 'Everyone can see that now you have changed.' She hesitated and then added: 'The feminist killjoy'. We both laughed at how the feminist killjoy made an appearance. The feminist killjoy can be how we signal to others *that* we have changed as well as *how* we have changed. Becoming the feminist killjoy can be how others witness that change; I think of those eyes rolling, again. You can't shed her, not only because you cannot unknow what you know, but because of how others can see what you know. The feminist killjoy, in giving us a name for a change we see in ourselves, can be how we see a change in each other.

KILLJOY SURVIVAL TIP 2:
BECOME MORE OF A FEMINIST KILLJOY

Why is my second tip on surviving as a feminist killjoy to become more of one? I think of this as a promise: once you become a feminist killjoy, it is hard to unbecome one. Promises do not always feel promising. Becoming more of a feminist killjoy points to how we accumulate killjoy experiences. The more you are known as one, the more you will be addressed as one. We carry those experiences around with us. Perhaps we put them in a *feminist killjoy bag*. However hard each experience might have been, when we put them together, this and that, memories becoming as tangible as things, they become a resource, helping you to make sense of a difficult world.

To think of the feminist killjoy as a resource is to show how much we learn from being given this assignment. We revisit the scenes in which we became the problem (for me, that scene was the family table; for you, it might be somewhere else). We make sense not only of the scene but of ourselves, realizing that if we became the problem because of what we exposed, we were not the problem. We problematize who becomes the problem (and who does not). We come to appreciate how we can be stuck in these dynamics. Understanding dynamics does not stop us from being stuck in them. But it might stop us from feeling we are the cause of them. One reader wrote to me, 'You turned "getting in the way" from being a "life-long shameful social inadequacy" to a calling.' Even when we are still the problem, we can change our relation to being the problem; we can find in it 'a calling'. From being a feminist killjoy, we learn that we don't have to take the blame, even when we are blamed. A student emailed me: 'Reading your work has helped me to take the blame for ruining the peace off my shoulders. I feel recharged and more assured that I should chart a path of my own.' The feminist killjoy helps us to lighten our load, it can be how we recharge ourselves, finding the confidence to chart our own paths. Becoming *more* of a feminist killjoy can actually be about *lessening* our sense of guilt or blame.

Even if understanding these dynamics does not automatically free us of them, it does not mean that understanding them cannot change them. If we change our relation to the dynamics, they can change. Or if we can, they can. We might feel lighter, less weighed down by history, less guilty, less responsible, less stuck. And if we enter conversations *as* feminist killjoys, we can sometimes have conversations *about* these dynamics. An academic wrote to me, 'Your book has prompted an incredibly in-depth conversation between myself and my sister about our strict Catholic/patriarchal upbringing, my father's mental breakdown during my adolescence, when I – the youngest of three daughters – was alone at home, and many other topics, not least of which was her acknowledgement that I was the feminist killjoy in a household where there was love but active discouragement of critical or ideological discussion.' With the feminist killjoy handy, we can have conversations about how some of us are stuck in or even by these conversations. To share an acknowledgement that some have been positioned as feminist killjoys allows a loosening of the hold of a history, a reorientation to the past as well as a different understanding of present relations.

That can happen. That does not always happen. It is important for me to stress that the story of a feminist killjoy is not a progressive one – becoming more of a feminist killjoy is not about getting better at being her or about how she can lighten the weight of a history. To survive as a feminist killjoy is thus to counter the assumption that you will grow out of her. The idea that maturing out of being a feminist killjoy assumes or hopes that feminism itself, or at least being that kind of feminist, the wrong kind, the one who always insists on making feminist points, who is angry, confrontational, a complainer, is just a phase you are going through.

KILLJOY COMMITMENT: IF BEING A FEMINIST KILLJOY IS A PHASE, I AM WILLING TO REMAIN IN THAT PHASE

Perhaps some assume the feminist killjoy is a battery: eventually it will run out, or she will or you will. We can refute that assumption but still feel like we are running out of energy. Becoming *more* of a feminist killjoy is not necessarily about killing joy *more*, at least when understood as a deliberate or willed action. If anything, the more experiences you have of being a feminist killjoy, the more you know how draining it can be. You know the energy it involves to speak out or to speak back, you know that some battles are not worth your energy, because there is no chance of getting through (although, remembering Audre Lorde's letter to Mary Daly, sometimes we might judge there's a point to making the point, even when we know we won't get through). If these experiences are resources, you carry them with you, becoming more skilled at detection, learning to tell when you are being wound up by somebody who is winding you up, learning when you need to leave a table, a conversation, because if that's the point, it is not yours. Radical psychotherapist Guilaine Kinouani offers a compellingly clear articulation of why refusing to debate is a good basis for our politics as well as ethics. She draws on Toni Morrison's argument that 'the function of racism is distraction', because when you refute one racist logic you will just have to refute another because they will keep coming up with new ones. Kinouani concludes, 'Engaging in debates is a waste of time. I repeat: engaging in debates is a waste of time. But more than a waste of time, it is psychologically taxing.'[9] Refusing to enter debates that have been set up in terms we would dispute is how we take time back for ourselves to talk in our terms.

Becoming more of a feminist killjoy is also a tip about time. Sometimes, when we receive something, it can be immediate, you can feel enraged. You might write a furious letter. Write it, express yourself, give your feelings a form. But then, give yourself time before you send that letter. Send it to yourself. Wait. Stay with it. Sit with it. Read it. You might decide not to send it. Or you might decide to send it. Either way, you will be glad you gave yourself time to decide. The more experiences you have of being a feminist killjoy, the more time you take. The more time you take, the more room you have. We had to fight for that room.

KILLJOY SURVIVAL TIP 3: FIND OTHER KILLJOYS

Being a feminist killjoy can be an isolating experience. And it can be hard not to be worn down and worn out by receiving this assignment. Finding other feminist killjoys can be crucial to surviving being a feminist killjoy. If some say, don't make a fuss, don't make it bigger than it is, you need to find others who see it, get it, see you, get you.

I think this is why so many readers have shared with me their own feminist killjoy stories. It is how we do the work of the killjoy, from *I*, to *you*; to *we*. One student wrote to me about being taught *Living a Feminist Life*, 'I first read your book in 2018 in a class called Feminism in Action. We read different chapters slowly throughout the semester and by the end we were creating our own feminist toolkits. Everyone in the class had deemed themselves killjoys, and bore the title proudly.' The feminist killjoy can be a collective action, how we rename ourselves. She told me that she read the book in another class. This time, she said, she was not looking for herself in my words. She wrote that reading it, 'was like talking to a peer and friend. A friend who validated and challenged us.' The feminist killjoy can be that friend, validating, also challenging us, telling us, reminding us, that we are not alone.

Another student wrote to me about how she shared the book with friends, creating a community of killjoys: 'I have been giving it to all of my girlfriends when they had their birthdays, and slowly, we are becoming a little group of killjoys.' We might use the term *consciousness raising*, to describe the collectivity of feminist becoming. In sharing killjoy stories, you realize you are not alone, that the problems you have, others have too. Finding other feminist killjoys can be how we raise our political consciousness. It can be therapeutic to share stories of being feminist killjoys, of being the problem because of what we point out.

Being part of a collective can help us as we go through difficult experiences, trying to process what is hard to process. Another student wrote to me about her experiences of complaint. She wrote from a very painful place, giving me a trigger warning for the content she was to share. She wrote at the end of her letter, 'My killjoy shoulder is next to yours and we are a crowd. I cannot see it at the moment but I know it's there.' I love the idea of a killjoy shoulder, becoming feminist killjoys as how we lean on each other. We cannot always see a killjoy crowd. But we know it's there.

Finding other feminist killjoys can be a research project as well as a life project. I have been helped by following the feminist killjoy around, looking for her in early feminist texts. In *Living a Feminist Life*, I suggested we create our own killjoy survival kits. I included many books in mine. At the end of this handbook, you will find a recommended reading list for feminist killjoys. It includes many kick-ass books by Black feminists, Indigenous feminists and feminists of colour that have been published since I first assembled my survival kit. They are in there now, doing their thing.

There are so many books that give killjoy inspiration! There will be more books to come. There will be more books to come because we need them. *Feminists need feminism to survive*. When finding feminist killjoys is a life project and a research project, these can be the same projects. Another feminist killjoy, Rajni Shah, wrote about their experience of setting up a feminist killjoy reading group in Sydney:

Several years later, the Feminist Killjoys Reading Group continues. Now there is a core group of five who meet regularly and organize monthly events at which anyone is welcome. It is a growing community. And creating this community is one of the ways of saying: it takes work to be a killjoy, and we need each other in order to be able to continue doing this work. In order for this work to exist, part of the work needs to be the work of finding solidarity and not parcelling each other up in the process.[10]

I love how a reading group is a meeting group, a space opened for other killjoys to join. As feminists, we put ourselves out there by putting ourselves into our work. The more we put out, the more we get from each other, the more we get each other. Remember the student who wrote that the feminist killjoy gave her the two words she needed to describe herself? She also said, 'Do bear with me as I write this to you. I know you'll get it. You'll get me, and what's happened and where one might go from here. You'll understand.' If the feminist killjoy gives us words to describe ourselves, there is understanding in description. Feminist killjoys can signal that we get each other; how we get each other. What leads us to the feminist killjoy leads us to each other.

KILLJOY SURVIVAL TIP 4: LISTEN TO THE FEMINIST KILLJOY AS IF SHE IS ANOTHER PERSON

Once you become a killjoy, and thus more of a feminist killjoy, it might be tempting to think you are always the killjoy, getting in the way of other people's happiness or just getting in the way. That is not the case. You might be a feminist killjoy in one situation, but in another be part of a 'we' whose happiness is deemed under threat. If we listen *as* the feminist killjoy, we stop listening *to* the feminist killjoy. In other words, by assuming we are her, we stop hearing her. If becoming a feminist killjoy depends on her exteriority, that exteriority is also her promise.

In introducing the feminist killjoy, I noted how Black women and women of colour often kill feminist joy because of what we bring up. When we speak about racism, we are heard as interrupting the conversation, as being divisive, as if before we spoke there was unity or common purpose. One way of telling the feminist story is telling of the loss of unity, solidarity, common purpose, because of who came in later; women of colour entered the room, lesbian women entered the room, trans women entered the room. Listening to the killjoy not only as another person but as someone who is already in the room gives us a different understanding of feminist history.

Let's take as an example Avtar Brah's contribution to the Black British feminist classic *Charting the Journey: Writings by Black and Third World Women*, which was first published in 1988 by Sheba Feminist Publishers. I will return to the importance of this well-worn book in my chapter on the feminist killjoy as poet. Brah describes her experience, as an Asian woman brought up in Uganda, of going to Nairobi for the UN World Conference on Women in 1985. She gives us a snippet of feminist history.

What some of us Black and brown feminists say, cannot help but think, others might try not to know. We can go somewhere, and be confronted by history; a history can be what you sip, a snip, a snippet; history can be pre-served as consciousness of a closed door, of a door even, of what you remember because of how you were barred. (I will turn to doors and why that matters later in this handbook.) Brah talks about how she became interested in feminism – by being introduced to Nanak Singh's novels by a neighbour.

I love that story; we can find feminism because of who we happen upon, led by a person to a book, to becoming part of a movement. Brah talks about how she became involved with the Southall Black Sisters and what became known as 'Black British Feminism'. Almost a decade after *Charting the Journey* was published, Heidi Mirza edited another collec-tion of essays that took that name, *Black British Feminism*, which included new essays as well as reprints of earlier classics, many with killjoy titles, such as Valerie Amos and Pratibha Parmar's 'Challenging Imperialism Feminism' and Hazel Carby's 'White Women Listen! Black Feminism and the Boundaries of Sisterhood'. In her introduction to this collection, Mirza describes Black British feminism as a movement that 'has its genesis over 50 years ago in the activism and the struggles of black women migrants from the postcolonial Caribbean, Africa and the Indian sub-continent'.[12] Black British Feminism was a name given to the political coalition formed by women of African and Asian descent united by their opposition to imperialism and capitalist patriarchy.

Sometimes we need a name not only for what we are doing but for what we are trying to bring into being. In an interview with Pratibha Parmar and Gail Lewis published in *Charting the Journey*, Audre Lorde reflects on the significance of the title of that book, '*Charting the Journey*, that's what you mean, isn't it? How we do we get from there to here? What you chart is already where you've been. But where we are going, there is no chart yet. We are brave and daring and we are looking ahead.'[13] *Charting the Journey* and *Black British Feminism* remain vital and important collections as they tell us something about where we have been and the struggles we have had to get here. In this interview, Lorde also comments on different uses of the term 'Black'. She says, 'our solutions are different. Take the issue of how we name ourselves, for example. In the United States, Black means of African heritage and we use the term Women of Color to include Native American, Latina, Asian-American women. I understand that, here, Black is a political term which includes all oppressed ethnic groups and Women of Color is frowned upon.'[14] I think that if we are to look ahead as bravely and with as much daring as we can, we might need to recognize that the use of Black as a political term is no longer tenable for many reasons, including the fact of continued anti-Black racism in Asian communities and because the experience of colonization by Britain does not provide a common reference point for all ethnic minority peoples in the UK.

To say *political blackness* is no longer tenable is not to suggest that the contestation over the term *Black* is recent. *How* it was embraced in the past might just have made it harder to hear the contestation. If it has become more difficult for some of us to know how to name ourselves, I understand that situation not as a loss but as another reason to be in conversation with each other about how to speak to and of each other. I know from these conversations that many do not want to use the terms that come from policy such as BME (Black and Minority Ethnic) or BAME (Black, Asian and Minority Ethnic), which are typically read out as acronyms, because of how they are *used more to do less*, how they avoid the trouble of race. You might have noticed that in this handbook I sometimes use the term *person of colour* and, at other times, *brown people*. If a problem with the former term is that implication that whiteness is neutral, an absence of colour, a problem with the latter is that it can be used to create a problematic parallelism to Black (this is why I have chosen not to capitalize *brown* to acknowledge but by no means resolve this problem). Ruby Hamad makes the point pragmatically: 'the lack of better terms necessitates their use at times'.[15]

The practical is theoretical. Returning to Brah, the practical difficulties she describes in her article about how to meet, how to organize, are feminist insights, how she is *doing* feminist theory. Brah shares a feminist memory:

> As a research student in Bristol in the 1970s when white women started organizing around women's gender oppression, I remember going to some consciousness raising sessions. But there was no room in this 'consciousness' for dealing with an Asian woman's experience in Britain. I attended the first national feminist conference organized by the white women's movement. There were only two other Black women there. In the workshop, we, the Black women, argued that feminist demands must be anti-racist, but the woman who reported back on the workshop, a feminist journalist, did not say a word about this at the plenary session We felt angry but being in such a minority we remained silent. After this experience I drifted away from consciousness raising groups.[16]

Avtar Brah is referring here to the 1973 Women's Liberation Conference held in Bristol. We learn from this story how you can become a Black or brown feminist killjoy, making that point, that anti-racism must be a core feminist demand, and be blanked. And so, we had to keep making that same demand. If our demands were included, it would change the nature of these demands. The first four demands produced by the Women's Liberation Movement conferences in the 1970s were for equal pay, equal educational and job opportunities, abortion on demand and free nurseries. These were demands *to* the state. If anti-racism had been included as a demand, we would demand a critique *of* the state. You cannot add our demands without changing them.

Our demands disappeared because we did. Blanking is teaching us something about how feminism became 'white feminism'. The word *blank* comes from white. Feminism became white not because Black and brown women were not there, speaking, knowing, creating, as feminists, but because we were blanked, *not recorded as being there.*

KILLJOY EQUATION: WHITE FEMINISM = BLANKING

For feminism to survive we need to recover this Black and brown feminist killjoy lineage, to hear our voices as a record, however broken. When snap is a moment with a history, to snap is to recover that history. A recovery is work. In my introduction, I described this handbook as a handle because it can help to know that others have been where we are. It can take a political effort to know where others have been because of how so many killjoys have been blanked. Feminist survival is thus also about relating differently to killjoys, listening out for them, knowing they were already there, at that event, part of the proceedings rather than arriving at some later point. It also means that if our research project, also life project, is to find other killjoys, we might have to look in the margins of so many feminist books.

There is more to it. When they do not record us, what we said, that we were there, we might end up removing ourselves from feminist spaces ('I drifted away from consciousness groups'). What is the point in being in those spaces if no one is listening to you? Another way of putting this is: some of us become strangers in feminism, drifting away from some of the spaces in which feminism happens. In one of my early books, *Strange Encounters*, I suggested that the stranger is not somebody we don't recognize, which is how we are taught to think of the stranger, but somebody we recognize (as a stranger). To be recognized as a stranger is to be seen as not from here or not belonging here, a 'body out of place'.[17] I will return later in the handbook to how those who are 'out of place' are seen as suspicious or dangerous. When we become strangers we end up in the edges of rooms, as well as conversations, not part of us, not like us, not with us.

To become a stranger is sometimes a matter of feeling, which is why the killjoy is often a stranger, estranged from a group. Listen to the following description from bell hooks:

> *a group of white feminist activists who do not know one another may be present at a meeting to discuss feminist theory. They may feel they are bonded on the basis of shared womanhood, but the atmosphere will noticeably change when a woman of colour enters the room. The white women will become tense, no longer relaxed, no longer celebratory.*[18]

A woman of colour just has to enter the room for the atmosphere to become tense. Atmospheres – they seem intangible, mostly. But when you become the cause of tension, an atmosphere can be experienced as a wall. The woman of

66

colour comes to be felt as apart from the group, getting in the way of a presumably organic solidarity. Think back to Avtar Brah's story, how her demands were not recorded. There are many ways we can be removed from the conversation. That removal creates a *feeling* of unity. That some feminist spaces are experienced as more unified might be a measure of how many are missing from them.

Atmospheric walls are tangible to those who are stopped by them. Blanking can also be about a bond ('they may feel they are bonded on the basis of shared womanhood'), which means blanking can also be a wall, noticeable to those who are missing. *Some had to insist that they were women.* We can think of Sojourner Truth, speaking as a Black woman and former slave, at the Women's Convention in Akron, Ohio, in 1851 saying, 'Ain't I a Woman?'[19] As Angela Davis notes, Truth in her speech referred to the strength of her own body, her labouring body, to challenge the 'weaker sex' arguments made against the suffragettes.[20] *Some had to insist that they were not women.* We can think of Monique Wittig, speaking as a lesbian feminist to the Modern Language Association conference in New York in 1978, saying, 'Lesbians are not women'.[21] This audacious claim was necessary for Wittig to show how the very category of *women* has historically functioned as a heterosexual injunction, how *women* came to exist, or were required to exist, in relation to men. To notice who records the conversation and who is missing from it is to learn how bonds can be binds. The word *women* too can be a bind as well as bond, a record of who is missing from the conversation.

67

KILLJOY SURVIVAL TIP 5: LET THE FEMINIST KILLJOY GO

It might be assumed that feminist survival depends upon holding onto terms such as 'women', as if without those terms being held tightly we would lose each other. To listen to the feminist killjoy, to give her a history, is to challenge that assumption. This also means that for feminism to survive, and I am referring here to the survival of a movement, we need to let the feminist killjoy go. I remember one time when a white feminist was called out for her use of racist language. She responded by claiming these criticisms were only directed at her because she was a 'difficult woman' with 'controversial opinions'. Holding on to the feminist killjoy, by claiming that opposition to your work is just because you are her, could function similarly, as a method for deflecting critique.

Feminist survival might depend upon loosening our attachments to our terms, including those that help make sense of our struggle. We can return to Audre Lorde's reflections on survival. She writes:

> *Those of us who stand outside the circle of this society's definition of acceptable women; those of us who have been forged in the crucibles of difference – those of us who are poor, who are lesbians, who are Black, who are older – know that survival is not an academic skill. It is learning how to stand alone, unpopular and sometimes reviled, and how to make common cause with those others identified as outside the structures in order to define and seek a world in which*

we can all flourish. It is learning to take our differences and
make them strengths.[22]

Lorde is suggesting that those who are least supported by existing structures are those who will be most inventive, because, for them, survival is 'not an academic skill', but a profoundly practical and urgent task. What follows her description is her famous line, '*The master's tools will never dismantle the master's house.*' Lorde is telling us something about feminist survival, and again, I am referring here not just to our own survival but the survival of a movement. Feminism can only survive as a movement if it is led by those for whom survival is not an academic skill but a struggle to exist on their own terms. The killjoy teaches us (as does Lorde) that these struggles are *internal* to feminism because some women are not seen as acceptable women by other women. When some women say to other women they do not accept them as women, they are not dismantling the master's house but becoming the master's tool.

This is why I want to name the problems of transphobia as well as racism as a matter of feminist survival. Take 'gender critical' feminism as an example. In the UK, 'gender critical' feminism has invested in the category of sex (defined more or less explicitly as real, material, immutable, biological), rather than gender and gender identity (defined more or less explicitly as cultural, immaterial as well as a matter of 'personal feeling'). A story often told both by some 'gender critical' feminists and the mainstream media is that feminists are being stopped from using the terms *sex* or *women* because of the agenda of trans activists and their misguided feminist allies. In my chapter on the feminist killjoy as activist, I will return to how 'gender critical' feminists often inflate the power of trans activists whilst minimizing the harms of transphobia. Perhaps some 'gender critical' feminists might imagine they are the feminist killjoys around the table, having to insist that sex matters. They are not. If anything, they have taken the place of the patriarchal father, because of how they use terms like sex, biology, nature or even reality, as if they are unproblematic. Feminists have *always* disagreed on these terms. Our task is *always* to problematize them.

By listening to the feminist killjoy as another person we learn not only that the category of *women* has always been disputed, but so too has *gender,* so too has *sex.* Let's take as an example the work of the feminist sociologist Ann Oakley. Her classic *Sex, Gender and Society* certainly made use of the sex–gender distinction, drawing on the work of psychiatrist Robert Stoller, with sex referring to biological differences, visible difference of genitalia and difference in procreative function, and gender referring to 'a matter of culture' and the social classification of people into 'masculine' and 'feminine'.[23] However, in Oakley's later work, she offers a strong critique of this very distinction: 'The distinction between sex and gender does not call into question how society constructs the natural body itself.'[24] Oakley suggests that to question how gender is constructed without questioning sex itself does not go far enough, given that gender helps to create the naturalness of sex. Or take the work of historical materialist Christine Delphy, who argues that 'gender precedes sex'. She explains: 'We have continued to think of gender in terms of sex: to see it as a social dichotomy determined by a natural dichotomy.'[25] If gender creates the effect of two distinct and immutable biological sexes, to make that effect our cause would reproduce the system we are trying to dismantle. Even feminist traditions sometimes assumed to be untroubled by the category of sex, such as radical feminism, have in fact been so. Andrea Dworkin's *Woman Hating*, for instance, offers a radical feminist critique of what she calls 'the traditional biology of sexual difference' based on 'two discrete biological sexes'.[26]

These critiques of the category of *sex* come from a wide range of feminist traditions. And they have been erased for a reason. Gender is turned into a stranger (yes, a category of thought can be treated as a stranger), as if it comes from the outside or from outsiders, an imposition on nature or biological reality. Women become *natal women*. The transformation of gender into the stranger allows *sex* to be positioned as *nature* or *natal* or even as *native*, as if all these categories are not themselves the product of labour, as if we do not have a hand in making and shaping them.

When the category of gender becomes a stranger, those who are assumed to rely on that category for their existence become strangers too. The use of terms such as *natal women* or *adult human female* are then used to exclude trans women from feminism, from the shelters and centres we created together to survive sexual violence, domestic violence, gender-based violence. If feminism is to survive as

71

a radical project, a project with a commitment to ending violence, we must refuse to use categories in this way. Perhaps if those 'outside the circle of this society's definition of acceptable women', to use Lorde's terms, were those whose theories of sex and gender mattered, heard for how they were interrogating the terms, questioning what was acceptable, we would not be here, having to do this, having to say this. But that is where we are.

Our terms are always provisional and contestable. A feminism that is too confident in its own terms or that places its own terms outside of history has already cost us so much. And so, if finding the feminist killjoy can be how we find our confidence, she also teaches us why we sometimes need to lose it. Yes, there can be strength in claiming the killjoy; we become part of a long line, a lineage, however hidden, or broken. We have to make sure that strength is not turned too quickly into conviction, leading us to become less sensitive to how we could be positioning other feminists as killjoys, getting in the way of our happiness, our occupation of space. In listening to the feminist killjoy, we might hear uncomfortable truths, difficult truths, **killjoy truths**, about ourselves. And so, we learn: activism might need us to lose confidence in ourselves, letting ourselves recognize how we too can be the problem. That can be hard if we have had a lifetime of being the problem.

KILLJOY SURVIVAL TIP 6: KNOW IT IS NOT ALWAYS UP TO YOU

Sometimes it might seem you have a choice, killing joy or not killing joy, saying something or not saying something. But killing joy can have nothing to do with what we say or do. It can be a relief to know that whether or not we kill joy is not always up to us. Recall bell hooks's description of what happens when a woman of colour enters a feminist meeting. For women of colour, turning up can be enough to bring race up. We don't have to say anything to cause tension.

This is not to say that sometimes we don't try to avoid causing tension. I began my academic career as a lecturer in Women's Studies. I remember one time I was in a taxi in Adelaide. I had just travelled from England. I was tired. The taxi driver asked me what I do. I said I was a lecturer. When he asked, in a friendly way, 'What do you teach?' I hesitated. I was used to strong reactions when I said I taught Women's Studies. Here are some more memorable reactions shared with me or directed at me: 'Women's Studies, I fancy a bit of that', 'Women's Studies, what do you teach, how to iron clothes?', 'You can study anything at university these days.' When you challenge sexism, sexism is the reaction to what you challenge. That *loop* is the life of a killjoy; we know it well. This time, I just couldn't be bothered to go there, so I said I taught Sociology. It turned out he had a very strong reaction to Sociology! Listening to what he said about sociologists, I laughed. My laughter was directed towards myself. I was laughing because I was learning how trying to wriggle out of something can get you back into it. We can't always wriggle out of being a feminist killjoy.

KILLJOY TRUTH: YOU CAN'T ALWAYS CHOOSE BATTLES; BATTLES CAN CHOOSE YOU

Learning means ending up somewhere unexpected. Sometimes, the feminist killjoy can be a place, can be what is unexpected. Sometimes, not arriving at that place can be what is unexpected. Sometimes when I said, 'I teach Women's Studies', and waited for *that* reaction, I was met instead with curiosity and interest. People can be surprising. And so, over time, despite my accumulated memories of being a feminist killjoy, or perhaps because of them (*Killjoy Survival Tip 2: Become more of a feminist killjoy*), I am less sure I will be met with the same old reaction. It is good to be less sure. I noted in my introduction how feminists are assumed to oppose something because they are being oppositional. I oppose this use of oppositional! But it is also important not to assume that all that we encounter will confirm what we oppose. If we make that assumption, we can stop an encounter from happening, the chance of it, the surprise in it. If I do encounter *that* reaction, the same old, same old, not only do I recognize it, I know how to explain it.

Knowing that we can kill joy without saying anything can free us from some burdens. We are not always responsible for how we are received. We don't have to try to change our words or soften our appearance or make ourselves seem smaller as if by doing that or being that we will no longer have that effect. To open up spaces we cannot not killjoy, that is, get in the way of how the space is being occupied. Yes, sometimes, we cause tension. This is not surprising. *Social change is tense.*

KILLJOY SURVIVAL TIP 7:
REMEMBER THERE IS ONLY SO MUCH YOU CAN DO

Even when you have achieved feminist consciousness, consciousness can still be hard. Simply put, it can be hard to be conscious of what is hard. It can be a problem to be conscious of a problem. Feminist consciousness can feel like being *on* is the default position: you are always turned on. It can be exhausting being on, which means sometimes we might switch off. *Feminism needs feminists to survive.* I have already suggested that a survival tip is a tip about time. In time, we learn to take time out. Time out *from* being a killjoy is necessary *for* a killjoy. Even when you claim her, she is not all you are, or all you do.

The histories that bring us to feminism are the histories that leave us fragile. There is trauma here. Many of us have experienced violence growing up, or experience violence still, because of where we are, who we are, what we want. To be traumatized is to hold a history in a body. You can be easily shattered. You might not be ready to take something

75

on because if you were shattered, you would not be able to put yourself back together again. Be careful, be cautious about what you take on, when you take it on.

KILLJOY TRUTH: THERE IS ONLY SO MUCH YOU CAN TAKE ON BECAUSE THERE IS ONLY SO MUCH YOU CAN TAKE IN

Our bodies speak to us. Your body might tell you it is not coping with what you are asking; and you need to listen. I used to have what I called 'the Dean's neck'. Every time, I met with the Dean who was behind a series of decisions that led to the closure of a Women's Studies degree to which I had been deeply committed, I would get the same pain in my neck. I would have to hold my neck in the middle of the meeting because it felt like my head was falling off. One time, much later, I met with a different Dean at a different university – I was being considered for a job – and I got that same pain in the neck. My body was telling me something. That I couldn't do that. That I couldn't go there. In this case, I didn't go there, although I suspect it wasn't only my neck that made the decision!

It is not always clear what our bodies are telling us. And we can't always follow their instructions. But we can keep listening. Our bodies often know something before we do. Sometimes, we put aside what is too painful, too close to the bone. That is why **killjoy truths** are often felt first in our bones. I have spoken to so many people about how their

bodies expressed the pain or trauma of a fight for existence –
from necks, backs, to legs, hands or skin.

KILLJOY TRUTH: WHEN YOU HAVE TO FIGHT FOR
EXISTENCE, FIGHTING CAN BECOME AN EXISTENCE

We need room to exist. And so, we learn not to expect too
much from ourselves or from others. I think of a student
who wrote to me about her experience of complaining
about harassment. She said,

> I felt tremendous guilt for 'not doing more', for having stayed
> there for so long, for having not stood up for myself enough.
> These are feelings I'm still dealing with, but reading your book
> has tremendously helped me deal with this guilt and see it from
> another perspective. To find less anger with myself, and more
> with the job I was at, and the culture in general that allowed all
> those things to happen.

From being a feminist killjoy, we learn that if we don't get
very far, or we don't get through, that is not a sign of our
failure, but a measure of how much we are up against. We
begin to change our relationship to what we do, to value
what might seem like small things. We learn to be suspicious of scale; something might be a big thing to one
person but be disregarded by another as slight or light.

Scale matters not only in perceptions of wrongs but in perceptions of opportunities for change. I think again of Lorde's

work; I am always learning from Lorde. She suggested that we be 'vigilant for the smallest opportunity to make a change'.[27] She is talking about revolution in talking about these smallest opportunities. By asking us to be 'vigilant for the smallest opportunity', Lorde is addressing *you* directly: do what you can, when you can, where you can. Opportunities for change can be closed like windows. To be a feminist killjoy is about looking for those openings, however small, when you might be able to say something, do something, get through to someone. Only so much can matter so much.

Looking after yourself can require stopping or stepping back when it is too much. Write yourself some permission notes – we might call these *no notes* – notes that say, sorry, I can't do that or sorry, I am not going to be able to make it. It can help to give yourself permission to say *no* to something before you are asked to do it. You might decide *not* to have that conversation with that person because of what happened before. You might decide *not* to fight for a programme because it is taking too much out of you. Or you might decide, like I did, to leave your post and profession. I will say more about why I resigned in my chapter on the feminist killjoy as activist. Let me say this here (as it's a question of survival), I resigned in protest at the failure of my institution to address sexual harassment as an institutional problem. I also resigned because I had just had enough: I couldn't do it any more, fighting so hard not to get very far.

That I could resign depended upon having material resources, security and another career path available to me as a writer, a feminist killjoy writer (maybe *this* handbook

78

is a product of *that* no!). But it did still feel like I was going out on a limb: I was leaving not only a job, an institution, but also a life I had loved and was used to. Resignation can sound passive, even fatalistic, as if you are just holding up your hands and resigning yourself to your fate. But resignation can be an act of feminist protest. By going you are saying: I will not work for an organization that is not addressing the problem of sexual harassment. By going you are saying: I will not reproduce what I cannot bear.

Resigning or leaving is not about giving up your projects but refusing to give them up, to give too much of yourself, your time, energy and labour, to what takes you away from them.

KILLJOY SURVIVAL TIP 8:
FEEL EVERYTHING INCLUDING KILLJOY JOY

If we become feminists because we are unhappy with the world, our unhappiness is a judgement about the world. Unhappiness can still be a feeling. That feeling is not an obligation. You might be pleased to know this: to be a feminist killjoy is not to be obliged to feel unhappy! We do, however, live with the assumption that we are unhappy. You do not need to counter that assumption by trying to show you are happy – that pressure to be happy can distance you from how you feel and can even make you unhappy. I will return to the pressures of happiness in the next chapter. The feminist killjoy is rather how we diagnose that assumption of feminist unhappiness. The feminist killjoy is close kin to the humourless feminist: the ones who cannot or will not get the joke.

We know from experience that when people keep making light of things there is something heavy going on. We refuse to laugh at sexist jokes; remember, that's a **killjoy maxim**. We refuse to laugh when jokes are not funny. In introducing the feminist killjoy, I differentiated laughing *at* something from laughing *it off*. We might laugh at something or in recognition of something, the absurdity of this world. I think of the time a diversity practitioner told me of when her friend asked, 'Are they related?' to a photo they were looking at of her management team. They were all white men. How we laughed at that question. When we see something that is so often reproduced by not being seen – how institutions reproduce themselves to create an impression of likeness, of sameness – it can be such a relief. Laughter can be how we bring something out, a shared experience, a pattern, a structure, *so it can be laughed at.* To laugh at something can be simultaneously to make something more real, to magnify it, and to reduce its power or hold over you.

Being a feminist killjoy is not necessarily about feeling bad, but it is about feeling. Feminist killjoys are often judged for being too emotional, letting our feelings get in the way of our judgement, or simply letting our feelings get in the way. It is not surprising, then, that feelings can be the site of rebellion. We might be angry, and that anger is directed *at* something. That anger is, as Audre Lorde describes, 'loaded with information and energy'.[28] But you might then be dismissed as being angry, an angry Black woman, an angry woman of colour. If our anger tells us something about what is wrong, our anger does not make us right. To assume our anger as right would turn anger into righteousness.

Our anger not only tells us something is wrong, or something about what is wrong, it gives us the energy to take it on. We are *on it*. But it is not only anger that gives us energy. In my book *The Cultural Politics of Emotion*, I considered wonder and hope as well as anger as crucial to the journey into feminism. Wonder can be how we marvel at the world as it takes shape; we might wonder at the form of social gathering, the shape of the family, say, or the couple, that curious form, wonder about whether we can gather in different ways. Hope gives us a sense that another world is possible or that there is a point to a struggle. That is not all there is to say about the politics of hope. My killjoy heart beats faster when I read Chelsea Watego's injunction to 'fuck hope', because she recognizes, as an Indigenous feminist living 'another day in the colony', another day, every day, how hope can be used to distract people from the violence of the present in an empty promise of what is to come, a 'change without change'.[29] To make change possible might require us to be angry about how change itself can be used to distance us from what we need to do *now*.

What makes us joyful, gives us pleasure, lightens our load, now, still matters. There can be energy (also learning) in living otherwise, being otherwise, inhabiting our bodies differently, by not trying to take up less space, by standing

81

our ground, or by taking our bodies back, 'our bodies, our-selves', to use the title of an old feminist book. I did not just put *books* in my survival kit. I put *bodies* in it. And I put *life* in it. To survive as a feminist killjoy is to find out what you need to live your feminist life. I think of the air we breathe, the food, how we nourish ourselves, how we carry our pasts, the smell of spices. I think also of who we need, our friends, our companions. I think of my survival and I think of Mulka, the horse who came into my life when I was a child, who gave me somewhere else to go, somewhere to be safe, and I think of Poppy and Bluebell, our precious dogs, what a joy it is to be their human, to walk with them.

It is not just that our bodies tell us the limits of what we can do, although they do that. It is through our bodies that *we do what we can*. We talk. We walk. We dance. I think of the Lesbian Lives conferences I have attended over the years; we talked so much, but the dancing is what I remember. I danced with my friend Nila at those conferences, dancing can be *queer*, also *crip*, how we move together in our different bodies. Nim Ralph in a beautiful memorial to Nila describes their dancing: 'Nila, committed to find-ing the joy of embodied movement and collective sweat, was the master of adapted dancing. I'd often look across a dance floor and see them expertly vibing in a chair, or making shapes assisted by their stick, frequently adding a point of leverage from the wall.'[30] Dancing can be how we throw ourselves into proximity with others, making queer shapes by reusing the technologies some of us need to assist a passage through our world. Or we might think of the anarchist Emma Goldman's famous statement: 'I won't join your revolution if I cannot dance.' She affirms the freedom to dance when she is told by a young boy 'with a solemn face' that 'it did not behove an agitator to dance'.[31] Goldman dances. And in dancing, she affirms dance as the affective rebellion from the requirement to be solemn. We become affect aliens not just when we do not participate in happiness, when we do not laugh in the right places, but also by being joyful when we are supposed to be sad or solemn. Perhaps we are told we are being silly. If the feminist killjoy is easily understood as too sad or too solemn, she might also be understood as silly. Silly originally meant blessed, happy or blissful. The word mutated over time; from blessed to pious, to innocent, to harmless, to pitiable, to weak and feeble. Yes, the word *silly* has a killjoy history.[32]

The figure of the feminist killjoy has so much to teach us about social feeling or shared feeling. This might seem surprising: the feminist killjoy might appear as an *anti-social figure*, pushing against others, that flow of human traffic. It is because the feminist killjoy teaches us to be cautious about the idealization of social experience that she models a different understanding of the social. We do not treat divisions as evidence of the failure of a social bond, what needs to be overcome if we are to be with each other, but as part of social experience, how we learn from each other. Proximity is sometimes offered as a solution to social antagonism, as if by getting closer, we would be as one. Proximity is not a solution but a situation. We are not fully present to each other, just as we are not fully present to ourselves.

The social nature of feelings makes them all the more complicated. To be an affect alien is to give these complications our full attention. We know the restrictions of the requirement to feel the same way that other people feel, or to feel joyful or sad at the 'right' moments. That does not mean we don't know the value of having other people to celebrate with us when things are going well or to be sad with us when they are not. We also know how some people might justify their distance from others, those who seem sad, are deemed sad, out of fear their sadness is contagious. We might hear that old expression *misery loves company* with concern, keeping our sadness to ourselves to protect our companions. That feelings are shared is how some end up more isolated. We learn to listen to other people's sadness, trying not to become sad ourselves, or at least trying not to appear so, to give other people room to express their sadness without being weighed down by concern it will travel. We learn to listen to our own sadness. We might call someone up because we want to be cheered up. Or we might experience someone's effort to cheer us up as pressure as if there is an acceptable amount of time to be sad or to grieve and we have gone beyond it. And so, in time, we learn to give each other time to explain what we need. We don't always get it right. We don't always get each other. Even if we share a killjoy project, or because we share it, we are aware of our differences.

To survive as a feminist killjoy is to make a commitment to the survival of other feminist killjoys. We don't try to smooth things over. We bump into each other. Solidarity is a bumpy ride. Two of the most-cited sentences from my own work are about solidarity. Let me share them again here:

Solidarity does not assume that our struggles are the same struggles, or that our pain is the same pain, or that our hope is for the same future. Solidarity involves commitment, and work, as well as the recognition that even if we do not have the same feelings, or the same lives, or the same bodies, we do live on common ground.[33]

To be in solidarity is not to be in the same place even when we cover the same ground. Solidarity has to be achieved, not assumed. In other words, solidarity requires changing our relation to killjoys. *They arrive before we do.*

There can be joy in arrival, joy in survival. We can return to Rajni Shah's description of setting up a feminist killjoy reading group. They wrote about survival: 'The other day, I spent time with some of the killjoys reflecting on the work we have done so far. One of the reflections was: We have survived. We took this as celebration. Survival as celebration. We all knew what this meant. To have continued, to have survived, means we are doing the work.' When we celebrate, when we are joyful, do we cease to killjoy? No. Joy too is part of killjoy survival, without any question. We need joy to survive killing joy. We find joy in killing joy. I think of all the letters sent to me by feminist killjoys, how we reached each other. I think of what I have learnt from picking the figure of the feminist killjoy up all those years ago, and putting her to work. When I think these thoughts I feel *killjoy*

joy. Perhaps we find *killjoy joy* in resistance, *killjoy joy* in combining our forces, *killjoy joy* in experimenting with life, opening up how to be, who to be, through each other, with each other. *Killjoy joy* is its own special kind of joy.

And finally, if I have given you some tips on how to survive being a feminist killjoy, let me affirm again that being a feminist killjoy can be how we survive. Reclaiming the feminist killjoy sounds empowering and energizing. *And it can be.* Reclaiming that figure sounds tiring, difficult and painful. *And it can be.* The feminist killjoy teaches us that these are not two different stories of feminism, one about empowerment and self-actualization, energy and hope, the other about pain, exhaustion and difficulty, but *two sides of the same story.* We are empowered and energized not by keeping our distance from what is painful, but by working through it, acquiring a clearer, sharper sense of who we are and of the world we want. *Killing joy is a world-making project.* It is what we show (the feminist killjoy as cultural critic), how we know (the feminist killjoy as philosopher), what we make (the feminist killjoy as poet); what we break (the feminist killjoy as activist). It is to these different ways of approaching killing joy as a world-making project that I now turn.

3/ The Feminist Killjoy as Cultural Critic

In introducing the feminist killjoy, I placed her where we often become her, around a table in the middle of a heated argument. Thinking of the feminist killjoy as cultural critic might seem to place her somewhere else, perhaps in a chair observing a film or object of some kind from a distance. But when the feminist killjoy becomes a cultural critic, she ends up at that table in the middle of yet another heated conversation.

I remember having one of these conversations about the film *Kramer vs. Kramer* (1979, dir. Robert Benton). The plot of the film is summarized thus: 'After his wife leaves him, a work-obsessed Manhattan advertising executive is forced to learn long-neglected parenting skills, but a heated custody battle over the couple's young son deepens the wounds left by the separation.' After seeing the film with my family, I remember questioning how the wife and mother was demonized, how her desires were presented as selfish. I made that point, that rather obvious feminist point. And then, the noise, the noise! 'Oh, can't you just let us enjoy this lovely, sweet film?', 'Oh, can't you see how special the relationship is between the father and son, those scenes over breakfast, how touching!', 'Oh, how cruel the mother is, to abandon them both and then expect to get custody of her child!' That first utterance is an explanation of what follows, to raise questions about how women are portrayed is deemed as not *allowing* other people to enjoy that portrayal. What is it about enjoyment that it is so dependent on other people giving their permission, so precarious that it can be dislodged even by a question? The feminist killjoy as cultural critic appears as the one who asks questions, or offers full-blown critiques, intended to stop others from just enjoying something.

Of course, we might reply that you can criticize something and still enjoy it. Or we might reply that if enjoyment requires not engaging fully with something, then enjoyment is superficial. To idealize something ('that lovely, sweet film') can be to miss so much that is in it. The feminist killjoy as cultural critic can say more because she is willing to question what is enjoyable. We learn about the politics of enjoyment from how the feminist killjoy turns up. When enjoyment is framed as *innocent*, the feminist killjoy appears as the loss of innocence. Feminist film critic Judith Mayne gives an account of her experience of going to see *Kramer vs. Kramer*:

> *Like most people at the movie theatre, I was invested in* Kramer
> vs. Kramer, *that is, I was intrigued by the film, moved at the*
> *appropriate moments. But by the time the house lights had come*
> *on at the film's conclusion, I began to think that I had been had.*
> *What interests me is that precise moment when, my nose still*
> *runny from that emotional investment, I say: This is appalling.*

I have just 'embraced' a film, and then there comes the moment
of disavowal. I suspect that the 'embrace' and the 'disavowal'
are, for many women viewers – feminists included – more inti-
mately connected than most of us realize.[1]

It can come to you in a moment. Whilst your nose is 'still runny', you realize you have been manipulated into feeling that way. For Mayne, that 'moment of disavowal' does not cancel out the previous embrace, but is 'intimately connected' with it. This intimate connection is a source of ambivalence; feelings that seem to take you in different directions, feeling appalled by how you are feeling moved, coexist in the same person. The arrival of the feminist killjoy can be a complication and a feeling of complication.

To be a feminist killjoy thus does not mean you no longer feel joy in relation to objects you question or critique. The feminist killjoy might be connected to what feminist author Roxane Gay calls 'the bad feminist'. In her moving account of her own feminist trajectory, Gay describes how she initially disavowed feminism because she assumed that to be a feminist would require giving up what she wanted: 'I had it in my head that I could not both be a feminist and be sexually open.' For Gay, being a bad feminist is messy: it is about questioning dubious gender politics whilst also enjoying music that has a dubious gender politics. Gay 'dances her ass off to music she knows, she *knows*, is terrible for women'.[2] I admire how Gay stresses what she *knows* as a feminist. You can know something is problematic without avoiding it. You can know something is problematic and enjoy it. To be a feminist killjoy is not to be positioned above or beyond what you question. When the lights are turned on, or when you hear the lyrics, you can still be hit by what you know. When you reflect back on what you are moved by, putting the stress on knowledge as Gay does, you learn more about it. To kill joy is how we learn about joy.

My final killjoy survival tip was **to feel everything**. Becoming a feminist killjoy critic often begins with feeling; we do not feel what others feel or we do not feel as we are supposed to feel. That's how we end up thinking about feelings, turning them into a resource. To turn feelings into a resource is to turn not inwards but outwards, *towards things.* We look more closely at something because we are not affected in the 'same' way or the 'right' way. This is why being a feminist killjoy can be thought of as a skill set. If we begin with a visceral reaction – a no, a questioning, an indignation, a refusal – in time, we learn to *explain that reaction.* Sometimes we explain that reaction by finding the feminist killjoy herself, who often appears in a story as an obstacle to its happy ending. In this chapter, I begin with a consideration of the narrative function of the feminist killjoy before turning to offer a sustained meditation on happiness, how it is turned into a story we tell about ourselves. We become feminist killjoy critics when we show what is removed from that story.

I rewatched *Kramer vs. Kramer* whilst writing this handbook. It felt rather like returning to the family table. And in rewatching it, I realized that Joanna Kramer is positioned as a feminist killjoy not simply because her unhappiness causes the break-up of a marriage and a family, but because her unhappiness is *explicitly* associated with feminism. I had not remembered that association, despite the arguments I had with my family, so many years ago!

In the film, there are minor references to feminism, but these are, in plot terms, major. Ted arrives home; Joanna says she is leaving him. He is angry, he has just had success at work, he was expecting a celebration. Joanna has a friend, a neighbour called Margaret. If the film starts with Joanna leaving, walking out of the door of the apartment, walking out on Ted, it is Margaret who gives Ted the reasons why. Margaret says, 'Joanna is a very, very unhappy woman.' Margaret also witnesses Ted's reactions; his response to Joanna leaving enacts the reasons she is leaving, making her departure a matter of how it affects him, how it deprives him of a celebration. When Ted explains to his boss the reason Joanna left him, he refers to Margaret: 'She got this from Margaret you know they [makes reference to chatter with a hand gesture], women's lib.' If Joanna is positioned as a killjoy, if her unhappiness has stopped her from caring for Ted's happiness, she has been infected, it is implied, by Margaret, and through Margaret, by feminism. Feminism is presented as infection, what causes misery to spread.

KILLJOY MAXIM: BECOME A FEMINIST INFECTION!

The figure of the feminist friend is thus pivotal. And, by the end of the film, Margaret has a conversion. It is she who listens to Ted; who becomes sympathetic to him. If Margaret is pulled from a concern with Joanna's unhappiness to Ted's happiness, that is how our sympathies too are pulled.

Despite pulling us away from Joanna, the film does give her a story, in glimpses. The glimpses are offered as speeches, the first of which is delivered to Ted, the second of which is delivered to the court in the custody case. When she and Ted have their first meeting, when she tells him she loves her son, she has a speech prepared: 'All my life I felt like somebody's wife, somebody's mother or somebody's daughter.' It is a serious speech about how women disappear by becoming relatives. It is also a killjoy speech about how caring for his happiness is predicated on her disappearance. It is Ted who 'loses it', throwing a glass against a wall. We hear it shatter. To hear it shatter can be to hear more than the sound of a glass breaking. Words can shatter, things too, relationships also.

There is so much you are not supposed to say if the project is to keep things together, to hold us together. And in fact, it was because of Meryl Streep's intervention in the telling of the story that we even have that much of Joanna's story. Streep had to fight for a different script, which meant in practice fighting the men who had control of the script, to offer even glimpse of another story:

When Dustin [Hoffman] asked her what she thought of the story, she told him in no uncertain terms. They had the character all wrong, she insisted. Her reasons for leaving Ted are too hazy. We should understand why she comes back for custody.

> *When she gives up Billy in the final scene, it should be for the*
> *boy's sake, not hers. Joanna isn't a villain; she's a reflection of a*
> *real struggle that women are going through across the country,*
> *and the audience should feel some sympathy for her.*[3]

Whilst Ted alludes to 'women's lib' as Joanna's reason for leaving, Hoffman refers to feminism as Streep's reasons for changing the script: 'Meryl, why don't you stop carrying the flag for feminism and just *act the scene*,' he said.[4] If Meryl Streep had to push for Joanna to be given more sympathy, she had to push in the same way Joanna had to push.

Perhaps that is why giving a critique of the film feels like pushing against a wall of sympathy. The word *sympathy* derives from *pathos*, sympathy as fellow feeling or feeling with. We are supposed to feel sympathy for Ted because the story is being told from his point of view, sympathy as 'him-pathy' to borrow a useful term from feminist philosopher Kate Manne.[5] Sympathy, in other words, is an arrange-ment, how the story is organized around Ted, his life, his love, his losses, what is near to him, near to us, far from him, far from us. To feel sympathy for feminist killjoys is *how* we become killjoy critics, how we allow ourselves to be infected by the misery of a situation to see the world from her point of view.

To give your sympathy in the wrong way, or to the wrong character, has consequences. Indeed, returning to Joanna's speech, the glass that is thrown at the wall was not in the script. It was Hoffman throwing something into the story, to get a reaction, an intrusion of the real into the fictional, the anger at the woman plotting to tell a story, or even just more of her story, expressed through an unexpected shattering. The *point* of shattering, this intrusion of the real, is punishment. The feminist killjoy operates as *an early warning system*. The fate of the feminist killjoy is used to discourage us away from feminism, as if to become a feminist is to head in a miserable direction. Warnings can be threats. To feel sympathy for her is to be threatened with the misery of her fate.

We learn so much about happiness from how we can be threatened by its loss. To become a feminist killjoy is thus to acquire *a happiness literacy*, we learn how to read happiness, which is how the scope of our critique extends beyond readings of films and other cultural objects to everyday life. What do I mean by *reading* happiness? I mean that happiness often takes the form of a story, with a beginning, an obstacle, an end. Happiness can be both the story and the end of the story. However various it has been as an idea, happiness is usually assumed to be what we all want, wish for or will. Economists Bruno S. Frye and Alois Stutzer make the argument in simple terms: 'Everybody wants to be happy. There is probably no other goal in life that commands such a high degree of consensus.'[6] Even when we want different things, it is assumed we all want happiness. Happiness becomes a container for the diversity of human wants.

Classically, happiness has been considered as an end rather than means. In *Nicomachean Ethics*, Aristotle describes happiness as the Chief Good, as 'that which all things aim at'.[7] Happiness is defined as an independent good we 'choose always for its own sake'. Other goods (such as honour, pleasure and intellect) are instrumental; we choose them 'with a view to happiness, conceiving that through their instrumentality we shall be happy'.[8] An instrumental good is what leads to happiness. Happiness can be understood as an end not just in the sense of the final part of a story, but in the sense of what we aim to accomplish, happiness as the point of an existence. The killjoy would be a deviation from the main point, the one who gets in the way of an accomplishment or prevents the realization of a desired end. That's quite a story.

It is the end-orientated nature of happiness that makes it such a powerful tool. Some things become 'good' because they *point* in the direction of happiness. Consider Mary Wollstonecraft's *Vindication of the Rights of Woman*, originally published in 1792. It makes a plea on behalf of women: 'Consider, I address you as a legislator, whether, when men contend for their freedom, and to be allowed to judge for themselves respecting their own happiness, it be not inconsistent and unjust to subjugate women, even though you firmly believe that you are acting in the manner best calculated to promote their happiness.'[9] I hear Wollstonecraft as a feminist killjoy critic, showing how the subjugation of women rests on men claiming to know how to promote our happiness.

Wollstonecraft's critique of the use of happiness to justify the subjugation of women was directed towards Jean-Jacques Rousseau and, in particular, to his book *Émile*, one of the most influential works of moral and educational philosophy of the time. In this book, Rousseau introduces us to two imagined pupils, first Émile and then Sophie, whose fate is to become Émile's wife. Rousseau offers a description of the virtuous woman, of who Sophie needs to become:

> she loves virtue because there is nothing fairer in itself, she loves it because it is a woman's glory and because a virtuous woman is little lower than the angels; she loves virtue as the only road to real happiness, because she sees nothing but poverty, neglect, unhappiness, shame, and disgrace in the life of a bad woman; she loves virtue because it is dear to her revered father, and to her tender and worthy mother; they are not content to be happy in their own virtue, they desire hers; and she finds her chief happiness in the hope of just making them happy.[10]

It would be hard to find a clearer example of the gendered nature of the moral economy of happiness. The good woman loves virtue as the road to happiness; unhappiness and disgrace follow being bad. For the daughter to be happy, she must be good because being good is what makes her parents happy, and she can only be happy if they are happy. *Conditional happiness* is how one person's happiness is made conditional upon another's. When some people come first, *their happiness comes first*. For those who come after, happiness means being directed towards other people's goods. The daughter puts her parents' happiness first by marrying, and then, when married, puts her husband's happiness first. That happiness is predicated on her disappearance was, centuries later, the subject of Joanna's speech.

At one point in this story, Sophie is misdirected. Her

imagination and desires are activated by reading too many books, leading to her becoming an 'unhappy girl, overwhelmed with her secret grief'.[11] In fact, the cause of Sophie's grief does not remain secret; we find out that she had become 'infatuated' with Telemachus, a character from a Greek myth. Implicit in the plot is a diagnosis of how girls reading books endangers their happiness, how in taking flight from reality, they withdraw their affections from proper objects. Sophie is given a solution: 'Let us give Émile his Sophie; let us restore this sweet girl to life and provide her with a less vivid imagination and a happier fate.'[12] Rousseau conjures the feminist killjoy only to put her to rest. Sophie's 'happier fate' is to be given away.

Rousseau claimed that the path of nature *is* the path of happiness; any deviation from it leads to unhappiness. Happiness was how restrictions of possibility were made necessary. These restrictions do not only relate to gender. Happiness was used to justify the restriction of education to different classes of people. For example, in Britain the Parochial Schools Bill of 1807, which would have enabled education for the children of the labouring classes, was defeated on these grounds. One politician argued that 'giving education to the labouring classes of the poor' would be 'prejudicial to their morals and happiness; it would teach them to despise their lot in life, instead of making them good servants in agriculture, and other laborious employments to which their rank in society had destined them.'[13] Happiness was assumed to enable acceptance of one's 'lot in life', and as being necessary to the maintenance of social order.

We can begin to understand why feminists have been so consistent in their critiques of happiness. The history of happiness can only be told *happily*, as a history of a good thing, by excluding these critiques, which is why feminist killjoys offer a distinct vantage point on this history.[14] Simone de Beauvoir wrote in 1949: 'We cannot really know what the word "happiness" means, and still less what authentic values it covers, there is no way to measure the happiness of others, and it is always easy to call a situation that one would like to impose on others happy.'[15] If happiness is assumed to be a good thing, but it is hard to say what happiness is, or to measure it, happiness can be how a situation is imposed *by making it seem good*. Ann Oakley argues that 'happiness can be a cover term for conservativism', and that 'countless evils', can be 'sanctioned' by its name.[16] The feminist killjoy as cultural critic does not simply offer another definition of what happiness *is*, from the point of view of those assumed to come second or after, but of what happiness *does* or is *used to do*.

That is what Beauvoir was doing. She showed how women came to experience happiness as freely chosen because of how it was imposed. This is the basis of her existential critique of happiness as bad faith; women learn to experience a restriction that is imposed on them as what they have chosen for their own happiness. Beauvoir explores how a woman might adjust to her situation by learning to enjoy housework: 'the little girl readily enjoys shining the silver, polishing doorknobs'.[17] In other words, the girl, in becoming a woman, also a wife, learns to love home-making: 'It is

98

through housework that the wife comes to make her "nest" her own.' For her to consent to the restriction of her horizon, housework 'must spark some joy or pleasure somewhere'.[18] In feminist killjoy fashion, Beauvoir concludes that the housewife 'wears herself out running on the spot'.[19] There can be so much energy expended in not getting anywhere. To adjust to a situation is to find happiness in it. When we are *adjusted* to the limits imposed by an existing arrangement, those limits are no longer even perceived as limits. We become feminist killjoys when we refuse to adjust ourselves to a situation that has been imposed upon us.

KILLJOY MAXIM:
BE MALADJUSTED, DON'T ADJUST TO INJUSTICE!

Of course, then, as discussed in my introductory chapter, feminists are positioned as the ones who are imposing change. Part of that story is the failure to recognize the imposed nature of what we try to change. Happiness is crucial to *that* imposition. We become feminist killjoys by not accepting a situation we have been told is necessary for our happiness. This means that even asking why happiness is expected *there* is sufficient to become a feminist killjoy. Just think how the wedding day is often described as 'the happiest day of your life' before it even happens! An expectation can be turned into a story, a fairy-tale story, that rewards good girls with a happy ending, arriving, often, in the form of a prince. As feminist killjoy critics, we might point out how old fairy-tale stories have been turned into romantic comedies, telling us, teaching us, that even if girls want many things, what would *really* make them happy is still finding their prince. Not all of us want what we are told will make us happy. We might not want a prince. We might want to be a prince. We might not want there to be princes.

We can return to the idea of conditional happiness. It is ordinary and understandable to want the happiness of those you love – or at least to want for them what they want for themselves. But what if you want somebody to be happy, but you do not want what would make them happy? Say what would make your parents happy would be for you to get married and to have children. Say you want to give them what they want even though that is not what you want. You might try and convince yourself that what they want *is* what you want.

KILLJOY TRUTH: THERE CAN BE NOTHING MORE UNCONVINCING THAN THE EFFORT TO BE CONVINCED

Trying to convince yourself to feel something is in fact close to what sociologist Arlie Hochschild called 'emotional labour'. One of her examples is the bride who does not feel happy on her wedding day: 'sensing a gap between the ideal feeling and the actual feeling she tolerated, the bride prompts herself to "be happy"'.[20] We learn from this example that it is possible not to inhabit fully one's own happiness, or even to be alienated from it. Maybe you labour to convince others that what they want, for your happiness or for theirs, will come later. You might say you do want to have children, but just not yet, trying to displace their hopes for happiness into a happily distant future. But you then might be asked questions, more and more questions. When are you getting married? When are you having children? Sometimes questions can be warnings: don't leave it too late, time is running out! Some of us, feminists and queer people included, want children. Some of us do not. If you say firmly, no, no, I don't want children, you might encounter the weight of mourning, as if you are depriving others of a future they had imagined or anticipated for themselves; as if you have stolen the grandchildren. Earlier in the handbook, I suggested that killjoys appear as those who have stolen the past. The killjoys also appear as those who have stolen the future.

Consider the speech act: 'I just want you to be happy.' When a parent says this to a child, it seems to mean: 'I want you to do *whatever* would make you happy.' And yet, my mother would often say to me, 'I just want you to be happy', in an exasperated tone, when she was, if anything, frustrated with what I was doing or saying. In other words, she seemed to express a desire for my happiness when my actions compromised her own. Even when someone says they want *your* happiness, it can be unclear *whose* happiness they are talking about. The desire for another's happiness can be directive by appearing to give them freedom to decide for themselves what would make them happy.

When I came out in my thirties, I began reading lesbian

and gay literature; as you do. And I kept noticing how often the phrase 'I just want you to be happy' is repeated by parents to their queer children. Take the following exchange from Nancy Garden's novel *Annie on My Mind*:

> 'Lisa,' my father said, 'I told you I'd support you and I will. And right now, I can see we're all too upset to discuss this very much more, so in a minute or two I'm going to take you and your mother and me out to lunch. But honey, I know it's not fashionable to say this, but – well, maybe it's just that I love your mother so much and you and Chad so much that I have to say to you I've never thought gay people can be very happy – no children for one thing, no real family life. Honey, you are probably going to be a damn good architect – but I want you to be happy in other ways, too, as your mother is, to have a husband and children. I know you can do both ...' I am happy, I tried to tell him with my eyes. I'm happy with Annie; she and my work are all I'll ever need; she's happy too – we both were until this happened.[21]

The father tells her he will support her. But he then makes a judgement that gay people can't be very happy. He is unhappy about his child being gay because he is unhappy about his child being unhappy. Being gay is assumed to be giving up what would make you happy, 'a husband, children'. But the daughter is happy. Her girlfriend too is happy. They were both happy, 'until this happened'. The father, by withdrawing his support for his daughter's decision out of fear of her unhappiness, creates the unhappiness he feared. Even happy queers become unhappy at this point!

If the idea that gay people cannot be happy is 'unfashionable to say', it is still widely shared. Some people distance themselves from homophobic judgements that there is something wrong with being gay whilst worrying about the unhappiness of children. One comment made to me at a table by a family member was, 'It is selfish for gay people to have children.' The family member who made this comment was concerned with how the children of same-sex couples would be teased. She would not agree with the judgement that gay people were sick or perverted. Rather, she was concerned that the children would be hurt because of how other people would make that judgement. This concern for the children can still be the basis of a judgement about gay people, that for us to want children would be selfish as it would put our happiness over theirs.

It might seem that concern about the potential unhappiness of children in queer families is less damaging than the homophobia that scripts gay people as perverts in need of discipline in the first place. To want happiness for children, after all, seems to derive from care for them. But the presumptions of perversion and unhappiness are intrinsically related. Psychologists Michael Schroeder and Ariel Shidlo, for instance, analysed how clinicians used this argument – that gay people will inevitably be unhappy – to justify sexual conversion therapy.[22] The violence of conversion was an attempt to redirect an unhappy queer child to become a happy heterosexual. In other words, conversion therapy was justified as care for happiness.

In the UK, there is still an ongoing battle to make conversion therapy illegal.[23] And a key set of actors resisting those efforts do so from a position of apparent support for lesbian and gay people, because they do not want to ban the use of therapies to redirect trans children away from their self-understanding as being trans. Trans feminist scholar and activist Julia Serano quotes a passage by historian and bioethicist Alice Dreger:

> If the clinician thinks the patient might be a gay boy – that the child might, with good familial and social support, grow up to be a well-adjusted gay man without the need for sex-altering surgeries or lifelong hormone replacement therapy – the clinician must not 'change or direct' the child's understanding. But by not 'changing or directing' the child's understanding – by 'affirming' a 'transgender' identity as soon as it appears – the clinician might actually be stimulating and cementing a transgender identity.[24]

As Serano shows, the only well-adjusted adult who appears in this passage is a gay man. A transgender woman, if she was to appear, would do so not only at a great cost, but falsely, 'cemented' by the failure to 'change or direct', that is, to redirect, the child. Rather than redirecting an unhappy gay child to be a happy heterosexual, the therapist, using conversion therapy, violence justified as care for happiness, redirects an unhappy trans child to be a happy homosexual.[25] This is how transphobia displaces homophobia *whilst taking its exact form.* So much violence can be justified as care for happiness.

The speech act 'I just want you to be happy' can sometimes be expressed as a desire to protect a queer or trans child from the pain of rejection. Take the film *Everybody's Talking about Jamie* (2021, dir. Jonathan Butterell), based on a play that was itself based on a BBC documentary, *Jamie: Drag Queen at 16*.[26] Jamie's mother loves and supports her queer son, who wants to be a drag queen. She says to her son, 'I just want you to be happy', not because she wants her child to be straight or to straighten himself out by giving up his desires and dreams. The mother loves her child not despite but for his queerness, his exuberance, his refusal to give up possibilities by following a narrow path. She says, 'I just want you to be happy' when Jamie is angry with her, when he learns that she has hidden from him his father's rejection, by writing letters and sending flowers as if they were from him. When she can't stop the father rejecting his son, when she can't stop him being homophobic, she tries to stop her son from learning about it. It doesn't work, not only because Jamie finds out his mother sent the letters, but because not knowing you are being rejected does not stop you from being rejected. There can be so much grief in rejection. We grieve for a relationship we did not have. We grieve for a relationship we will not have. There can be grief in the need not to be overwhelmed by grief. We need to work through it, even let ourselves be overwhelmed by it.

The effort to protect someone from unhappiness does not lead to happiness. Audre Lorde's work helps us to understand why. Lorde suggests, 'Looking on the bright side of things is a euphemism used for obscuring certain realities of life, the open consideration of which might prove threatening or dangerous to the status quo.' She moves from this observation to a wider critique of happiness as an obscurant: 'Let us seek "joy" rather than real food and clean air and a saner future on a liveable earth! As if happiness alone can protect us from the results of profit-madness.' She writes that the very idea that our first responsibility is for our own happiness must be resisted by political struggle: 'Was I really fighting the spread of radiation, racism, woman-slaughter, chemical invasion of our food, pollution of our environment, and the abuse and psychic destruction of our young, merely to avoid dealing with my first and greatest responsibility – to be happy?'[27] Lorde has given us the answer to her question.

KILLJOY TRUTH: IF HAPPINESS REQUIRES TURNING AWAY FROM VIOLENCE, HAPPINESS IS VIOLENCE

This is Lorde's truth. In *The Feminist Killjoy Handbook*, we are learning from Lorde. Lorde was writing as a cancer patient about the injunction to be positive as if you could make yourself better by feeling better. The other side of this moral argument is that if you don't get better, it is because you failed to make yourself better. The injunction to be positive makes an individual not only the problem but the solution, as if you can stop yourself from being ill or poor or discriminated against by acquiring a more positive outlook. The injunction to be positive is cruel. When 'obscuring certain realities of life' is performed out of care, care is cruel. In *Zami*, she gives us an example of how her mother used to pretend that the people spitting at her daughter were 'spitting into the wind'. Lorde writes:

> It never occurred to me to doubt her. It was not until years later once in conversation I said to her: 'Have you noticed people don't spit into the wind so much the way they used to?' And the look on my mother's face told me that I had blundered into one of those secret places of pain that must never be spoken of again. It was so typical of my mother when I was young that if she couldn't stop white people spitting on her children because they were Black, she would insist it was something else.[28]

Lorde's mother tries to protect her child from the pain of racism by obscuring it. When Audre asks her mother, 'Have you noticed?' she has ventured into that secret place of pain. Happiness is sometimes used to cover over those secret places of pain. So much comes out when the cover fails.

The cover fails. Let's think again about the familiar image of the happy family. An image can be *polished*. Polishing is an activity, a form of labour. To cover is to labour at an appearance. Recall Beauvoir's description of how girls come to enjoy polishing furniture. It is important to note that Beauvoir was talking about middle-class women who did not have to work outside the home. Anne McClintock, in her book *Imperial Leather*, makes class explicit in her description of polishing: 'Middle-class women who did indeed spend their days scrubbing, cleaning, polishing and scraping went to incongruous lengths to disguise their work and erase its evidence from their hands.'[29]

Polishing is about more than the removal of dust and dirt; it removes evidence of itself. Claudia Rankine describes how one of her difficult conversations about race was ended by a white woman 'turning our attention toward the dessert tray'. She explains: 'Hers is the fey gesture I have seen exhibited so often by white women in old movies – women who are overcome by shiny objects.'[30] A shiny object can be how we are distracted from something, or by something. If we refuse to polish the surfaces, *we encounter what is real*, all that has been removed to create that impression. By seeing happiness, not just seeing it but seeing through it, we come to see so much else. Reality can intrude as or in what Lorde calls 'the secret places of pain'.

To polish is to create a shiny reflection. A smile too can be sheen. I think of all the times I was told I had ruined the photograph because I did not smile enough or because I looked how I probably felt, grumpy. So many dinners ruined; so many photographs too! For the family to appear happy, I would have to contain how I felt. As I have been writing this handbook, I have been thinking more about how much can be invested in a happy appearance.

When my parents broke up, for me, it was such a relief. My father would no longer be there. After he left, my mother agreed with him that we would go to his new house with his new partner for Christmas. It was presented as if it was a gift to us, the children, so that we would not have the holiday ruined by a break-up. I wanted to tell her how

I felt, how I did not want to be there, to go, but I did not. I could not, perhaps, because I felt she would not be able to take it. I remember the grief of that day, to be back there, at the table, that place.

I know this story well. Still, sometimes by revisiting the past, we tell other stories. My mother was a housewife. Her task was to care for the happiness of others, her husband and her children. And she became a housewife because she had to give her up her own career, her vocation as a nurse, after becoming ill in her late twenties. I think my mother could cope with her own unhappiness, finding solace in experiencing it as sacrifice. Earlier I suggested that it can be hard to tell exactly whose happiness someone wants when they want your happiness. For my mother, the possibility of her own happiness seemed to rest on ours. Perhaps she needed the illusion of family happiness, and of our happiness in it, or with it, to feel that there was a point, a purpose, to what she had given up. I think, looking back, that is why she found it hard when I stood up or spoke back to my father. It shattered the illusion. For my mother, to give up the illusion of our happiness might have been to give up too much.

I don't think my mother was ready for the illusion of family happiness to be shattered. Perhaps having everyone together one more time was how she held herself together. In thinking of what she might have needed to do, I feel I have more room; I can breathe as I remember that day. There were many stresses and strains on my parent's marriage: her illness, living in a country without any extended family, being a mixed-race, mixed-religion couple, him a

Pakistani Muslim, her a white Christian woman. When my parents divorced, my mother became a disabled pensioner with limited means; my father remained a wealthy man of many means. Another time, at another table, a family table, someone else's father said, 'Divorce discriminates against men.' This was one of the memorable comments I mentioned in my introduction. I felt such rage when he said that, because I knew from his daughter that it wasn't true for him, and it most certainly wasn't true for my father. I reference these untruths because sometimes we know them by feeling them. It wasn't true. I was a feminist killjoy by calling already by this point. I knew that if I expressed what I thought it would not end well. I could not use a permission note. I could not stay silent. I expressed myself. That conversation didn't end well.

Sometimes it is right for things not to end well. Another of the memorable comments that was made to me by friends, family or acquaintances was: 'This is what happens when you marry a Muslim.' The comment was in fact made to my mother by a friend of the family, after my father had left, in the mid-1980s. When my parents were together, the friend had not said anything about my father being Muslim. When my parents broke up, he said something. Perhaps he did not say anything before out of politeness. *Polite racism* is a racism that is masked, sometimes only barely, by the veneer of politeness. The word *polite* shares a root with the word *polish*, to make smooth, to smooth over. Racism comes out very quickly when the masks slips, when something is not working, things are no longer running smoothly.

Racism can then be used as an explanation for what did not work, what broke, as if my mother, by marrying a Muslim – marrying out – brought this upon herself.

It can be painful to be told that a break-up was an inevitable consequence of a commitment you made. That break becomes your fate. And it can be hard not to take it in, not to begin to explain difficult things that happen to us in the terms given to us. It was my mother who said to me many years later, 'Enoch Powell had it right.' When she said it, I heard Powell's words, his infamous Rivers of Blood speech, his racist prediction of the dire and dreadful consequences of immigration. My mother said this to me just after I had given a talk on multiculturalism and the promise of happiness at a conference. I had been so excited, full of *killjoy joy*, as it had been the first conference I had ever attended in Australia where I had been one of many people of colour (rather than being, as I was used to, the only person of colour). Aboriginal scholars had not only been present but they had given keynotes. I was shattered when she said this.

Some years later, my mother said that what I had heard was not what she said, or at least not what she meant. She spoke of the racism she and my father had experienced as a mixed-race couple in 1960s England. Sometimes to make sense of these difficult spaces, when whiteness is at home but you are not white, it helps to listen and to learn from others. Black feminist scholar Gail Lewis wrote an article about her relationship to her white mother, which she addressed to her mother. I have learnt so much from Lewis over the years, not least the lesson about how intimacy in mixed families is 'messy and ambivalent', involving solidarity, but other stuff, too, 'racial cleavage and antagonism' that do not just come from outside.[31]

Other stuff, too. So much stuff. Families can be contact zones, where many differences collide. And I think again of my mother and what it might be like for her to have three daughters who went to university, when she had not. I wonder if my killjoy joy on that day, the intellectual buzz I had from that event, could have spilled over, into over-confidence, a lack of awareness of how much space I was taking up. These are speculative thoughts, cautious remembering. My mother has her own story to tell. Her story is not mine to tell. And yet, in telling our stories, we tell stories of each other, of the words shared between us. Yes, some sentences can hit you. Maybe that sentence did not come *from* her, but *to* her, an echo of what others had said, what that friend of the family had said, a break coming from marrying the wrong person, the wrong kind of person, too much and too many of the wrong kind of people, mixed, mixed up, the breaking apart of a nation, the breaking down of a marriage, the loss of a relationship, of a hope for happiness, of whiteness, rivers of blood, coming home.

Yes, it was shattering to hear. In time we pick up the pieces, finding in their sharpness, insight. To see through happiness, beyond its polished surfaces, for me, was to see how whiteness was at home. We see whiteness when we see through happiness, which is why *seeing whiteness* becomes a central task of the feminist killjoy critic. I think of Toni Morrison's *The Bluest Eye*. The novel tells the story of Pecola, for whom 'the bluest eye' signifies what she cannot have, who she cannot become, as if being estranged from whiteness, a stranger to whiteness, is not to be beautiful, not to have what would or could make you happy. Pecola sees herself as black and ugly. She sees herself through the lens of whiteness, which is the same lens as anti-Black racism, which makes blackness distance from whiteness, distance from light, from knowledge, from happiness, too. She sees herself how the world has taught her to see herself.

We learn about Pecola from Claudia, our narrator. Claudia could be described as a Black feminist killjoy. In one scene, she reflects on being given a doll:

> It had begun with Christmas and the gift of dolls. The big, the special, the loving gift was always a big, blue-eyed Baby Doll. From the clucking sounds of adults I knew that the doll represented what they thought was my fondest wish ... what was supposed to bring me great pleasure, succeeded in doing quite the opposite ... [I] traced the turned-up nose, poked the glassy-blue eyes, twisted the yellow hair. I could not love it. But I could examine it to see what it was that all the world said was lovable ... I destroyed white baby dolls.[32]

Claudia knows from the adults clucking that she is supposed to love the white baby doll. She is not affected that way, the right way; she is even affected in the opposite way. She pokes and twists the doll rather than clucking, a way of handling it that would, I have no doubt, be deemed violent and aggressive; as disaffection, disloyalty, ingratitude. Not loving the doll means Claudia can examine the doll to learn 'what the world said was loveable'. We learn what is supposed to make us happy when it does not make us happy. The happiness formula that Morrison explores in order to challenge it is *happiness = proximity to whiteness.*

With this formula to hand, we can explain so much. It is not just that we can find the figure of the feminist killjoy being employed to do certain things when we become cultural critics. Rather the feminist killjoy as critic *of* culture appears *in* culture. We can return to Sissie, our sister killjoy, from Ama Ata Aidoo's novel of the same name. We follow Sissie as she travels from Ghana to Germany then to England. In Germany, Sissie wanders around a market. She sees 'polished steel. Polished tin. Polished brass.' Sissie 'saw their shine and their glitter'.[33] Something becomes shiny because of what is not seen. Sissie sees what is not seen. She then sees how she is seen:

> *Suddenly, she realized a woman was telling a young girl who must have been her daughter: 'Ja, das Schwartze Mädchen'. From the little German that she had been advised to study for the trip, she knew that 'das Schwartze Mädchen' meant 'black girl'. She was somewhat puzzled. Black girl? Black girl? So, she looked around her, really well this time.*[34]

When she is referred to as the Black girl, she is puzzled. But then she sees that it is she they see. Reading this passage, I was reminded of revolutionary psychoanalyst Frantz Fanon's discussion of being seen as a Black man by a white child in *Black Skin, White Masks*. Fanon shows how to be seen as Black is to be made fearsome in the present and to be given a history woven 'out of a thousand details, anecdotes, stories'.[35]A history can make it hard to breathe, a circle 'drawing a bit tighter'.

When Sissie sees herself seen as a Black girl, she looks around. It is then that she sees whiteness, 'And it hit her. That all the crowd of people going and coming in all sorts of directions had the colour of the pickled pig parts that used to come from foreign places to the markets at home.'[36] For Sissie, seeing whiteness is about refusing to be drawn into it. She becomes more herself, our sister killjoy, closer to home, in conversations she has with other Black people about why they stay in Europe. Sissie listens to an eminent doctor who says he stayed in Europe 'to educate them to recognize our worth'. Sissie asks by 'them' does he mean 'white people' and he says, 'Well yes.'[37] Sissie can hear the violence of that *yes*, of having to demonstrate one's worth to those who have denied it. Sissie's critique of the injunction to be positive is a critique of what those who have been colonized have to do in order to be recognized by the colonizers as being worthy, what they remove from themselves.

The implication is that some end up having to polish themselves, make themselves more palatable, appearing grateful, smiling, or putting on a 'white mask', to borrow terms from Fanon, in order to be included. We are back to that formula, *happiness = proximity to whiteness*. Happiness can function as a technology of inclusion. Consider how diversity is used to create a picture of organizations as being happy, those glossy brochures of colourful faces that are instantly recognizable as images of diversity. People of colour are asked to provide these smiling colourful faces. Perhaps the word *diversity* is a smile, a smoothing out of an appearance; diversity as another kind of white mask, diversity as *masking whiteness.*

Or we could describe diversity as *institutional polishing*. I interviewed a diversity practitioner who told me she did not use the word diversity even though it was on her job description. She said, 'Diversity is like a big shiny red apple, right? And it all looks wonderful, but if you actually cut into that apple there's a rotten core in there and you know that it's actually all rotting away and it's not actually being addressed. It all looks wonderful, but the inequalities aren't being addressed.' When I heard her talking about the shiny red apple I was reminded of Betty Friedan's critique of the image of the happy housewife whose beaming smile hides an infection.[38] When diversity is a way an organization can appear happy, diversity is how inequalities are 'not actually being addressed'.

If diversity is what we see, there is so much we do not see. Diversity can be a way of not seeing whiteness. People of colour become the polish, helping to create a shiny reflection. Earlier I mentioned a conference where I gave a talk on multiculturalism and the promise of happiness. The talk had focused on the film *Bend it Like Beckham* (dir. Gurinder Chadha, 2002). This film was in fact one of the reasons I decided to write about happiness in the first place. I was so struck and – OK, I am going to say it – *appalled* by the happy ending. The explicit politics of this film is that the daughters should be free to find happiness in their own way. As the father says, 'Two daughters made happy on one day, what else could a father ask for?' Jess, his daughter, is not a killjoy by inclination. She wants to play football. But she also wants to make her parents happy. They do not want her to play football. So, she plays football in secret. Many second-generation children of migrants might hear something of their own experience in Jess's story; we know how much our parents gave up for our happiness.

As killjoy critics, we have learnt to notice where the obstacle to happiness is located. In the film, it is the father who stops Jess from doing what would make her happy. He is thus positioned as the killjoy in the film. The father gives two speeches to his daughter. In the first speech, he says, 'When I was a teenager in Nairobi, I was the best fast bowler in our school. Our team even won the East African Cup. But when I came to this country, nothing. And these bloody gora in the club house made fun of my turban and sent me off packing . . . She will only end up disappointed like me.' The father's memory of racism is what stops him from letting her play. He does not want her to suffer like him. By the end of the film, the father has a conversion. In the second speech, he says, 'When those bloody English cricket players threw me out of their club like a dog, I never complained. On the contrary, I vowed that I would never play again. Who suffered? Me. But I don't want Jess to suffer. I don't want her to make the same mistakes her father made, accepting life, accepting situations. I want her to fight. And I want her to win.' If, in the first speech, the father says she *should not play* in order not to suffer like him, in the second, he says she *should play* in order not to suffer like him. The second speech suggests that the refusal to play a national game is the truth behind the migrant's suffering: you suffer because you do not play the game; not playing is read as self-exclusion. To let Jess be happy, he lets her go. By implication, he is not only letting her go, he is letting go of his own suffering, the unhappiness caused by accepting racism.

When the father stops holding onto his hurt, he lets the daughter go. Jess goes to America to take up her dream of becoming a professional football player. She also falls in love with Joe, her white football coach. Interracial love can be framed as the problem. It can be a problem when it is framed as the solution. The acceptance of interracial heterosexual love is in fact a conventional narrative of reconciliation, as if that love can overcome past antagonisms (love as polishing, perhaps). The final scene is a cricket scene. Jess's father is batting. Joe, in the foreground, is bowling. He smiles as he approaches us. This is the last scene, but the first cricket scene of the film. The implication being, of course, that the father can now play cricket again. It is the white man who is presented as the agent who brings the melancholic migrant back into the national fold.

The film, despite its effort to give a brown girl her own story, her own desires, wishes and wants, ends up using the same happiness formula Morrison and Aidoo dissected through their Black feminist killjoy critics, Claudia and Sissie: *happiness = proximity to whiteness*, or to be even more specific, *happiness = proximity to a white man*. Of course, at one level, Jess's story is a story of an unconventional Indian girl, who is bending the rules that tell her what she can do and who she can be. The story of an Indian girl who wants to bend the ball like Beckham (rather than 'cooking Aloo Gobi') is a conventional story, a national story, of how an immigrant daughter can be freed from the past or from the restriction of her culture, by identifying with the nation, with its promise of happiness, by playing its game.

KILLJOY TRUTH: THE UNCONVENTIONAL DAUGHTER OF THE MIGRANT FAMILY IS A CONVENTIONAL FORM OF SOCIAL HOPE

Reading this film as a killjoy critic has helped me to explain why I found the ending of the film so problematic. Racism comes up as what the melancholic migrant is attached *to*, as an attachment to injury that allows migrants to justify their refusal to participate in the national game ('the gora in their club house'). We are told to let go of the pain of racism by letting go of racism as a way of understanding that pain. Racism is framed as a memory that, if it were kept alive, would just leave us exhausted. If the figure of the feminist killjoy implies that to speak of an injury is *to make it bigger than it is*, the figure of the melancholic migrant implies that to speak of racism is not to get past it.

KILLJOY COMMITMENT:
I AM NOT WILLING TO GET OVER WHAT IS NOT OVER

The figure of the melancholic migrant implies that to be concerned with race, let alone racism, is to be too attached to oneself or one's own particulars. Happiness itself becomes universal. Consider this description of happiness written by V. S. Naipaul in an article, 'Our Universal Civilization':

> It is an elastic idea; it fits all men. It implies a certain kind of society, a certain kind of awakened spirit. I don't imagine my father's Hindu parents would have been able to understand the idea. So much is contained in it: the idea of the individual, responsibility, choice, the life of the intellect, the idea of vocation and perfectibility and achievement. It is an immense human idea. It cannot be reduced to a fixed system. It cannot generate fanaticism. But it is known to exist, and because of that, other more rigid systems in the end blow away.[39]

The grandparents are figured here not only as the ones who cannot enter the universal, who are too particular to 'get it', but also as those who need to be given up to enter the universal. Herein lies another happiness formula: *white universal, brown relative*. If some of us have to give up our particulars, the universal is not quite so elastic; it does not quite fit 'all men'. Or maybe the universal is an elastic band; it snaps when it is stretched to fit everyone.

The figure of the melancholic migrant circulates not

only in literature and popular films but in wider political discourse. In 2020, in part in response to Black Lives Matter protests, the British government set up a new commission to investigate 'race and ethnic disparities in the UK'. The Sewell Report that followed argued not only that there was no evidence of institutional racism in the UK, but that 'the success of much of the ethnic minority population in education and, to a lesser extent, the economy, should be regarded as a model for other White-majority countries.'[40] The report locates racism not only in the past, but in the minds of those it suggests have held onto the past: 'For some groups historic experience of racism still haunts the present and there was a reluctance to acknowledge that the UK had become open and fairer.' The report implies that racism only exists in the minds and memories of those who are haunted by history, not as what stops some groups from participating but as how some groups stop themselves from participating. Being positive is treated as objective and neutral and forward-thinking; being negative, as subjective and biased and stuck in the past. As killjoy critics, we have learnt to read the distribution of positives and negatives. The report uses them to describe the attitudes that determine outcome not only for individuals, but for different ethnic groups:

> *Those groups, particularly Indian and Chinese ethnic groups, who have the most success in British society tend to see fewer obstacles and less prejudice. And those groups that do less well, Black people and Pakistani and Bangladeshi Muslims, tend to*

*see and experience more of both, though Black African people
are considerably more positive than Black Caribbean people.*

The report even tries to 'see the positives' in slavery: 'There is a new story about the Caribbean experience which speaks to the slave period not only being about profit and suffering but how culturally African people transformed themselves into a re-modelled African/Britain.' Yes, even the transatlantic slave trade, which caused the death and dispossession of millions of African people, can be turned into a positive story of self-empowerment.

I think back to Lorde's critique of happiness, to the *cruelty* happiness obscures, to the *cruelty* of that obscuring. Earlier, I referred to Anne McClintock's discussion of how the labour of polishing within domestic interiors, creating shiny surfaces, erased the signs of labour. McClintock also shows how bourgeois morality and the imperial mission turned cleanliness into instruction, with reference to the Pears' Soap advertising campaign. Soap was credited not only with 'bringing moral and economic salvation to Britain's "great unwashed" but also with magically embodying the spiritual mission itself.'[41] White became pure, and also clean; labour and blackness, dirt or dirty. The text of one advert quotes Kipling's 'the white man's burden', as 'teaching the virtues of cleanliness', via the soap, 'a potent factor in brightening the dark corners of the earth'. There is a picture of 'a native', gratefully, happily, receiving the soap from a white man, standing above him.

Empire could be described as *world polishing*. A happy picture of empire is created by the removal of violence and the removal of evidence of that removal. One utilitarian philosopher described the imperial project thus: 'The pace of civilisation would be quickened beyond all examples. The courts, the knowledge, and the manners of Europe would be brought to their doors, and forced by an irresistible moral pressure on their acceptance. The happiness of the human race would thus be prodigiously augmented.'[42] When empire is told as a happy story, it is being told in the same terms it was justified. By *world polishing* I am referring to how much is obscured by this way of telling the imperial story, including the mass extraction and exploitation of resources from the colonies. I am also pointing to how empire brought with it an affective injunction to keep telling the happy story of imperial progression. That view of empire is enforced through citizenship, by which I mean, to become a citizen is to learn that view and be required to repeat it. The Home Office guide for citizenship tests, *Life in the United Kingdom: A Journey to Citizenship*, mentions empire a few times and always in positive or glowing terms. In one instance, the guide mentions empire as what brought 'regular, acceptable and impartial systems of law and order' to 'Indigenous peoples in Africa, the Indian subcontinent and elsewhere'.[43]

When Indigenous peoples are asked to tell this happy story of imperial progression, they are being asked to celebrate their dispossession. Consider how when 26 January, the date of the landing of the First Fleet into Sydney Cove in 1788, was made Australia Day, colonial conquest was turned into an annual celebration. Indigenous Australians in renaming that day Invasion Day, sometimes Survival Day, made it a day not for celebration but protest and mourning. Indigenous feminist Celeste Liddle stresses the importance of Invasion Day 'remaining a day of Indigenous protest and the assertion of sovereignty'. She suggests that the best response to protests would not be to change the date or to include more Aboriginal and Torres Strait Islander people in celebrations but for other people to 'find out why so many of us do not consider this a day of celebration'. She adds, 'I have always been optimistic that in a country which prides itself on the notion of a "fair go for all", all that I mention is not an impossible dream. I think we owe it to the future generations. But until some hard conversations are held and people start listening, it will unfortunately remain something I am unlikely to witness in my lifetime. And that truly is a reason to mourn.' [44] We mourn the reason to mourn. We need to keep having 'hard conversations' about colonialism even, or perhaps especially, during times of celebration.

If in recent times there has been a concerted effort *not* to keep telling the idealized story of empire, that polite story of well-mannered colonizers, *not* to keep polishing away the violence, that effort has been met with resistance. The killjoy as cultural critic helps us *to explain this resistance*. Let's return to the Sewell Report. It describes (and dismisses) the political movements that challenge these idealizations of colonial history, and of the history of slavery, as being 'negative', in other words, as killjoy projects. For instance, it contrasts 'being positive', about British heritage and history to 'the negative calls' for decolonizing the curriculum: 'Neither the banning of White authors or token expressions of Black achievement will help to broaden young minds. We have argued against bringing down statues, instead, we want all children to reclaim their British heritage.'

This equation of decolonizing the curriculum with banning white authors is frequently made in the media. Here is one example: 'students at a prestigious London university are demanding that figures such as Plato, Descartes and Kant should be largely dropped from the curriculum because they are white.'[45] If you consulted the university's decolonizing the curriculum initiative, you would learn that the students did not propose the dropping of any authors (let alone 'because they were white'). Decolonizing the curriculum is about *widening* the curriculum beyond a narrow body of thought. Students were asking for more philosophy from outside the West to be included; and they were asking for more discussion of the colonial contexts that shaped eighteenth- and nineteenth-century European philosophy. Asking about, say, the role of racism in Enlightenment philosophy teaches us more, not less, about that philosophy. I will return to what it means to position the killjoy as philosopher in the next chapter.

The critique of a canon is framed *as the failure to revere it.* You just have to say that a canon is not a simple expression of quality or worth, that these 'great texts' are not simply there because they are 'great texts', and responses will be that you are 'flushing great literature down the drain', to quote from one best-selling author,[46] or that you will end up 'reading cereal boxes instead of Shakespeare', to quote from a cultural studies scholar who admits to being relatively sympathetic to this concern.[47] A critique of something is judged as destroying it. To question who or what is idealized is to be deemed damaging, to become vandals, 'wilful destroyers of the venerable and beautiful'.[48]

KILLJOY COMMITMENT: WHEN CRITIQUE CAUSES DAMAGE, I AM WILLING TO CAUSE DAMAGE

Note the negativity belongs to the judgement rather than the action. Killing joy becomes a world-making project when we refuse to be redirected by a judgement away from an action. Instead, we expose how the judgement has a defensive function. We acquire the resources to explain why so many conservative defences of culture and history exercise the figure of 'the woke'. One article by a conservative politician, titled 'What is Wokeism and How Can It be Defeated', begins by stating 'Britain is under attack. Not in a physical sense, but in a philosophical, ideological and historical sense. Our heritage is under a direct assault – the very sense of what it is to be British has been called into question, institutions have been undermined, the reputation of key figures in our country's history have been traduced.'[49] He refers to Black Lives Matter and the decolonizing movement as examples of 'assaults' on what it means to be British. These movements, he suggests, are 'not motivated by positivity. Quite the reverse.'

Positivity is tied to preservation. This is why the judgement of negativity does so much work; why it is more than a story of motivation. By locating negativity in the outsider, whether the killjoy or the 'woke', culture and history are stabilized, treated as if they are a shared substance. This author adds, 'words that have been universally understood for millennia, such as "man" and "woman" are now emotionally charged and dangerous.' Of course, this statement is not true, words change, language does; as we do. To show how the meaning of words is not decided including, yes, *man* and *woman*, is treated as closing down a line of communication, depriving people of their ability to speak to each other. Another conservative politician stated, 'We want to confront this left-handed culture that seems to want to cancel our history, our values, our women.'[50] Just as asking for more philosophers from outside the West to be taught is treated as cancelling white philosophers (summarized as cancelling history), asking for more inclusive language, such as *pregnant people* (in recognition that not all people who are pregnant are *women*), is treated as cancelling *women*. The argument that *women* are being cancelled, expressed with that old sexist possessive ('our women'), draws loosely from the 'gender critical' argument that the term *gender* has replaced *sex*. Perhaps we are supposed to treat *sex* like a statue, what you have to affirm as being there, what is supposed to stand up or to stand firm.

There is so much we refuse to affirm. I began these reflections by suggesting that when feminist killjoys become cultural critics, we are not at a distance from something, observing it. We are in it. Let me end with that proximity. For many of us, empire was not long ago or far away. I was brought up with my father's stories of Partition. A hard train journey, a country breaking in two, a family for whom the past would be another country. We tell stories. We carry them. We are them. Race for me was never an object of study, something I approached from a distance. I was hired as a lecturer in Women's Studies in 1994 to teach a core course on gender and race. The appointment was the result of a recognition that feminism needed to take race seriously, as a primary not secondary category. Even if that recognition was right, some of us can end up embodying a category, becoming the *race* person, becoming *race*.

I designed a new course, Gender, Race and Colonialism. The course had to be approved, forms filled in. At the final stage of the process, I was asked to attend the university committee. We are seated around a table. Most of the courses are approved without much discussion. My course comes up. And a professor from another department begins to interrogate me. I was there, seated at the same table, a young woman, a person of colour, the only brown person in the room. No one else said anything. Perhaps the white man next to him nodded: I seem to remember a murmur of agreement. Everything in what he said, and how he said it, expressed his anger, his distaste, his revulsion that I could be there, where he was, saying what I was saying, doing what I was doing. I can't remember everything he said. But the word in the course description that triggered his reaction was the relatively uneventful word 'implicated'. That

I had used that word was a sign, he said, that I thought colonialism was a bad thing. He then gave me a lecture on how colonialism was a good thing, colonialism as modernity, that happy story of railways, language and law that is so familiar because we have heard it before. As I was listening to him, I heard how he saw not just me, but the course, my terms, the work, through the lens of whiteness, how I was seen as a sad, brown relative, an ungrateful recipient of that gift of modernity.

Perhaps they cannot bear it when the objects speak, when those pictured as willing recipients, taking it in, all of it in, say *no*. He heard a *no* in the word *implicated*. I turned that *implication* into a theory, making *no* the implication of my work. When we say *no*, we show what we know. We might even turn *no* into philosophy. And it is to killjoy philosophy I now turn.

4/ The Feminist Killjoy as Philosopher

Who do you picture when you picture a philosopher? A picture can be part of a story.

When we picture a philosopher, what comes to mind, who comes to mind, might be an old bearded white man; how wise he appears, how solemn. Where do you think philosophy originates? You might think of ideas as what comes to mind in a one-to-one encounter between man and an object, the law of gravity as what hits the philosopher on the head like an apple falling from a tree. If we think of philosophy as happening in that way, philosophy seems to happen somewhere other than where feminist killjoys are doing their thing, in the heat and the happening of everyday encounters we have with others.

But philosophy does not have to evoke him or happen like that. In considering the feminist killjoy *as* a philosopher, I will not be positioning her in relation to the academic discipline of Philosophy (later, when I come to doors, I explain why). Why talk about her as a philosopher, then? The word *philosophy* comes from knowledge, a love of knowledge. Considering the feminist killjoy as a philosopher is to make a point about knowledge, how we know, how much we know, from our experiences of killing joy. Considering the feminist killjoy as a philosopher changes our image of who a philosopher *is* as well as our understanding of what philosophers are *doing*.

I remember one time I was introducing a film about Angela Davis to a live audience. I was describing her importance as a Black feminist activist, an abolitionist, a freedom fighter. And suddenly, my hand, holding a piece of paper, banged the table next to me, almost as if it had a will of its own. I said, Angela Davis is a philosopher. I said it loudly; I might even have shouted it, 'Angela Davis is a philosopher!' Davis was trained as a philosopher, but that's not why I was so insistent. So often work by Black women and women of colour, whether activists and freedom fighters or not, is *not* understood as philosophy, or general knowledge, but as just a particular story, a personal revelation made by someone.

Those lodged as particular have so much to teach us in general. Angela Davis teaches us that activism, trying to change the world, is how we know it. Just take the well-used word 'intersectionality'. That word came from the important work of Black feminist legal theorist Kimberlé Crenshaw, who uses it to capture how discrimination works, 'like traffic through an intersection'.[1] Before the word there was the work. As Davis explains, 'Behind this concept of intersectionality is a rich history of struggle. A history of conversations among activists within movement formations, and with and among academics as well.'[2] Following Davis, we can show how knowledge is not a one-way traffic system; it does not come *from* academia or academic disciplines and then go out *to* the world to be used by ordinary people and activists in our daily lives. We create new concepts by trying to change old worlds. Maybe I banged the table because the table is where philosophy happens. To think of the feminist killjoy as a philosopher is to bring philosophy to *that* same table, to the heat of a conversation, to activism, to the effort to build more just worlds. In this chapter I reflect firstly on how we notice worlds because of our alienation from them (there are tables in those stories), to what we come to know from being stopped (there are doors in those stories), to what we come to know about institutions from our efforts to transform them (there are walls in those stories).

To say that the feminist killjoy becomes a philosopher *around the table*, might make the table our philosophical object. But the table was already a common philosophical object. In fact, tables appear everywhere in philosophy. So, for example, analytical philosopher Bertrand Russell opens his classic *The Problems of Philosophy* with a table, describing where he is, what he is doing, and what he can see: 'It seems to me that I am now sitting in a chair, at a table of a certain shape, on which I see sheets of paper with writing or print.'[3] There is nothing odd or surprising here. Russell notes if any other 'normal person' were to come into the room, then 'he will see the same chairs and tables and books and papers that I see', and would confirm that the table that is seen is the 'same table', as 'the table pressing against my arm'. Russell complicates this rather simple story by returning, again and again, to the table, how it looks, how it sounds when he taps it, how it feels when he touches it; its surface, its texture. Is it the same table or a real table, apart from these impressions? How do we know? Russell suggests that 'it becomes evident that the real table if there is one is not the same thing we immediately experience by sight or touch or hearing.' The 'familiar table', which 'roused but the slightest thoughts in us hitherto', has 'become a problem full of surprising possibilities'.[4]

However much the table is filled with surprising possibilities, Russell leaves it behind. What follows his rather tantalizing descriptions of the table is a discussion about how different philosophers and philosophical traditions deal with the kinds of questions about matter, reality, truth that the table allowed him to pose. In Russell's final chapter on the value of philosophy, the table does not appear at all. It would not be surprising to those trained as philosophers that the table disappears. When the point of the table is to provide an example, it points elsewhere. That the table is the example still tells us something about the orientation of philosophy. As literary critic Ann Banfield observes, 'Tables and chairs, things nearest to hand for the sedentary philosopher, who comes to occupy chairs of philosophy, are the furniture of that "room of one's own" from which the real world is observed.'[5] Tables show the orientation of philosophy not only because they are 'nearest to hand' to the philosopher, but because to occupy the chairs of philosophy is to be given the time and resources to ask questions about tables, most often in conversations with other philosophers.

When we become feminist killjoys around the table, we

are not simply conversing about it or pondering the nature of reality through it. And yet I want to show how those conversations we have around tables can lead us to become philosophers. When we are alienated by a conversation at the table, or withdraw from that conversation, we *notice the table*, not only as a thing, but as what we are gathered around; we notice how we are gathered, who gathers. If philosophers withdraw from something *in order to* inspect it, the killjoy as philosopher inspects something *because* we are withdrawn from it.

To explore the significance of how and why we inspect things, let me return to two killjoy stories discussed in earlier chapters. Recall Claudia, our narrator and Black feminist killjoy critic from Toni Morrison's novel *The Bluest Eye*. It is because Claudia does not want the white doll that she inspects it closely. She looks at how it is made, noticing the turned-up nose, the glassy blue eyes, the yellow hair. Claudia is not just learning about the doll. She is studying the world. She is studying whiteness. The doll becomes a mirror to a world. And, by seeing 'what the world said was lovable', she sees a reflection so different from her own.

KILLJOY TRUTH: THE LESS WE SEE OURSELVES REFLECTED, THE MORE WE SEE IN A REFLECTION

Claudia teaches us how alienation can be studious. And if Claudia is a Black feminist killjoy critic, by virtue of what she sees, or how she sees, Toni Morrison could be described as a killjoy philosopher. In *Playing in the Dark: Whiteness and the Literary Imagination*, Morrison offers a profound inspection of whiteness. She is very clear in the opening of this text that by reflecting on her situation as an African-American writer, her 'gendered, sexualized, racialized world', she is generating knowledge, counter-knowledge, challenging how the world has been known through whiteness as if, for instance, the category of American literature is 'free of, uninformed by, and unshaped by' the presence of Africans and African Americans.[6] Whiteness is not only evident when Africans and African Americans are represented in the literary landscape. Morrison uses the analogy of the fishbowl: when we see what is in the bowl, distracted by the detail, the flash, the movement of what is inside, we don't see the bowl.[7] She shows how whiteness is what is seen through, and thus how whiteness is not seen.

To think of the killjoy as a philosopher is to consider what we know of the world by not being given a place in it. Remember the student who started to 'stand out in that way', because she did not laugh at a sexist joke? She appears 'that way' because she did *not* participate in something. When you are not in agreement, you stand out. When things are in agreement, they recede from view. Smiling can be a way of being in agreement; laughter too. Because she stood out, she became a target around a lunch table. She left the table. And by leaving the table, I am not just referring to an actual table: she also left the university. She left in part because of what she learnt about the university by how it made her the problem. She described the process:

'I lost my rose-tinted glasses, the way I saw those spaces being a place of excellence. I thought they were welcoming of difference. I had worked really hard to get to that space. When you come from the kind of background I have – no one had been to university to do a degree.' She had seen the university as a space of excellence but also as 'welcoming of difference'. Diversity is often used as a welcoming address to students from non-traditional backgrounds, including working-class students. And so, if she saw the university through rose-tinted glasses, it is because they were handed to her. Diversity is what you see through the glasses, a happy table, a shiny table, creating the impression that everyone can participate in the conversation. She *sees through that reflection*, to what it does not show, who it does not show. This is how the table comes into view, when we don't have a seat at it or when we are alienated by the conversation around it, no longer distracted by the detail, our immersion, the flash and the movement.

That process can start with what you notice. You might notice how you are noticeable. And in noticing how you become noticeable, how you stand out, you come to see what you otherwise would not see if you participated in something, or what you could not see from the vantage point you previously enjoyed. This is why I think of noticing as political labour. In noticing the world, we hammer away at it.

KILLJOY EQUATION:
NOTICING = THE FEMINIST KILLJOY'S HAMMER

If the feminist killjoy turns noticing into a hammer, she could be understood as a feminist phenomenologist. Phenomenology, the study of phenomena, of what can be perceived, has been a useful resource for feminism because of, as Judith Butler describes, its 'commitment to grounding theory in lived experience, and to revealing the way in which the world is produced through the constituting acts of subjective experience'.[8] To ground theory in lived experience is about reflecting not on oneself but on the world *as it is given to us*. Simone de Beauvoir and Judith Butler, already referred to in this handbook, as well as Iris Marion Young and Sandra Lee Bartky, who I cite later in this chapter, all make use of phenomenological methods. What I find useful about phenomenology is the method of bringing to the front of consciousness what usually recedes into the background. But my point in calling the feminist killjoy a phenomenologist is not so much to locate her within this intellectual tradition, but to show how she is one by virtue of what she is doing. If to be a killjoy is to stand out, we bring to the front what is *not* perceived, what is around us or surrounds us.

Of course, there is only so much we can notice. You might walk into a room. It is familiar. When everything is as it should be, you don't notice it; it is just there. But, perhaps, something catches your attention. You look up, you look around. Perhaps something is missing; a vase, say, that is usually on the mantelpiece. If the vase was where you put it, where you expect it, you might not notice it. What deviates from an expectation of what is there or what should be there, is *striking*; it gets your attention. We too can deviate from an expectation. We too can be striking. You might appear odd, out of place, disturbing the picture, if you do not appear as expected. If you notice some absences, what is not there, like that missing vase, you might notice some presences, what or who is not supposed to be there.

You might notice being noticed. Think again of Sissie: it is only when she is referred to as 'the Black girl', that she sees whiteness: 'she looked around her, really well this time'. She regrets 'when she was made to notice differences in human colouring'.[9] But once she has noticed it, she can't unnotice it. Nor can she be comfortable. Whiteness can be comfortable for those who inhabit it. I think of comfort, and I think of an armchair that is all the more comfortable when used by someone who usually uses it. A social space can be like an armchair. When spaces become comfortable for some by being repeatedly used by them, they become less comfortable for others. Comfort can be the promise of a sinking feeling, a way of inhabiting space by the accumulation of gestures of sinking into it.

KILLJOY TRUTH: DISCOMFORT IS REVEALING OF WORLDS

Having worked in universities in the UK for most of my career, I got used to whiteness, to opening a door and encountering it. I stopped seeing it. But, every now and then, it would hit me, usually because of how I was addressed. One time, I was seated around a coffee table with friends and colleagues. A white feminist admired for her work on cultural difference was sitting opposite me. She leaned forward, as if peering at me closely. 'Sara, I didn't know you were Oriental.' I winced at that word, how it was pointed, its colonial legacy.

We are told who we are, assigned a place in history. Or, if we don't meet an expectation, we might be asked who we are. You might be stopped and questioned because of how you appear: who are you, where are you from, where are you *really* from? You can be Black or brown and born here and still be asked that question. One time I was asked that question when I was walking down a street in Cardiff. I answered I was born here. 'That's not what I meant,' the man said. 'I was brought up in Australia,' I replied. He became angry. I knew what he meant. He wanted me to explain myself, to give an account of how I ended up brown. The question 'where are you from?' can be how you are told you are not from here or you don't belong here. If you are seen as *not* from here, perhaps you become *not*, experienced as negation, pressing against something, intruding on somebody.

The stranger is noticeable. The stranger notices. I mentioned earlier in the handbook how I understand strangers not as those who we do not recognize but as those we do. I defined strangers as 'bodies out of place'. This formulation was an adaptation of the anthropologist Mary Douglas's definition of dirt as 'matter out of place'.[10] To define dirt as 'matter out of place' is to show how the perception of something or someone as dirty depends upon a set of prior expectations about what (and who) belongs here. That some people become 'bodies out of place' is not only how they are designated as dirty, unwanted or undesirable, but it provides justification for their removal. Neighbourhood Watch could be considered a system for recognizing strangers, those who seem suspicious, who loiter without a legitimate purpose, as potentially causing damage to property. Indeed, the injunction to be suspicious of strangers is often predicated on the protection of property.

The stranger is the one who appears because they are not expected. Or perhaps strangers don't appear as expected. You might be assumed not to be a philosopher, for instance, or not to be a professor, because you do not appear how a philosopher or professor usually appears. I walk into a lecture theatre with a white man; we are both professors. I feel the gaze land upon him: plop, plop. And then, he is addressed as the professor. When you are unexpected, you know who is expected. I know more about being a professor, or what it means to be a professor, from not having been seen or addressed as one.

KILLJOY TRUTH: THOSE WHO ARE NOT 'AT HOME' IN CATEGORIES TEND TO KNOW MORE ABOUT THEM

If I was to say, 'Hey, I am a professor, too', I would be heard as drawing attention to myself or even as being self-promotional. We don't even have to say 'Hey, I am a professor' to draw attention to ourselves. Heidi Mirza describes a conversation at her inaugural lecture as professor: 'A white male professor leaned into me at the celebration drinks and whispered bitterly in my ear "Well, they are giving chairs to anyone for anything these days."'[11] When a woman of colour becomes a chair, chairs lose their status and value. So, yes, when those designated as strangers get in (to a profession or a place), they are often judged as causing damage to property.

It can be the point of these kinds of utterances, to remind some of us we do not belong here. You do not get to feel *at home*, to move around easily, you don't get the promise of that sinking feeling. You are made suspicious, as if you are up to something. To be made suspicious is to end up under more scrutiny. A woman of colour academic describes the impact of this scrutiny: 'To retain your post you have to be whiter than white. You are not afforded any good will. You have no scope for error. You don't have any scope for being a bit foggy. The level of scrutiny is so high.' The expression *whiter than white* is telling us something: how whiteness becomes clean, good, pure, yes, but also for people of colour, how you have already failed to be those things, or how easily you come to fail, because when you are under scrutiny, anything can be used as evidence of failure, any mistake you make can be confirmation that you are not meant to be here.

KILLJOY TRUTH:
TO BE GIVEN ROOM IS TO BE GIVEN ROOM FOR ERROR

For some, norms can be roomy, how you are given more room. A norm tells you what to expect, who to expect. You might be asked whether you are in the right place if you do not appear as expected. You might enter the women's toilets. But if you do not appear as a woman is expected to appear, you might be told you are using the wrong facility. You might be told: you are not supposed to be here, directed towards another facility. When your use of a facility is questioned, you are questioned. When you are questioned about your right to occupy a space, you are being questioned about your right to occupy a category. A category too can be assumed to be closed; a door can be used to close the category 'woman', for instance. Becoming a stranger can mean being questioned, turned into a question, asked to debate your existence, to explain yourself. Questions can pile up, becoming a mountain, what you have to go up, to get around. Some more than others are *called upon to explain themselves*: who are you, what are you, why did you turn out like this, are you a boy or a girl, what's wrong with you, where are you from, no really, why do you look like that, why did you want that, why don't you want this?

KILLJOY TRUTH: FOR SOME, TO BE IS TO BE IN QUESTION

Or you might be invited to join the table only to become the question or the topic of conversation. A trans student of colour made a complaint about sexual harassment and transphobic harassment from their supervisor, who kept asking them deeply intrusive questions about their gender and genitals. These questions were laced in the language of concern for the welfare of the student, predicated on judgements that they would be endangered if they conducted research in their home country. Racist judgements are often about the location of danger 'over there' in a black or brown elsewhere. Transphobic judgements are often about the location of danger 'in here', in the body of the trans person: as if to be trans is to incite the violence against you.

When they complain, what happens? 'People were just trying to evaluate whether he [the supervisor] was right to believe there would be some sort of physical danger to me because of my gender identity,' they describe. 'As if to say he was right to be concerned.' The same questions that led you to complain are asked because you complain. These questions make the concern right or even into a right; a right to be concerned. So much harassment today is enacted as a right to be concerned. We have a right to be concerned about immigration (as 'citizens'); we have a right to be concerned about sex-based rights (as 'adult human females'). A right to be concerned is how violence is enacted, a violence premised on suspicion that some are not who they say they are, have no right to be where they are.

You can see why it is important to refuse to join some tables, to enter into debates where you are the question or the topic of conversation. I think back to how, when tables are used as examples within philosophy, they disappear. When you are asked to debate your existence around a table, you are asked to witness yourself disappear. In her aptly named article 'When Tables Speak', trans feminist philosopher Talia Mae Bettcher suggests that the problem of how tables appear in philosophy can be related to how philosophy has dealt with social and political issues. She notes: 'I'm afraid there's a tendency among some philosophers to suppose that philosophical investigations into race, gender, disability, trans issues, and so forth, are no different methodologically from investigations into the question of whether tables really exist.'[12] When some of us enter a philosophical conversation about 'race, gender, disability, trans issues', *it is akin to the tables speaking*: when we embody the issue, we cannot abstract it from our lives or our activism.

It is not surprising we keep speaking about tables. Maybe we keep speaking about tables because we know what it is like to be made an example. The phrase *made an example* can mean to punish someone as a warning to others. The figure of the feminist killjoy is used as an example in this sense. I discuss another philosopher, the phenomenologist Edmund Husserl, in *Queer Phenomenology: Orientations, Objects, Others*, which was the last book I wrote before the feminist killjoy turned up and became one of my central preoccupations. I sometimes call it my 'little table book'. In the introduction I describe how it came to be so:

Once I caught sight of the table in Husserl's writing, which is revealed just for a moment, I could not help but follow tables around. When you follow tables, you can end up anywhere. So, I followed Husserl in his turn to the table, and then when he turns away, I got led astray. I found myself seated at my table, at the different tables that mattered at different points in my life. How I wanted to make these tables matter![13]

I can hear how my feminist killjoy sensibilities led to this obsession with tables. Writing about tables was how I *set the table* for the feminist killjoy, enabling her to appear in my own work.

The table can be where we are asked questions, or where we become the question. To be a killjoy philosopher is to turn the questions *out.* We question who is made questionable and who is not. In my introduction to this handbook, I noted how asking someone to use the right pronouns for you or your partner is sufficient to become a killjoy not only in the sense of being a nuisance but also in the sense of imposing a requirement upon others. Perhaps in the past it was assumed (or perhaps we assume this about the past) that you could tell the difference; there she is, there he is, hello, sir, madam. Perhaps in the past it was assumed that she was she, she was with he, he was he, he was with she. To be part of a movement – a feminist, queer and trans movement – is to open up the world, open ourselves up, by refusing to make these assumptions. We don't assume we can tell the difference, or assume that she or he are all that is available; we don't assume who is who or who is with whom. *We ask each other how to address each other.*

Even a question can be treated as an imposition, as a restriction on freedom. In fact, as anyone involved in trying to challenge norms and conventions to enable them to be more accommodating discovers, you will be quickly judged as *imposing* restrictions on the freedom of others. A norm is a restriction that can feel like freedom to those it enables. To challenge a norm is thus almost always treated as restricting other people's freedoms. To turn pronouns into questions or preferences rather than assumptions or assertions is to become killjoys, all over again. Even asking for such small changes, such as being asked to be she or he or they, can produce such big reactions, as if you are asking for a world change. Maybe, just maybe, we are. As Lauren Berlant suggests, 'Even the smallest claim, such as not to be addressed by one's state-sanctioned name and the pronoun convention-ally attached to it, has been called "too much".'[14] In asking for minor modifications in the routine of address, we become, in Berlant's terms, 'inconvenient to the reproduction of norm-ative life, the conventions and institutions of that life'.

KILLJOY COMMITMENT: I AM WILLING TO BE INCONVENIENT

Refusing to make an assumption about another – about their gender, for instance – can be how we loosen our attachments to a world. An assumption is also a habit. When something has become a habit, you don't have to think about it. Habits can be useful: that you don't have to think about driving the car allows you to think about other things when you are driving the car. But if we think of social assumptions as habits, we learn how they might seem natural, obvious, inevitable, how we do things as how they are, because they have become unthinking. To challenge an assumption is to ask us to think about it, to turn every word, every term through which we communicate with each other, into something to be thought through or thought about or thought out.

To be a feminist killjoy philosopher is a commitment to think what is unthought, what is turned into an assumption or presumption by the habits of everyday life. Every category becomes an occasion for more thought, every practice questioned because we have put the old tired explanations – nature, culture, history, biology – out of work. Even to throw open the world with questions is to become the object of so much hostility. That, too, is how we learn; we learn how much is invested in not questioning an arrangement. I suggested earlier histories can be made to seem natural or inevitable because they become habits; they ease our passage through life by allowing so much to be done without thought. To become conscious of what was previously habitual can thus be to become alienated from your own history.

We can return to feminist critiques of happiness. If happiness is how a restriction of possibility is justified as necessary, becoming a feminist leads you to become conscious of possibilities. Sometimes we become conscious of a possibility when it is no longer possible.

148

KILLJOY TRUTH: TO BECOME CONSCIOUS OF
POSSIBILITY CAN INVOLVE MOURNING FOR ITS LOSS

It is not surprising, then, that the journey to feminist consciousness can lead us to the feminist killjoy; you can end up
feeling like you have to kill your own joy. To become feminist can be to become conscious of what we have already
given up. Iris Marion Young discusses how some girls learn
to 'throw like girls', they learn not to get themselves behind
an action, exhibiting what she calls 'inhibited intention-
ality'. She describes how girls often 'lack confidence in their
capacity to do what needs to be done'. She goes on to note:
'We decide beforehand – usually mistakenly – that the task
is beyond us and thus give it less than our full effort.'[15] Decisions we make about our capacities are not always our own.
We receive messages all the time that tell us who can do
what (and who cannot). If you are told you can't do it, that
girls can't do it, you might doubt whether you can do it; you
might not put all of yourself into it. And then when you
don't manage it, you don't pull it off, the judgement that
you are not capable is confirmed. Gender norms sometimes
work through a reversal of sequence: we assume we do it
because we can, or don't because we can't, but often we can
do it because we do it, or we can't because we don't. Over
time, girls learn to inhabit their bodies with less confidence,
assuming what they cannot do as a restriction of a horizon
of possibility.

It is not just possibility that is restricted. Some of us are taught to take up less space. The less space you take up, the less space you have. Conversations can be spaces. I have suggested that we become feminist killjoys if we take up too much of that space, which can be a judgement made about some of us for saying anything at all. This might be why becoming *more* of a feminist killjoy is about acquiring *more* confidence. The journey to becoming a feminist can be about learning how we have been taught to take up less space (and thus how we come to know we could have had more space than we have). I think of a conversation I had with a professor about her experience of harassment when she was a student. She described how difficult it was to protect herself: 'A tutor at my college had been harassing me verbally, well, it was more a case of going up to that line beyond which it would be pretty clear what he was trying to do. It was just a case of trying to push that line and inveigle his way into my confidence, in getting me to meet him off campus. I was not comfortable with it. He still found ways of talking to me, and presented it very much as "I am just being friendly here". We are always taught, aren't we, to be polite and considerate and the least troublesome as possible.'

Who you are taught to be, *how* you are taught to be, polite, considerate, not troublesome, as a girl, as a student, is how you become more vulnerable, less willing or able to stop someone from pushing the line you need to protect yourself. When you know that to say *no* is to be judged as antisocial, it is hard to say *no*. To say *no*, *no* to the harasser, but also *no* to the structure than enables that harasser, requires a refusal to be what we are told is a right or good way to be. But that you say *no* also means you become conscious of how you were taught. When you become conscious of gender as *a lesson*, you are unlearning gender, you become estranged from what was previously a habit.

To think of the feminist killjoy as a philosopher is another way of thinking about the time it takes to acquire a feminist consciousness. As Sandra Lee Bartky notes, 'to be a feminist, one has first to become one'. Bartky describes becoming a feminist not only as 'developing a radically altered consciousness of oneself and others', but also as changing one's consciousness of what she calls 'social reality'.[16] This process of alteration does not stop happening. Even after we have identified as feminists we still have to work on ourselves, to notice something, which is why the feminist killjoy often appears just ahead of ourselves. An MA student began her new programme with high hopes. And then 'it started': 'It started, I would say, in the second or third lesson I had with Prof X. There were certain signs that rang alarm bells for me and my first reaction is stop being paranoid, stop being . . . a feminazi where everything is gendered, you know, you are probably reading too much into this, you need to take a step back.'

The sound of an alarm bell announces a danger in the external world even if you hear the sound inside your own head. We don't always take heed of what we hear. She starts questioning herself rather than his behaviour. She tells herself off; she gives herself a talking to. In questioning herself, she also makes use of stereotypes of feminists as feminazis, distancing herself from her first reaction by distancing herself from feminism, even though she identified as a feminist. But she keeps noticing the behaviour because it keeps happening: 'He left any thinker who wasn't a white man essentially until the end of the course.' He introduces a woman thinker as 'not a very sophisticated thinker'. She comes to realize that her first impression that something was wrong was right: 'And then I was like, no, no, no, no, things are wrong not just in terms of gender, things are desperately wrong with the way he is teaching full stop.' When she realizes she was right to hear that something was wrong, those *no*s come out. I think of all of those *no*s, 'no, no, no, no', the sound of an increasing confidence in her own judgement.

KILLJOY MAXIM:
GET A *NO* OUT SO THAT OTHERS CAN FOLLOW!

You can become a killjoy because of what you refuse to take in. We could describe sexism as *received wisdom*. It is not that sexism is wise but that sexism is what you are supposed to take in; you are supposed to take the professor in, how wise he is, how wise he is assumed to be; the canon in, the curriculum in, what he says, whatever he says. It is not only that we are supposed to *revere* the canon, as I suggested in the previous chapter, we are supposed to *ingest* it. So, when she tells him she wants to write her essay on gender and race, he says, 'If you write on those fucking topics you are going to fucking fail my course, you haven't fucking understood

152

anything I have been talking about if you think those are the correct questions for this course.' If you ask the wrong questions, you hear the violence of correction. And then she hears how he writes her off: 'But then he says, "Wait, you know what, you're so fucking old, your grades don't really matter, you're not going to have a career in academia, so write whatever essay you wanted to write. You are going to fail, but it doesn't matter."' She becomes not only a nag but a hag, the feminist who gets the questions wrong, the old woman who might as well be wrong, who is too old for it to matter whether she got it wrong, because she can't proceed, she won't proceed.

She did not proceed. Towards the end of her testimony, the student told me that she had begun her MA with the hope she would go on to do a PhD. But then she said, 'That door is closed.' I discuss in more detail what led to *that* door being closed in my chapter on the feminist killjoy as activist. Let me pause on this expression, 'That door is closed.' This is quite an ordinary expression. But when she said it, I heard the sound of a door being shut. I noticed the door. When feminist killjoys become philosophers, we turn the table into a door. Noticing tables is about how we can see something because of our alienation from it. Why notice doors, then? We are more likely to notice what stops us from doing something. We are more likely to notice doors when we can't open them.

Doors matter. They matter as metaphors; to say 'That door is closed' is to say that a path has closed or an opportunity has been lost. Doors matter as ordinary, familiar things that swing on hinges. A door is a border, an entry point, but also an exit point, a means to control who is coming and going. Doors can be, to borrow from the title of Audre Lorde's famous essay, 'The Master's Tools', how some are given the right to enter a building, how others become trespassers. To be a gatekeeper is to 'hold the door' to an institution or profession. Philosophy, for instance, has doors that you have to go through to become a philosopher. A definition of philosophy can be a door. Once I asked Judith Butler about their relation to philosophy. They answered:

> *The way philosophers tried to exclude one another from the definition of philosophy was actually part of their professional practice and should enter into any sociological description of the field. There was always something grave and authoritative about the claim that someone else was not 'really' a philosopher. Sometimes it was said with an air of superiority and other times it was delivered as an act of derision.*[17]

We learn so much from disciplines from those deemed as not 'really' doing them. My own story of becoming obsessed with a philosopher's table might have told you I am not 'really' a philosopher. Feminists often have a *killjoy relationship* to academic disciplines, including philosophy, we are not quite at home in them. This is why to think of the killjoy *as* a philosopher is not about claiming she 'really' *is* one.

That doors keep coming up is telling us something about how worlds are built, what you have to do to get through them. I spoke to another student who was being harassed by her supervisor. She's a queer woman of colour: she is from a working-class background; she is the first in her family to go to university. She's had to fight really hard to get here. She is being advised by someone she admires. Having fought to get here, she is where she wants to be. Still, something is not right. She is feeling more and more uncomfortable. Her supervisor keeps pushing back boundaries, wanting to meet off campus, then at coffee shops, then at his house. She tries at first to handle the situation. She describes: 'I tried very hard to keep all of the meetings on campus, and to keep the door open.' She keeps the door open, an actual door, at the same time as she closes another kind of door, we might call this door the door of consciousness, trying to shut out what he is doing: 'I thought I would take myself down by admitting to the kind of violence he was enacting.' Take myself down: to admit to violence can feel like becoming your own killjoy, getting in the way of your own progression. To admit can mean to confess a truth as well as to let something in. Doors hold a contradiction: to keep the office door open is an admission of a truth she handles by not letting it in. But handles can stop working.

'I was sitting with another colleague at another lunch another day and he started texting me these naked photos of himself and I think I just hit a critical mass of, like, I just can't handle it any more. I said, Just look at this, and she was just like, you know like, completely speechless . . . And then like it suddenly started to seep into me, into her, in this shared conversation about, like, how horrible and violent that I am having to receive these things, right, and so that basically put a process in motion.'

A handle is sometimes what we use to stop the violence directed at us from seeping or leaking into us. When the handle stops working, the violence seeps not only into her but also into her colleague; into a conversation, into the space in which they are having that conversation. When violence gets in, a complaint comes out. A critical mass can be what has to be reached before things can be set in motion.

It can be difficult to admit something. To let the violence in would mean to give up so much. It can be hard to recognize harassment even though it is happening to you, or because it is happening to you. It might be that it has to reach a certain point such as the sending of naked photos, such that you cannot not see what is happening, although then, even then, it is still possible to excuse the behaviour, or to allow others to excuse the behaviour ('It was a mistake', 'That's what he's like', 'It didn't mean anything'). Those excuses after all exist all around you, they surround you. An excuse can be how a door is shut before something even happens. *We inherit closed doors*, ways of not seeing something, of shutting it out. This is why opening a door is never completed by one action. You might admit what happened was wrong, but then when you try and share the story, as the student did, you will hear those excuses, those justifications, more doors being shut.

Remember this **killjoy truth**: there is only so much you can take on, as there is only so much you can take in.

Sometimes we can't take something in because of what we have taken on. We might keep the door shut because we know what is behind it. A woman attends a meeting for senior managers. She is the only woman around the table. She is used to this; it is business as usual. But then one of the men at the table makes a sexualizing comment about chasing a woman around a dark room. She described how the comment became a bonding moment between men: how the atmosphere in the room changed, laughter, interest, as if they had been brought to attention. Even when you are used to it, it can hit you, the sexism, the heterosexism, bubbling away at the surface of so many encounters. She did not say anything. She did not do anything.

After expressing her feelings to me, of alienation, disappointment, also of sadness, she said, 'You file it under "Don't go there".' And that is what many of us do: to keep doing our work, we file away what is hardest to handle. Note that these files are full of what we have already noticed. The file 'Don't go there' tells us where we have been. The killjoy philosopher opens that file, looking closely at what has been put away by being put here. And note, too, that if you open that file, you don't only see what is in the file. *You see what is not seen because of what is in the file.*

Sometimes we try not to notice something because to notice it would be to stop us from doing our work. At other times, we notice something because it is stopping us from doing our work. You might not have the key to the door. A key can be an actual thing, made exactly to specification so only that key can unlock that lock. A body can be a key.

A door can be shut because you can't open it; perhaps it is too heavy for you to pull or too narrow for you to get through. Many doors are not usable to those who have mobility restrictions. An access sign is used to give information to disabled people about where or how to enter. As Tanya Titchkosky says, 'a white stick figure against a blue background', has become a 'symbol of a wheelchair user'. Titchkosky also notes that if you have to use a sign to indicate access, then 'There must be an assumption of a general lack of access.'[18]

A world can be built around an assumption. A table, a door, assumes the bodies using it. As Aimi Hamraie notes, 'Examine any doorway, window, toilet, chair or desk . . . and you will find the outline of the body meant to use it.'[19] When you can't use something, you are more likely to examine it, to become conscious of it; to notice its weight, its size; to apprehend its qualities. You put things under inspection when you cannot make use of things to do what you are supposed to do. We put things under inspection when our involvement in the world, stepping forward or towards it, is made difficult or becomes a crisis.

KILLJOY TRUTH: YOU NOTICE WORLDS WHEN THEY ARE NOT BUILT FOR YOU

So much work in disability studies captures what I am describing as killjoy philosophy. Rosemarie Garland-Thomson describes misfitting as follows:

A misfit occurs when the environment does not sustain the shape and function of the body that enters it. The dynamism between body and world that produces fits or misfits comes at the spatial and temporal points of encounter between dynamic but relatively stable bodies and environments. The built and arranged space through which we navigate our lives tends to offer fits to majority bodies and create misfits with minority forms of embodiment, such as people with disabilities'.[20]

In an earlier article, Garland-Thomson describes misfitting as 'an incongruent relationship between two things: a square peg in a round hole.'[21] When you try to fit a norm that is not shaped to fit your body, you create an incongruity, or become one.

We might become more conscious of our bodies when we try and fit ourselves into a space that is not built for us. Killjoy philosophy gives us another way of *thinking about thinking*. We are thinking with and from our bodies. Even our exhaustion can be insightful, the physicality of a strain and a struggle; we learn from what we keep coming up against. That we become conscious of our bodies teaches us as much about the world as it does about our bodies. We philosophize *because* we are not accommodated, we philosophize *when* we are not accommodated! We become square pegs, misfits, killjoys, when we have to keep demanding different entry points in order to get in.

I spoke to a disabled student about the work she had to do to secure reasonable adjustments so she could complete her degree: 'They experienced my need for adjustment as making their lives a complete pain in the ass and they wanted at the very least grovelling gratefulness on a daily basis in order to continue providing it, preferably considerably more than that. I think if I had turned up with some kind of cheerleaders for them, I think then maybe they would have thought it was acceptable.' Asking for accommodations is framed not only as causing inconvenience to others but as *being* an inconvenience. You have to smile as if in compensation for the inconvenience. As feminist philosopher Marilyn Frye observed, 'it is often a requirement upon oppressed people that we smile and be cheerful. If we comply, we signify our docility and our acquiescence in our situation'.[22] Not smiling, not showing signs of gratitude, not being a cheerleader for the organization, is sufficient to be heard as a killjoy, as not being compliant, as complaining, being demanding.

If you point out that a room is inaccessible you are heard not only as a killjoy, but as potentially depriving others of a room of their choice. And you might have to keep pointing out that the room is inaccessible because they keep booking rooms that are inaccessible. A disabled academic shared with me what it felt like to do this work: 'I worry about drawing attention to myself. But this is what happens when you hire a person in a wheelchair. There have been major access issues at the university.' She spoke of 'the drain, the exhaustion, the sense of why should I have to be the one who speaks out?' You have to speak out because others do not; and because you speak out, others can justify their own silence. They hear you, so it becomes about you, 'major access issues' become your issues. If you have to keep saying it because they keep doing it, it is still you who is heard as repeating yourself. You are heard as a broken record, stuck on the same point.

The feminist killjoy as a broken record: we hear something here. Think back to that scene from *Arlington Park*, how Juliet is heard as strident even though she is interrupting somebody else who is 'going on and on'. That some of us are heard as repeating ourselves is about what (or who) does not come into view. I am reminded of a conversation I had with a student who made a complaint about sexual harassment. She described how by complaining 'you draw attention to the inequities, the power situations that are present, the things that you know people should see, but the minute you draw attention to them the attention is drawn to you.' When drawing attention to a problem draws attention to yourself, the problem doesn't come into view *because you do*. When this student sees how she is seen, she also sees that other people do not see, 'the inequities, the power situations that are present.'

We can return to our **killjoy equation, noticing = the feminist killjoy's hammer**. To be a killjoy is to learn *how* some things remain unnoticed. The disabled academic who worried she was 'drawing attention to herself' in addressing 'major access issues' noticed the door that made a room inaccessible to her. She probably also noticed that the people who could open the door did not notice it was not accessible. But she also learnt *how* people kept not noticing the door by seeing her as the one with the problem when she

161

pointed it out. It can be exhausting to have to keep ham-mering away at the door, not just an actual door, but the door of other people's consciousness. And so, more doors are shut by how some people are made responsible for opening them in the sense of making events or institutions more accessible. This is why to be a killjoy is to see through diversity, which is often represented not only as a happy table but as an open door. An open door can be evoked by a tag line: we are back to that welcoming address, minorities welcome, come in, come in!

KILLJOY TRUTH: JUST BECAUSE THEY WELCOME YOU, IT DOES NOT MEAN THEY EXPECT YOU TO TURN UP

Some of us are assumed to bring diversity with us. Perhaps by turning up, we come to realize we are not welcome or that we are welcome on condition we don't try and change things too much. This academic described how she 'was brought in to assist with some cultural change, to bring in diversity and a progressive curriculum'. When an organiz-ation appoints someone 'to assist with some cultural change', it does not necessarily mean those within the organization are willing to be assisted. She described her experience thus:

'I found being the only woman in a senior management group quite a distressing experience. I found there were lots of sexualized conversations. I felt like I was in a latrine. They were really over the top; inappropriate. There were also racialized conversations. They always referred to "the Black

162

boy". . . . The dean . . . is a really high flyer and crash hot about feminist stuff, feminist politics and scholarship; he had a double kind of life. I thought someone from a diverse background would actually make a difference, which is why I took up that position. I was the most senior person with a visible disability in the university.'

You find a gap between the official commitment to diversity and equality, and the kinds of conversations that are routine; between a senior manager who is 'hot about feminist stuff' and the conduct of that manager. She came to realize that hiring someone from a 'diverse background' does not make a difference, that her arrival did not make a difference, even though they could and did use her arrival as a sign of having made a difference. Even if your difference does not make a difference, you are still supposed to be positive, which means overlooking so much negative stuff; all those sexualized conversations, all those racialized conversations. The requirement to be positive can mean covering over the hostility of an environment. Another woman of colour described her department to me as a 'revolving door': women and minorities enter only to head right out again, whoosh, whoosh. You can be kept out by what you find out when you get in.

Doors can be shut by appearing to be open. A Black woman told me about how she was racially harassed and bullied by a white woman who was her head of department: 'I think what she wanted to do was to maintain her position as the director, and I was supposed to be some pleb. You know what I mean: she had to be the boss, and I had to be the servant type of thing. That was how her particular version of white supremacy worked, so not just belittling my academic credentials and academic capabilities, but also belittling me in front of the students, belittling me in front of administrators.'

How do you know it's about race? That's a question we often get asked. Racism is how we know it's about race; we come to know whiteness – or let's call it what it is, as she did, white supremacy – intimately, as it is what keeps coming up. To have got there – a Black woman in a white institution, a lecturer, a senior lecturer, on her way to becoming a professor (she is now a professor) – is to be understood as getting above her station, above herself, ahead of herself. To belittle someone can be a command: Be little! To refuse that command is to exceed your position, to become too much. The feminist killjoy, remember, is seen as making something bigger than it is. We are also seen as trying to make ourselves bigger.

She added, 'I had put down that I would like to work towards becoming a professor, and she just laughed in my face.' That laughter can be the sound of a door being slammed. Some of us, in becoming professors, become trespassers; you are being told you need permission to enter by being told you do not have permission. We can become Black and brown feminist killjoys by wanting more for ourselves, because our own ideas of what we can do, or who we can be, exceed their estimations. Perceptions can be doors; you can be stopped because of how you are seen. This is not to say we are always stopped, but that some of us have to work harder, do more, to get through the door of perception. When perceptions are doors, the doors are not perceived by those who are not stopped by them. This is important: if you are stopped by a door, and the door is not perceived, it can seem like you have stopped yourself.

We know how the world is built from how we are stopped. Not fitting can be about the effort and energy required for some to complete what might seem to be an easy or simple action, like opening the door.

What about fitting, then? Fitting can mean less time, effort or energy is required to complete that same action. When the world is built for you, there is so much you do not have to think about, so much you do not have to do.

KILLJOY EQUATION:
PRIVILEGE = AN ENERGY-SAVING DEVICE

Some might view the institution as open because it was open to them. That view of the organization, I would add, corresponds to, and is confirmed by, the official view: the door is open, anyone can enter. Openness can then be assumed to be a quality of a thing rather than a relation to it. It is not just that some do not need to notice doors. They might be *invested* in not noticing doors. To be invested in not noticing doors is about protecting a *relation* to an institution.

I think back to how, when we ask questions about gender and race, they become the wrong questions. We might question who is here and who is not here. We might ask why are our professors not Black or why are all the best-paid people men. We point to the structures that enable some to fit the criteria for promotion; how they have doors opened for them because of how they speak, how they act, because of their connections. Those who fit might hear 'fit' as self-description, evoking as muscle memory Herbert Spencer's retelling of Darwin's theory of evolution as a story of the 'survival of the fittest', as if the fact that they have done well or are valued more is evidence that they are more fit rather than they fit more.

KILLJOY EQUATION: SURVIVAL OF THE FITTEST = SURVIVAL OF THOSE WHO FIT

To be a feminist killjoy philosopher is to give an explanation of structure. The word structure might seem rather abstract. What do I mean by it here? A structure can be used to refer to a complex arrangement between different parts. In my book *What's the Use? On the Uses of Use*, I began to think about fitting in terms of structure in a precise sense. I explored how Darwin made use of 'use' in explaining natural selection. Darwin uses the metaphor of a building that is built without a design or plan. That this or that stone is selected is described by Darwin as 'accidental', the stone used is the one that happens to fit. The word *accident* might make us think of events like car crashes. But the word accident can simply mean something that happens by chance, unintentionally or unexpectedly. If it is an accident that this stone fits, the selection of the stone still references its material qualities; its size and shape.[23] An institution, too, is shaped by processes of selection. It might appear as if the moment of selection is accidental: that this person or that person just happens to fit the requirements, the way this stone just happens to be the same size as that hole in a wall. Once a building has been built, once it has taken form, more or less, some more than others will fit the requirements. The same people will keep having the qualities referenced as being necessary to fill the vacancy when the vacancy was created with them in mind. It can then appear as if some people just happened to fit, rather than they fit *because of how the structure was built.*

That appearance is turned into an argument. When you point out the structure, they reply it was an accident: we are here because we just happened to meet the requirements. This is how a structure can disappear by accident. We – let's call ourselves the killjoy philosophers – reply, You meet the requirements because you made them. Institutions are reproduced by stabilizing the requirements for what you need to survive or thrive within them. They might reply, more forcefully, perhaps using the word *merit,* that they are where they are, higher up, because they are better or even the best. I recall a time when I was a visiting scholar at an elite institution. I kept noticing how colleagues kept using the word *best* for everything, the best wine, the best this, the best that. Perhaps they were trying to convince themselves or perhaps they were hoping the word *best* would eventually stick. The killjoy as philosopher is attuned to who defines what; in other words, to what sticks. We reply, You are not here or higher up because you are the best, you are the best because you are here or higher up; in other words, you have defined the best around yourselves.

Diversity is often framed as helping those who are not the best, diversity as the back door, diversity as assistance. But those assumed to be where they are on the basis of merit are often those who are most assisted. The assistance given to some by a structure disappears along with the structure. It can then seem as if those who go further or go faster do so of their own volition. This is why statements such as 'It is easier to get a job if you are a person of colour' or 'You have to be a diversity hire to be hired' can be uttered in organizations dominated by white men. This is how 'equal opportunities' is treated as discriminatory. The structure that makes it harder for some to get in or get through is the same structure that eases the passage and progression of others. It is not surprising, then, that we encounter such resistance when we point out structures, when we try to make more visible for whom the doors are opened (and for whom they not).

KILLJOY TRUTH: THE MORE WE CHALLENGE STRUCTURES, THE MORE WE COME UP AGAINST THEM

When structures disappear by accident, we still catch a glimpse of them, because of how they are turned into statues, monuments of individual achievement, stories of who should be revered or admired. Think statue, think that old block. The expression 'chip off the old block' is most commonly used to refer to paternity, how the son is like his father, but it also helps to capture how institutions reproduce themselves in his image. The killjoy as philosopher: *we keep chipping away at the old block.*

It takes work not to keep reproducing the same thing. Many organizations appoint equality or diversity practitioners to do this work. But even when organizations appoint people to transform them, it does not mean they are willing to be transformed. One diversity practitioner described her work as 'a banging your head against the brick wall job'. A job description becomes a wall description. Banging your head against a brick wall, the sore point of repetition; you have a sense of coming up against the same thing, over and over again. So although she was appointed by the organization, she experiences it as a wall, blocking her efforts. Perhaps her efforts are blocked not just despite being given an appointment but through it.

KILLJOY TRUTH: WE LEARN ABOUT INSTITUTIONS FROM TRYING TO TRANSFORM THEM

Institutions can stay the same by appearing to commit to change. I spoke to one lecturer about her experience of appointment panels. Her university had introduced a numerical system for evaluating the performance of job candidates in an effort to ensure equality of treatment. She described what actually happened during the appointment process: 'Someone would say, that woman's presentation was outstanding, but, really, he's the guy you'd want to have a pint with, so let's make the figures fit.' The figures are made to fit when a person is deemed to fit. Fitting can also be about *fitting in*. The person most likely to be appointed is still the one who can participate in a shared culture; 'the guy you'd want to have a pint with', who you can relate to, whose company you would prefer. Earlier I suggested that habits save time and energy. Institutions too have habits. Hiring can be a habit, how the same sorts of people keep being appointed, reflecting back who is already there. When new policies and procedures are introduced to break that habit, they do not always stop what is habitually done from being done.

That wall comes up because of what you are trying not to reproduce. A diversity practitioner told me a long story about how she managed to get a new policy agreed requiring all academic members of appointment panels to be diversity trained. This policy was not especially ambitious: she knew that requiring diversity training wouldn't necessarily lead to more diversity in who was appointed.

The story is long because the resistance to the new policy came from different actors within the organization. The policy was agreed by the equality and diversity committee, but the agreement was removed from minutes of the meeting by the head of human resources. But when the minutes went to another committee, a higher-up committee, a member of that committee who was also a member of the equality and diversity committee noticed the removal. And then they had to take the minutes back to the committee to get the minutes amended. After all this effort, the policy was eventually agreed. But then other people in the institution acted as if the policy had not been agreed. The practitioner keeps making the same point in meetings. When her colleagues keep referencing the old policy, she has to keep saying there is a new one and that the Council haven't changed their view since. 'I said, I can give you the minutes, and they just look at me as if I am saying something really stupid. This went on for ages, even though the Council minutes definitely said all panel members should be trained. And to be honest sometimes you just give up.' In my tips on surviving as a feminist killjoy, I noted how a history of killjoys can be hard to give because of how we are blanked. This diversity officer is blanked not despite the evidence but because of it. It is only because there is a new policy that they have to pretend it does not exist. And because they blanked her, and also the policy, they kept doing what they were doing, appointing the same people in the same old way.

Those who worked to create a new policy know the work it took not to get anywhere. It is only the practical effort to bring about transformation that *allows the wall to be apparent*. To those who do not come up against it, the wall does not even appear; perhaps the organization appears as happy as its mission statement, as its diversity statement. What makes the brick wall so hard is that it is not even perceived by others. If there was an actual wall, you could at least point to it, although even actual things can be made to disappear. An actual wall is made out of hard material.

In physics, hardness refers to the resistance of materials to change under conditions of force. We encounter the materiality of resistance to transformation when we try to transform what has become material. If you were to throw a little object against the wall, it would shatter. What would happen to the wall? Perhaps there would be a scratch on the surface. This is what trying to transform institutions can feel like: scratching at the surface, scratching the surface. We can be the little objects. We throw ourselves against the brick wall only to shatter, which is one reason there is so much shattering in killjoy stories.

Those who don't come up against walls experience those who talk about them as *wall makers*. Feminist killjoys are positioned as wall makers. When we point out problems we are treated as bringing them into existence. Another wall comes up in the reframing of walls as *immaterial* as phantoms, as how we *stop ourselves* from doing something, or how we stop ourselves from being something. And so, we learn: what is real, what is in concrete terms the *hardest*, is not always available as an object that can be perceived or touched even by those seated at the same table.

KILLJOY TRUTH: WHAT IS HARDEST FOR SOME DOES NOT EXIST FOR OTHERS

We can be at the same table and in a different world. Same table, different world: oh, how feminist killjoys know this! We know this because we live this! We can explain why,

172

also how, in accounting for *that* scene, around the table, disturbing the atmosphere, feminist killjoys became philosophers. Same table, different world.

We have gone from tables, to doors, to walls, and back to tables. The table, too, matters. Not everything that is material can be perceived by everyone. If those with privilege are those who philosophize, *so much material will be missing.* No amount of critical reflection, wondering or pondering will bring some things into view. Some things are *not* perceived because of what some people do not have to force into existence. Feminist killjoys appear all the more forceful because of what we have to do to get through. There is a connection, then, between *how we know* and *what we do*. I bang that table, thinking again of Angela Davis, showing us how to philosophize by trying to change the world. To try to change how things are is to know how things are. That is why, also how, feminist killjoys know so much.

5/ The Feminist Killjoy as Poet

In considering the feminist killjoy as poet, I am thinking of our need to find new forms of expression. I noted earlier in the handbook that you can be heard as a killjoy without saying anything, by not laughing or smiling, not showing your compliance with an existing regime. But sometimes, to be a feminist killjoy, you have to work to express yourself. To express can mean to *press out*. I learn from the sense evolution of the word *expression*. It came to mean 'to put into words or to speak one's mind via the intermediary sense of how clay under pressure takes a certain form.'[1] When I imagine that clay, I imagine not only how we give shape to something, but how we ourselves are under pressure to take a certain form. To express ourselves, to get something out of ourselves, or even to get ourselves out, can require resisting that pressure. By 'the feminist killjoy as poet', I am not suggesting that feminist killjoys simply write poems to express ourselves as if poems are tools being applied to a task at hand. Rather, poetry is a way of thinking about what makes it possible to speak our minds, to give shape to our thoughts and feelings, *given* the pressure we are under to comply.

Not everyone who writes poems appears as a poet.

Claudia Rankine, critic, also poet, also philosopher, refers directly to the racialized history of the poet. In her poetic, experimental text *Just Us*, Rankine has a section, 'Notes on the State of Whiteness', which is a reproduction of part of an old book, *Notes on the State of Virginia*, from 1888.[2] Only some sentences of this old book are visible in her book. Other sentences are blacked out. Sentences, highlighted by not being blacked out, hit you. Here are some: 'Misery is often the parent of the most affecting touches in poetry – Among the blacks is misery enough, God knows, but no poetry . . . it could not produce a poet.'[3] Poetry as high culture is deemed to come from higher people, from white people. There can be a hierarchy to suffering: the white poet might be melancholic, yes, but his suffering is profound, just as his happiness is virtuous.

KILLJOY TRUTH: WHEN BLACK AND BROWN PEOPLE BECOME POETS, WE ARE FIGHTING AGAINST HISTORY

To create we might have to push against an idea of who creates or an idea of ourselves as not somebody who creates. If to create is to make something that does not yet exist, we do so, we can do so, because of who is behind us. I think of my own family history, of my auntie, Gulzar Bano, who was a poet. She wrote poems as forcefully and furiously and fiercely as she lived her life. My aunt was an unmarried woman, a Muslim feminist, doing what she could do to create a less harsh and less hostile world for women, especially for poor women, in Pakistan, a country created from the scattered remains of a violent imperial history. My aunt was not afraid to express her opinions. She might even have been called opinionated.

KILLJOY EQUATION: OPINIONATED = WHEN SOME OF US EXPRESS OUR OPINIONS

Becoming close to Auntie, with her passion for feminism and for what she called in our family biography 'WOMAN POWER', gave me a different political orientation, a different way of thinking about my place in the world. She did not have a child of her own. In a conventional genealogy, women who do not have children of their own would be an end point.

Snap, snap: the end of the line.

In a feminist killjoy genealogy, created by those who do not follow straight lines, who wander away from what they are told they should do or be, life unfolds from such points.

Snap, snap: begin again.

As a feminist killjoy, as a brown feminist killjoy, I inherit so much from my Auntie. I dedicate these reflections on the feminist killjoy as poet to my Auntie. I begin this chapter with a reflection on wilfulness and creativity, and on the material resources we need to create as well as to communicate, before turning to the poetry and projects of two writers who have influenced my own killjoy trajectory, Adrienne Rich and Audre Lorde (a discussion that moves from doorframes,

177

to doors, to doorways), and finally, to an exploration of how there is poetry in killing joy, a rearranging of worlds as well as words, breathing life into arrangements.

Thinking of the feminist killjoy as a poet is a way of showing the creativity of being a feminist killjoy; we create something in part by what we refuse to do or be. Feminist killjoys are creative not *despite* being killjoys but *because* of being killjoys. And yet, creativity might seem far from the life situation of the feminist killjoy, whose *modus operandi* might appear to be rather destructive. Let's consider again Claudia's inspection of the white baby doll she is supposed to love in *The Bluest Eye*. She dismembers the doll to learn how it is put together. In one way, the work of the killjoy does require destroying something. What we pull apart, we cannot put back together in the same way. Nor would we want to. After all, the doll itself can be thought of as destructive; the equation of happiness with whiteness makes so many feel wrong, not beautiful, not wanted; not loved. To destroy what is destructive is to create something that would allow more of us to see ourselves reflected in the world.

We pull something apart so we can put it back together again in another way, and in so doing, we may be putting ourselves back together again, too. This is why the same action, whether understood as destructive or not, is not only a method, a way of studying, of writing, but a way of living *strangerwise*. *Strangerwise* is an odd word for an old wisdom, the wisdom of strangers, those who, in being estranged from worlds, notice them.

In the previous chapter, I suggested that noticing is the

feminist killjoy's hammer. If we notice the vase because it is missing, if what is odd or out of place is striking, there is poetry right there. Noticing can be a hammer, but also a pen or a keyboard, writing as fine-tuning, moving words around so things appear differently. I think of how *The Bluest Eye* begins with a story of a happy family from children's books. 'Here is the family. Mother, Father, Dick and Jane live in the green-and-white house. They are very happy.'[4] Morrison then removes the punctuation and spaces between words so that the story no longer makes sense. This is the creativity of her poetic attention: rearranging words to change our relation to what they depict. So much of the work of the killjoy is to change the usual sequence. To stop something, we stop it from making sense, maybe some words need to get stuck, not roll off our tongues quite so easily.

KILLJOY MAXIM:
STOP THE WORLD FROM MAKING SENSE!

Or maybe to become a poet is how other words roll off our tongues more easily, including the word *poet* itself. Poet can be an answer to a question of what you want to do or be. Ama Ata Aidoo, a poet as well as a novelist, answered such a question:

> At the age of 15, a teacher had asked me what I wanted to do for a career, and without knowing why or even how I replied that I wanted to be a poet. About four years later I won a short story competition but learned about it only when I opened the

newspaper that had organized it, and saw the story had been published on its centre pages and realized the name of the author of that story in print was mine. I believe these moments were crucial for me because . . . I had articulated a dream . . . it was a major affirmation for me as a writer, to see my name in print.[5]

The poet can be claimed in a reply to a question of what you want to be, who you want to be. You can claim to be one before you are one. A poet can claim you and, in claiming you, a poet can be how your name and your words end up in print.

I think, too, of Sissie, our sister killjoy, how she travels, how she goes places, how she gets her words out and about. She gives serious speeches. She writes an unsent letter to her lover, addressed as 'my Precious Something'. She begins with his instruction, 'Yes I remember that I was going to be positive about everything. Since you reminded me that the negative is so corrosive.'[6] But when she reflects on his reminder of the corrosion of negativity, which he compares to cancer, she makes an analogy with the West:

I nodded agreement, my eyes lighting up at how profession-ally clear you always are. But I remember too when I attempted to grasp your point better by suggesting a political parallel, that negativism then must be like the expansion of western civ-ilisation in modern times, because it chokes all life and even eliminates whole races of people in its path of growth, you said laughing: 'There you go again, Sissie, you are so serious.'[7]

The feminist killjoy or sister killjoy is often caught by that word *serious*. Serious is a *wilful* word. Alice Walker describes a 'womanist' in the following way: 'A black feminist or feminist of color . . . Usually referring to outrageous, audacious, courageous or *willful* behavior. Wanting to know more and in greater depth than is considered "good" for one . . . Responsible. In charge. *Serious*.'[8]

We can be wilful because we know too much, say too much, because we exceed other people's expectations of what will do us good. Black feminists and feminists of colour are often called wilful because or when we exercise our will. Walker highlights both the words *wilful* and *serious*. These words are killjoy companions, ways of being *in charge*. A judgement can be understood as a negative charge. To turn a judgement into a project is to end up charged up. It can be electric; we are back to that snap, snap, sizzle.

KILLJOY MAXIM: IF YOU ARE CHARGED WITH WILFULNESS, ACCEPT AND MOBILIZE THAT CHARGE!

Sissie accepts that charge. Perhaps we could call her a sister killjoy poet even if she appears in novel form. Sissie is not given a linear story. Some sentences appear all alone, finding their companions on other pages. Some pages appear like poems with jagged edges, allowing words to be sharper, clearer, more illuminating. A chapter turns out to be that letter that she has written but not sent to the addressee. As readers, we become the recipient of the unsent letter.

181

The thoughts she has, killjoy thoughts, spill onto the pages. Perhaps a killjoy character needs another kind of book. Or perhaps she writes one. She might also read one.

I think of writing another kind of book and I hear Black feminist critic, also poet, also philosopher, bell hooks 'talking back', writing about writing, as

> a way to capture speech, to hold onto it, keep it close. And so, I wrote down bits and pieces of conversations, confessing in cheap diaries that soon fell apart from too much handling, expressing the intensity of my sorrow, the anguish of speech – for I was always saying the wrong thing, asking the wrong questions. I could not confine my speech to the necessary corners and concerns of life. I hid these writings under my bed, in pillow stuffings, among faded underwear.[9]

The paper is cheap; it wears out because of how it matters. Writing is how she spills out, spills over, the intensity of sorrow, filling it up, stuffing it where she can, where she is, the places she has, under the bed, in the pillow cases. In putting her writing there, her thoughts and feelings tumbling out, what she hears, 'bits and pieces of conversations', she exceeds the space she has been given, the concerns she is supposed to have, allowed to have, the corners, the edges of the room. We are asking the wrong questions when we question a world that gives us such little room. In writing, bell hooks refuses to be confined, spreads her words, herself, all over the place.

To create another kind of book is to create another kind

of self. Queer Chicana poet and theorist Gloria Anzaldúa describes her book *Borderlands / La Frontera: The New Mestiza* as follows: 'The whole thing has had a mind of its own, escaping me and insisting on putting together the pieces of its own puzzle with minimal direction from my will. It is a rebellious, willful entity, a precocious girl-child forced to grow up too quickly'.[10] A book can have a life of its own, because it has a mind of its own, a wilful entity, a will of its own, a wilful will.

KILLJOY EQUATION:
WILFUL = HAVING A WILL OF YOUR OWN

What comes out of us is wilful when we are. Different parts of us can inherit that wilfulness. Gloria Anzaldúa describes a dentist who, when cleaning the roots of her teeth, says to her with 'anger rising in his voice' that 'we're going to have to do something with your tongue' and that he'd 'never seen anything as strong and stubborn'.[11] All the materials the dentist, concerned with health and hygiene, puts in her mouth, are pushed right out again, as if her tongue is refusing to be cleaned, as if her tongue is spreading an infection. Anzaldúa describes many attempts to tame her tongue, to make her 'speak English'.[12] Latinx Studies scholar Lorgia García Peña describes her own rebellious nature through the failure to tame her hair: 'As soon as my mom styled my hair into five perfect (and extremely tight) coils, I would pull them out, letting my kinks fly wild.' When the nuns at her school tried different methods to get her to tame her hair, Peña concludes, 'nothing worked'.[13] We express something about ourselves when we refuse to be straightened out. Wilful is what we become when deviate from the straight paths we are supposed to follow. The word *error* comes from err, to stray. We stray, we wander away. Just a small deviation can be enough to make something for ourselves. In our failure to be corrected is creation. Our creations too become wilful. Marilyn Frye uses the adjective *wilful*, 'The willful creation of new meaning, new loci of meaning, and new ways of being together, in the world, seems to me in these mortally dangerous times the best hope we have.'[14] To create new meaning is to create new ways of being together.

The need for new words is not new. In thinking of the feminist killjoy as poet, I imagine an alternative communication system, for those who are not supported, who do not have the publishing houses or institutional positions that enable the delivery of words to worlds. A vehicle can be vital. To recall the vitality of the killjoy, the poetry of her, in her, as a resource for the present is to stay attuned to that effort required for other worlds to be built. If you are not supported you have to find other ways of getting yourself out there. I think of Black feminist and feminist of colour classics such as *This Bridge Called My Back*, first published in 1981, and *Charting the Journey*, first published in 1988, which I referenced in my chapter on surviving as a feminist killjoy. We need books to survive because we need them for our survival. Both collections included poems as well as prose, fiery texts full of passion as well as insight. *This Bridge* is now

184

in its fourth edition. In 'Catching Fire', her well-named preface to that edition, Cherríe Moraga writes that 'in the twenty years that *Bridge* stayed in, and went out of, publication over 100,000 copies were sold. It has also been read by thousands more. Early edition copies, dog-eared and coffee-stained, have been passed from hand to hand, borrowed then borrowed again, and "liberated" from library shelves.'[15]

I love this idea of feminist books being passed around, worn and weathered, liberated books, liberating books. Books can be feminist fire; how we 'catch fire'. I think of all those feminist fires being lit, lit up, imaginations ignited, desires enflamed, rage too. Literary critic Michele Cliff, in *If I Could Write This in Fire*, describes how she was enflamed by reading *Our Sister Killjoy*, 'In her pellucid rage, Aidoo's prose breaks apart into a staccato poetry – direct, short, brilliantly bitter – as if measured prose would disintegrate under her fury.'[16] Cliff shows how Aidoo's story of our sister killjoy Sissie, with its 'rage against colonialism', freed her to 'direct rage outward into creativity', so that if she could write this in fire, she would. And so, she did. To write in fire is to write fire. Audre Lorde describes her own commitment to writing whilst she was dying as writing fire: 'I am going to write fire until it comes out my ears, my eyes, my nose holes – everywhere. Until it's every breath I breathe. I'm going to go out like a fucking meteor!'[17] And so, she did. Writing fire can be how you go out. Moraga's poem 'The Welder', in *This Bridge*, points to how fire and heat can be used to melt old shapes, make new shapes, 'the intimacy of steel melting, the fire that makes sculpture of your lives, builds buildings'.[18] From the fire of feminism, especially Black feminism and feminism of colour, we build. We have to build our own buildings when the world does not accommodate us.

Books can be our buildings. We write ourselves into existence. Feminism: we cite each other into existence. But we have to find ways to send the work out so it can be shared, catch fire, our imagination. *Charting the Journey* was published by Sheba Feminist Press, an independent collective founded by six women in London in 1980. They described their mission as giving

> *priority to the work of women writers who continue to be marginalized. That means more than simply being ready to publish writing by women of colour, or lesbians, or working-class women; it means recognizing the multiplicity of voices within these communities – a multiplicity which is frequently overlooked by a world quick to categorize and dismiss. Sheba has built its reputation around its commitment to diversity, to difference, and to open and critical debate.[19]*

In addition to classics such as *Charting the Journey*, so important to the emergence of a collective we called Black British feminism, Sheba published Audre Lorde, bringing her writing to the sweaty hands of feminist readers in the UK for the first time. Another of their publications, *Turning the Tables: Recipes and Reflections from Women*, includes recipes from feminist writers such as novelist Angela Carter and film maker Pratibha Parmar as well as reflections on the politics of domestic labour such as cooking.[20] Sue O'Sullivan describes how the idea for the book 'came out of some wonderful, exhausted, tipsy talks that three of us from Sheba had while unwinding after hot, hard work at the 2nd International Feminist Book Fair in Oslo last June'.[21] The book is a collection of recipes but also gives space for contributors 'to contextualise their recipes in daily life'. The expression 'turn the table' can mean to change a situation, often by reversing a power dynamic. They turn the table by turning to the table, so that cooking becomes not about the happiness duty or unpaid labour, but something we claim back for ourselves.

It is not surprising that feminist publishing turns to the table. The second edition of *This Bridge* was published by Kitchen Table Press. Barbara Smith describes why the Kitchen Table Press, dedicated to publishing the work of women of colour, took its name, 'We chose our name because the kitchen was the centre of the home, the place where women in particular work and communicate with each other.'[22] She describes the commitment of this press: 'Our work is both cultural and political, connected to the struggles of freedom of all of our peoples. We hope to serve as a communication network for Women of Colour in the U.S. and elsewhere.'[23] The places where we gather, meet and greet become a communication network, a vehicle for sending information out.

A kitchen table becomes a publishing house. In my book *What's the Use?*, I explored what I called *queer use*, how things can be used in ways that were not intended or by those for whom they were not intended. To queer use, to turn a kitchen table into a publishing house, is collective and creative work. If I showed how the story of the feminist killjoy as philosopher begins in the same place where the story of the feminist killjoy begins, that's where the story of the feminist killjoy as poet begins too, around that table, where we sustain each other. Maybe we write *on* the table, allowing it to record our intimacy. Iris Marion Young writes: 'The nick on the table here happened during that argument with my daughter.'[24] When we tell stories about tables, they tell stories about us – that nick, that argument.

We create from where we are. We might have to fight to create because of where we are, who we are. Consider Adrienne Rich's account of writing a letter:

> *From the fifties and early sixties, I remember a cycle. It began when I had picked up a book or began trying to write a letter . . . The child (or children) might be absorbed in busyness, in his own dream world; but as soon as he felt me gliding into a world which did not include him, he would come to pull at my hand, ask for help, punch at the typewriter keys. And I would feel his wants at such a moment as fraudulent, as an attempt more-over to defraud me of living even for fifteen minutes as myself.*[25]

I think back to how tables became topics of conversation for those who occupied chairs. Rich keeps being pulled away from her table. She has to battle to have time to write and read, time for herself. And it is a battle because even if she is committed to writing she cannot (also would not) suspend her other commitments even if those commitments can be experienced as 'fraudulent'. She creates something for herself in the little time she has. We can see from the point of view of the mother, who is also a writer, a poet and a philosopher, how you can be pulled away from the writing table. This loss of time for writing is the loss of time for yourself, your own time, as you are returned to the work of giving your attention to the children. It is not only that some might have to fight to be seen as poets, for their work to be valued and read as poetry, but also that they might have to fight for the time and space to write. Time and space matter all the more to those who have less of them: the less time you have, the more time matters, the less room you have, the more rooms matter, a 'room of your own', to evoke Virginia Woolf. Audre Lorde suggested that as poems are more economical than prose, they might also be a preferred form for those who are poor, working-class and of colour, 'A room of one's own may be necessary to writing prose, but so are reams of paper, a typewriter and plenty of time.'[26] To write more is harder for those with less.

We begin with the material. Rich turns this starting point into an instruction: 'Begin with the material,' she says, with 'matter, mma, madre, mutter, moeder, modder'.[27] Rich describes her process thus: 'Piling piece by piece of concrete experience side by side.'[28] To begin with the material is to begin with the body, and with what is near to hand. What is concrete becomes more complex. To begin with the material, for Rich, is to 'pick up against the long struggle against lofty and privileged abstraction'. If a white, masculinist model of creativity is premised on transcendence (what Rich calls 'a false universal'), the feminist killjoy as poet creates from immanence. Rich names one collection *The Fact of a Doorframe*. She explains the name: poetry is 'hewn from the commonest living substance' as a 'doorframe is hewn from wood'.[29] The commonest thing – the wood of the doorframe, the wood of the table – is the stuff of poetry. As historical materialism also taught us, matter is not simply there, inert; it is dynamic, taking form. In *Capital*, Karl Marx describes use value thus: 'It is absolutely clear that, by his activity, man changes the forms of the materials of nature in such a way as to make them useful to him. The form of wood, for instance, is altered if a table is made out of it. Nevertheless, the table continues to be wood, an ordinary, sensuous thing.'[30] The wood can be made into a door or a table. The material is the connection.

Words, too, are materials: we use them, we shape things, make things. Rich suggests that for poets, given that words are their wood and language their material, they must refuse to use that language to dominate, but instead 'bend and torque it into an instrument for connection'.[31] And feelings, too, are materials. Rich uses poetry as a vehicle not only to express feelings, such as anger that many women have been encouraged to suppress, but to reflect, to philosophize, about feeling. One of her poems is entitled 'The Phenomenology of Anger'.[32] The last stanza reads:

> *Every act of becoming conscious*
> *(it says here in this book)*
> *is an unnatural act*

To become conscious is an action with revolutionary implications, implying that not being conscious of something is how we learnt to put up with it. In this poem, Rich describes the effort to light a log 'that's lain in the damp as long as this house has stood', to try to start something from what is to hand that has become hard to use; trying to make something grow out of what has been diminished. In the poem, anger does not simply come from a subject, but is felt by objects. One line is a question: 'How does a pile of rags the machinist wiped his hands on / feel in its cupboard, hour by hour?' Perhaps it is those who have been treated as objects, used to keep someone's hands clean, wiped on, wiped up, or made into examples, who also ask how objects feel. A person is not just at the table, making use of it, like an instrument, but near the table, by it, with it: 'Table. Window. Lampshade. You.' To change the sequence is to get to you in a different way, through juxtaposition.

The objects that are near become our companions. Objects can be how we tell killjoy stories about how we are freed from containers. Objects too can be wilful. Any will would be wilful if you are not supposed to have a will of your own. The opening stanza reads:

> *The freedom of the wholly mad*
> *to smear & play with her madness*
> *madness write with her fingers dipped in it*
> *the length of a room*
>
> *which is not, of course, the freedom*
> *you have, walking on Broadway*

> *to stop & turn back or go on*
> *10 blocks; 20 blocks*

Rich reflects on the freedom of the 'wholly mad', evoking the old figure of the hysteric, whose frenzy or excitement is deemed to be caused by exercising her imagination. She wants too much; she is too much. Her freedom is a freedom that explores the length of the room, a freedom that *smears* the walls, those containers; they are no longer clean, no longer shiny. A container can be turned into a page upon which you write. You write on it, fingers dripping, getting something out of yourself, a feeling, a thought, an idea. If you direct anger *at* something, your anger is *in* it, gets over it. There is freedom in that. In a later stanza, freedom is described as an awakening:

> *many sleep*
> *the whole way*
> *others sit*
> *staring holes of fire into the air*
> *others plan rebellion:*
> *night after night*
> *awake in prison, my mind*
> *licked at the mattress like a flame*
> *till the cellblock went up roaring*

Those feminist fires are being lit again. In those same spaces, sleeping, still, sitting, constrained by gender, domesticity, a house of happiness as prison, you are setting things alight, catching fire, igniting something. You are plotting an escape. To plot an escape is to escape in your mind. If the killjoy is *in it*, that's why she is trying to get out of it, to find a way out of it, to counter history, to get the feelings out, to give them somewhere to go.

I think of getting out, going somewhere, and I think of all the books I have picked up that have expressed something that I didn't have the words for. I find myself returning to old favourites, poems as well as poets, texts worn from past use, poems as old friends. I find myself picking up Audre Lorde, again, Lorde a poet as well as a philosopher, a theorist, a writer, a librarian, a maker of books, a keeper of them. Lorde had a way with words; marching with them, demonstrating through them. I often think of Lorde's way with words as being about what she makes audible. It is not just that many of her published articles began as speeches but that her writing is speech-like. The word *speech* shares a root with the word *strew*, the scattering of words. She said, 'What I leave behind has a life of its own. I've said this about poetry. I've said it about children. Well, in a sense I'm saying it about the very artifact of who I have been.'[33] Poetry, motherhood and the self are presented as akin to each other, as unflinchingly optimistic gestures that come out of, rather than being at the expense of, a profound recognition of the difficulty of survival.

Lorde is inviting us to participate in her survival, by keeping her alive, keeping her words alive, giving them more lives. Consider her short essay 'Poetry is not a Luxury'. The title is a claim. Lorde is making a claim about what poetry is not, perhaps because she is challenging an assumption about what poetry is.

For whom would poetry be a luxury? Lorde responds by saying that poetry is not *that*, not a luxury, that poetry is necessary; as necessary, perhaps, as bread. Poetry is what we need to sustain ourselves. It is 'through poetry', Lorde suggests, 'that we give name to those ideas which are – until the poem – nameless and formless – about to be birthed, but already felt'.[34] Poetry is giving birth to new form. Feeling, for Lorde, is giving form to something.

KILLJOY TRUTH: THOSE WHO DON'T FIT THE OLD FORMS NEED TO CREATE THEIR OWN FORMS

If we need to create our own forms, we don't yet have what we need. Perhaps that is why we need each other. It is important that Lorde here is not separating how we express ourselves, how we feel, from how we live. She says, 'As we learn to bear the intimacy of scrutiny and to flourish within it, as we learn to use the products of that scrutiny for power within our living, those fears which rule our lives and form our silences begin to lose control over us.'[35] Remember Sissie: we see so much from seeing how we are seen. Later Lorde describes that scrutiny in terms of what we are 'socialized to fear'. She suggests we can still fear the 'withdrawal of those approvals that we have been warned to seek for safety'.[36] Lorde is suggesting that the challenge for living in accordance with one's own feminist principles, not seeking

194

the rewards that follow proximity to social convention, is that you also have to give up an attachment to what you have been told would make you safe. You need to be willing to forgo approval from those whose approval you have been told you need to be someone, or to go somewhere.

As I write this, I feel this. When I left my post and profession, I left a path. Just after I left, I received a letter inviting me to submit my CV so I could be considered as a Fellow for an elite organization. Even though this position is not something I would have wanted if I had stayed on an academic path, I still felt a pull, a sense of having given something up, recognition, reward even. In the letter it was stressed that only some of those who submit their materials will become Fellows. I knew what I was being told. I should be glad, grateful, honoured to have the opportunity to submit my materials, myself even, but that it might not be enough, I might not be enough.

We are constantly being sent reminders that this is a competition; that to do well is to do better than others, to get what others do not get. I am glad of what I left behind. But I think again of how the feminist killjoy can be a feeling of complication. Despite being glad, I sometimes still feel a sense of loss for what might have been. Lorde is showing us what many of us know, but we don't always know what to do with what we know: that even if we reject the world that rejects us, we can still experience that rejection as pain; we can fear missing out on what might have followed the paths we do not take. I have noted how the feminist killjoy herself can operate as a warning: from her, too, we learn what (also who) we are socialized to fear. We are told that to leave the safety of a brightly lit path – the happiness path, the straight path – would be to cause your own misfortune, steal your own future happiness, such that if something happens, if the worst happens, and let's face it, shit happens, then you have brought this upon yourself.

Lorde lists some of the accusations that can follow when we don't follow the straight path: 'Women see ourselves diminished or softened by the falsely benign accusations of childishness, of nonuniversality, of changeability, of sensuality.'[37] Even if we come to know what those accusations are doing, how they are working, creating the 'white man', as universal, not particular (how self-centred!), as adult, not child, as mind, not body, not emotion, not sensuality, we can see ourselves being diminished by them. We need to claim what might be, from a certain viewpoint, including even our own viewpoint insofar as it is hard not to see oneself as others see oneself, diminishing. It is a leap of faith to head towards what we are taught to fear. We don't follow them, 'the white fathers', and say, 'I think therefore I am', she suggests. We follow her, and say, 'I feel therefore I can be free.'[38] Lorde replaces not only 'think' with 'feel,' but also 'I am' with 'I can be free'. The point here is not simply to assert what is, or who one is, but to open up who one can be. Freedom is not then something we have, but something we are doing: we are freeing ourselves from the weight of history.

We might have to feel that weight before we can be free of it. Recall Audre Lorde's experience of racist violence, how her mother had tried to protect her from racism by not naming it as racism, as if the violence was just random. In her essay 'Eye to Eye', she describes *racism* and *sexism* as 'grown-up words'.[39] We experience racism and sexism before we can name what we experience. To return to your past with words such as racism is to see something that you did not, could not, see at the time. This is why some of the work we do as feminist killjoys in giving problems their names could be understood as poetry. The past becomes alive with new meanings. You become estranged from the past; you rearrange it. To rearrange the past is more than rearranging furniture, although it can feel like that, creating a different sense of space. A killjoy rearrangement of the past brings us closer to the truth, **killjoy truths**. We open the door to the past, we let it in, because of what we did not see in what happened as it happened, the violence, the structure of it, the repetition, the pattern.

To open the door, we sometimes have to stop what we are doing. In an interview with Adrienne Rich, Lorde describes how she was so sickened with fury about the acquittal of a white policeman who had murdered a Black child that she wrote the extraordinary poem 'Power'. In Lorde's own words:

> *I was driving in the car and heard the news about the cop being acquitted. I was really sickening with fury, and I decided to pull over and just jot some things down in my note book to enable me to cross town without an accident, to continue functioning because I felt so sick and so enraged. And I wrote those lines down, I was just writing and that poem came out without craft.[40]*

We could think of this poem as a wilful poem, coming out of Lorde almost as if it had a will of its own. It is striking that the poem or the book, the object, is here the subject, the one creating as well as being created. If for Lorde the poem came out without craft, she still has to let it out.

> *She stopped the car to get her feelings out.*
> *She stopped the car and a poem came out.*
> *She stopped the car because it would come out*
> *one way or another way*
> *an accident or a poem.*
> *A poem is not an accident.*

We learn from the how of an arrival, how a poem comes out is what a poem is about. What we create is shaped by how it comes into existence. Sometimes we have to stop what we are doing to feel the true impact of something, to let our bodies experience that impact, the fury of an escalating injustice, a structure as well as an event; a history, an unfinished history. We don't always know what will come out when we stop to register the impact of something. Registering impact can be a lifelong project. The poem 'Power' begins with a shattering stanza:

> *The difference between poetry and rhetoric*
> *is being*
> *ready to kill*
> *yourself*
> *instead of your children.*[41]

This poem enacts the violence it depicts. To read it is to be hit by it. In reflecting on the feminist killjoy as philosopher, I discussed how hard it can be to admit violence. When violence gets in, it can get everywhere. Lorde lets the violence in. The poem gets the violence out. Getting the violence *out* is what the poem is *about*. And Lorde gets it out by first telling us what poetry is *not*: poetry is *not* rhetoric; it is *not* empty. The emptiness of rhetoric, words that do not do what they say, is how violence is reproduced, how the future will be the same, the killing of children. A poem is how you show you are willing to kill yourself, destroy your own world, the calm interior of where you might hear about the violence, rather than the children to come. She evokes the Black woman who sat on the jury that acquitted the white police officer as lining 'her own womb with cement, to make a graveyard for our children'.

Lorde uses an image of what poetry is not, how poetry is about not letting our power 'lie limp and useless as an unconnected wire'. To get the violence out, Lorde uses words like electricity, snap, snap, sizzle; when the words come out, the violence does, too. To express oneself is to keep a connection alive. This image of power as an electric connection is telling us something about how to pass a message down a line, from one to another. We keep a connection alive so that others can receive something from us.

We receive something when we pick up an old book. In her interview with Adrienne Rich (there is so much in this interview; so much opened up by or as a conversation between poets), Lorde talks about a poem by Walter de la Mare, 'The Listeners'. She had been telling Rich a story about finding old books, used books, in a library in Harlem; books that were in 'the worst condition'. How I love how she finds those books! And not just them, she finds a poem there, too, this poem, 'The Listeners', a poem about a traveller who rides a horse up to the door of an empty house. This is the poem, in Lorde's words:

> *He knocks at the door and nobody answers. 'Is there anybody there?' he said. That poem imprinted itself on me. And finally, he's beating down the door and nobody answers, and he has a feeling that there really is somebody in there. And then he turns his horse and he says, 'Tell them I came, and nobody answered. That I kept my word,' he said. I used to recite that poem to myself all the time. It was one of my favorites. And if you asked me what it was about, I don't think I could have told you. But this was the first cause of my writing, my need to say things I couldn't say otherwise, when I couldn't find other poems to serve.*[42]

It is important to follow Lorde, to go where she goes. When we are fascinated by something we do not always know why. What captures your attention, causing you to write, might not have the crispness or the edges of an about. Lorde keeps reciting the poem; she says 'it imprinted' on her. I think of that imprint; the print of a poem on a person. Lorde can hear something in this poem, which is about listening; it allows her to express something, say something she could otherwise not say. To hear a knock on the door is to hear the door. The door could be the door to the master's house, how violence is shut in, or the door of consciousness, how violence is shut out. We knock on the door not to demand entry, but to create a disturbance, to disturb what or who lingers there, because of the violence that has not been dealt with.

A door, a doorway, a space to linger. In her poem 'A Litany for Survival' Lorde evokes for us a 'those of us', who 'love in doorways coming and going in the hours between dawns'.[43] A door becomes a doorway, not a barrier that stops some of us from entering, but a place we gather, those who live and love on the edges of social experiences, in shadows, who fall like shadows fall, the fallen, for whom coming into full view would be dangerous. Not coming into full view, remaining in the shadows, might be how some of us survive. To stay alive can be another view, another way of coming and going. Black feminist critic Saidiya Hartman echoes Audre Lorde in giving an intimate history of Black girls, of their wayward loves and lives; she describes how Black girls 'loved in doorways' and 'peered out of doorways'.[44] A doorway becomes a viewing point, a meeting place. Living and loving in doorways, we stop, linger, at the borders, in the shadows, on the edges.

So many doors, so many doorways. In *Map to the Door of No Return*, Black feminist poet Dionne Brand teaches us to hear more in the door. You can find the Door of No Return in the 'The House of Slaves', a museum to the Atlantic Slave Trade in Gorée Island, Senegal. Brand writes, 'I have not visited the Door of No Return, but by relying on random shards of history and unwritten memoirs of descendants of those who passed through it, including me,

I am constructing a map of the region, paying attention to faces, to the unknowable, to unintended acts of returning, to impressions of doorways.'[45] The Door of No Return is a *memorial door*, a door that remembers the exit point for millions of African people. For Brand, the door of no return 'was the door of a million exits multiplied. It is a door many of us wish never existed. It is a door which makes the word *door* impossible and dangerous, cunning and disagreeable.'[46] A door can be saturated by history; a history is what you can hear when you hear the word *door.* Brand approaches the Door of No Return as consciousness, as well as haunting: 'Black experience in any modern city or town in the Americas is a haunting. One enters a room and history follows; one enters a room and history precedes.'[47]

Doorways become places you visit in accounting for a history that haunts the present. Doorways leave or make impressions ('impressions of doorways'). Black British writer Joan Anim-Addo evokes 'another doorway' in an article about how Black women, as members of the Caribbean Women Writers' Alliance (CWWA), 'undertook a rewriting of the local museum experience so as to insert a hitherto largely absent presence, that of the Black woman, into the museum context'.[48] As a group, they organized workshops at the Horniman Museum, their local museum in south-east London. Another doorway then becomes, in Anim-Addo's hands, a poem, about how Black women are missing from the museums of history, how Black women have to enter museums differently, through the doorways, not the front door. She explains the use of the doorway motif as follows: 'The original line of thinking was cognisant of doorposts signifying homes where women are to be found even if nowhere else, despite the refusal on the part of collectors, exhibitors, or curators to render such presence visible.'[49]

Anim-Addo explains that her poem was inspired by carved wooden door panels from south-eastern Nigeria that are 'believed to have come from a Yakü elder or chief'.[50] The story of how the door panels got into the museum (like so many stories of objects in museums) is an imperial story: they were collected and donated by a British anthropologist and Africanist and his wife. She makes the door matter *strangerwise*, a way of making Black women's presence felt. Anim-Addo's 'another doorway' has a 'missing sign', 'Welcome here we women', a sign that points to how women are here, busy, pounding maize, concocting relishes, cooking dishes. Her 'another doorway' has 'an alternative sign', a sign that also points to how women are here, leaving gifts of food for those who are journeying, who are burying their dead. The last lines:

> So, where the bodies?
> Who take way the bodies?
> Somebody point us to
> the body thieves
> the spirit thieves
> for wheresoever they wander
> we have promised
> always to follow, follow.

To find 'another doorway' is to account for the many who are missing. Another doorway not only points to an absence, but makes those who are absent, present. A doorway becomes a stranger way of expressing oneself; a stranger way, a stranger's way. Lorde's poem 'A Litany for Survival' in evoking doorways, comings and goings, hours between dawns, also speaks of the necessity of speech. She says for those who 'were never meant to survive', it is 'better to speak'. When the world does not make you safe, makes it hard, and harder still, to survive, it is 'better to speak', because, again in Lorde's words, 'your silence will not protect you'.[51]

'So it is better to speak.' In her contribution to *A Fly Girl's Guide to University*, Muslim feminist poet Suhaiymah Manzoor-Khan describes the first time she performed a spoken-word poem at Cambridge. She describes her surprise at how easy it was to 'impress' her audience.[52] To express herself she makes an impression. She spoke her poem 'Token', which I would call a killjoy poem, a poem about being Muslim, a woman and Asian.[53]

> At first, they encourage you up
> The steps, the ladder
> smiling
> You smile back
> Unaware that their smiles
> are not for you.

The poem expresses something, just as she does in performing the poem, about how you might as a brown Muslim woman be encouraged or enabled by the very systems that block you, how even the smiles that surround diversity that appear to be for you are not for you. Even getting up, moving up, can be used against you. And yet, she expresses that poem, she puts herself out, she gets her words out. From her point of view, that expression matters: 'It was exciting. It was exhilarating to force people to hear my story, force them to imagine what it was like to not find it so simple and straightforward at Cambridge.'[54] Note her use of that word 'force', how to counter a history, an expectation of who would be here, who should be here, of what it is like to be here, can require becoming forceful, getting a poem out as forcing yourself in.

A poem, a life, can express what is not so simple, not so straightforward, coming out of the friction, coming out as friction, that square peg, that round hole, inhabiting spaces not meant for you. It can be about how you are seen. It can be about how you are not seen. A queer experience: you are seated with your partner, two women at a table; waiting. A straight couple walks into the room and is attended to right away; sir, madam, over here, sir, madam. Sometimes if you do not appear as you are expected to appear you do not appear. This is not so much about being seen, but being *seen to*, having your needs *attended to*: after all, when sir, madam becomes a question, 'Is that sir, or madam?', or an apology, 'Sir, oh I am sorry, madam!' you are being seen, your body turned into a spectacle. Some have to become insistent to be the recipient of a social action; you might have to wave your arm furiously to be noticed at all.

KILLJOY TRUTH:
SOME HAVE TO INSIST ON WHAT IS GIVEN TO OTHERS

If you have to wave your arm furiously, it is not surprising you appear furious. Maybe, just maybe, you are as you appear. A history can become concrete through the repetition of such encounters, which require you to put the whole of your body, as well as your arm, behind an action. Maybe these actions seem small. Maybe they are small. They can accumulate over time.

Actions that seem small can also become a wall. They feel like a hammering, a chip, chip, chip, against your being. It can feel like bits of you are coming off. No wonder they keep finding chips on our shoulders. Maybe killjoy poetry is how we turn it out, transforming the hammering into a hammer, or a pen, chipping away at that old block. Chip, chip, chip, who knows, eventually it might come right off. A chip as a poem, a sharp splinter, telling us something.

When insistence is political labour, what some have to do to be, insistence is also a craft, how we become more impressive. An arm can be a poem, waving around rather impressively. You turn up at a hotel with your girlfriend and you say you have booked a room. A hesitation can speak volumes. This reservation says your booking is for a double bed, is that right, madam? Eyebrows are raised; a glance slides over the two of you, catching enough detail. Are you sure, madam? Yes, that's right; a double bed. You have to say it, again; you have to say it, again, firmly.

KILLJOY EQUATION:
RAISED EYEBROWS = LESBIAN FEMINIST PEDAGOGY

Really, are you sure? This happens again and again; you almost come to expect it, the necessity of being firm just to receive what you have requested. Disbelief follows you wherever you go, still. One time after a querying, are you sure, madam, are you sure, madam, you enter the room; twin beds. Do you go down; do you try again? It can be trying. Sometimes it is too much, and you pull your two little beds together, you find another way of huddling. When you are blocked, when your very existence is viewed with general suspicion or even just raised eyebrows (yes, they are pedagogy), we have to become more resourceful.

We become each other's resources. I think of furniture, beds, tables, how we use them in queer ways, furnishing our lives for ourselves. We might tell other stories about chairs, too, when they are no longer understood as the seat of a profession, no longer so comfortable. Perhaps those who don't fit don't just notice worlds, as I described in the previous chapter; they create different impressions, different shapes. We wiggle around, our bodies, words, too, in the effort to create just a little room for ourselves. We might find a queer use for doors. Judith Butler in *Undoing Gender* talks about being in the basement of their house 'having locked the door', and in the 'smoke filled' airless room, finding books that once belonged to their parents, or at least passed through their hands, philosophy books that ignited their own desire.[55] Spaces that might seem like closets, or containers, airless, suffocating, can be where queer things happen, where we pick somebody or something up that gives us somewhere else to go.

We give ourselves somewhere else to go. In chapter 2, I reflected on how we become family when we are cast out by our families. When we call our queer gatherings *family*, we are reusing that word for our own purposes, that word so often used to create an illusion of happiness, also used to make our own ties seem lighter and lesser. Trans scholar Susan Stryker offers a beautiful description of what was opened up for the 'queer family we were building', when her partner gave birth to their child. She describes: 'We joke about pioneering on a reverse frontier: venturing into the heart of civilization itself to reclaim biological reproduction from heterosexism and free it for our own uses.' Stryker adds: 'We're fierce; in a world of "traditional family values", we need to be.'[56] When things are used by those for whom they were not intended, the effect can be queer. When we laugh at the effect, that laughter is not unrelated to how we rage against the machinery of the family, which, as Stryker shows, renders some offspring deviants and monsters. And that rage itself can be transformative: 'through the operation of rage, the stigma itself becomes the source of transformative power'.[57]

It takes work to reclaim biological reproduction 'for our own uses' just as it takes work to reoccupy the family, to make the familiar strange. And it takes work to rearrange our bodies, to rearrange ourselves. Stryker offers her own rearrangement by refiguring transgender embodiment as an affinity to monsters, to those who have been deemed monstrous, speaking back to Frankenstein in words sharpened by rage.

KILLJOY MAXIM: BECOME MONSTROUS!

To make the family strange, creating different kinds of families, combinations, slants, we loosen the hold of the family, that norm, that form. We spill out of it, spill all over the place. I think of Alexis Pauline Gumbs's *Spill: Scenes of Black Feminist Fugitivity*, her ode to the work and wisdom of Black feminist literary critic Hortense Spillers. Gumbs attends to Spillers' words with love and care, to what spills, to words that spill, to liquid that spills out from a container, to being somebody who spills things. Spillage can be a breaking, of a container, a narrative, a turning of phrases so that 'doors opened and everyone came through'.[58] Spillage can be, then, the slow labour of getting out of something. A poem too can be what spills. Gumbs, herself a poet, a philosopher, a theorist, a writer, a weaver, teaches us to read *as* poets, by hearing connections between words and worlds. In *Undrowned*, Gumbs teaches us to learn from marine mammals, to learn about what we need to breathe, to live, despite what is diminishing. We can be captured by the net of language, by names and pronouns, by how we are called into being. To free ourselves, we invent ourselves. We don't demand recognition, to be seen, in accordance with an existing

209

regime. We create something when we cast our hopes elsewhere. Gumbs writes: 'What becomes possible when we are immersed in the queerness of forms of life that dominant systems cannot chart, reward, or even understand?'[59]

Dominant systems make so much and so many impossible. We have to fight for possibility. We have to fight for some of us to be possible. So much that has come to be is wrapped up by fatalism – gender fatalism, institutional fatalism: girls will be girls; boys, boys; institutions, institutions. Judith Butler suggests that 'for those who are still looking to become possible, possibility is a necessity'.[60] Possibility is built out of a system. I think again of Lorde, who picked possibility up, too, possibility as taking time. Lorde wrote, 'Poetry is not only dream or vision, it is the skeleton architecture of our lives. Possibility is neither forever nor instant. It is also not easy to sustain belief in its efficacy.'[61] Possibility can take the longest time because to make something possible requires dismantling what makes it not so. This is why possibility is not plucked out of thin air. Possibility comes from intimacy with what has thickened in time, the walls, the doors, how rooms are occupied, making it hard to breathe. History is stale air. A poem, a breath of fresh air. To make something is to make it possible.

KILLJOY TRUTH: WHAT WE CREATE IS FRAGILE BECAUSE WE NEED IT TO SURVIVE

This sentence, like many of the killjoy truths in this handbook, is reused. This one first appeared in my book *What's the Use?*, which was an ode to used things, old things, worn things; it is full of jugs that fly off their handle, rather like we do.

Perhaps that is how I came to killjoy poetry. I came to words, tired and worn, from things, also tired, also worn. I wrote in that book about my old bag, worn out from how much I used it to carry stuff around, its zipper broken. In my chapter on surviving as a feminist killjoy, I suggested that we carry our experiences of being a feminist killjoy with us, putting them in a feminist killjoy bag. In approaching the feminist killjoy as a philosopher, I suggested we sometimes file away what is hardest to handle. Bags and files are both containers, used to hold things. When they break, what they hold spills out. The feminist killjoy is a leaky container, she too spills things, letting them out. Maybe we can turn her into a feminist warning: be careful, we leak! She is an old bag, that old bag, speaking out as spilling over. I think of *flying off the handle*, a killjoy expression. To fly off the handle means to lose it, to lose your temper, to snap. We can end up broken. The broken can be queer kin.

The feminist killjoy as poet does not start anew, with the light, the bright, the white, the upright. We start with

211

the brown and the down; the weary and the worn; the teary and the torn. Sometimes we get used to what makes it hard to bear. At other times, we snap under the weight of it, because of the weight of it. There is a connection not only between survival and creativity, but between snap and creativity. A breaking point can be a making point. Lauren Berlant teaches the ethical value of loosening our hold on things. Words can be things, sentences, too. To *let loose* can also mean to have a strong emotion or expression.

KILLJOY MAXIM: LET LOOSE!

Maybe our writing becomes looser as we refuse the requirement to express ourselves in a certain way. I think of how, in time, my own writing has changed. As I have worked more on feminist killjoys, with them, bringing them to you, my language has loosened. I have become more conscious of words, how they matter, the sound of them, using rhyme and repetition so that in the language, at least, I can breathe. Maybe we lighten a load through loosening the words. This handbook, a feminist killjoy handbook, is only loosely a handbook. I have loosened the form of it; there are no simple steps, no easy solutions. Yes, we can disappoint an expectation by loosening a form. To be a feminist killjoy is about changing our expectations, turning disappointment into an opening, a window of opportunity.

And so we leave our ends loose, flopping and fraying. We write, like we love, like we live. We tell tales, we leave trails. The more we leave behind us, the easier it is to find us. And by us, I mean each other.

I am reminded of the pansy project by the queer artist Paul Harfleet. Harfleet planted pansies in all the places he knew that homophobic violence and abuse had taken place.[62] Pansies are flowers; the word *pansy* a slur. We make something by repurposing what has been used against us. To be a killjoy poet is to plant something, a possibility, a new growth of some kind, to mark the site of violence, to tell us what happened here. The site of violence is the site of protesting it, of saying *no* to it. Pansies, little flowers, can be little poems, planted all over the place.

There are so many ways of saying *no*. Maybe a poem matters because we cannot quite get the words out or because to get a *no* out we have to find a way to make ourselves heard. I hear a poem by Sikh feminist poet Jasmin Kaur:

> SCREAM
> *so that one day*
> *a hundred years from now*
> *another sister will not have to*
> *dry her tears wondering*
> *where in history*
> *she lost her voice.*[63]

I hear the first line of this poem, a word can be a line, as a demand, a plea, loving and urgent, to scream so that others can hear us. I say loving as well as urgent as the poem teaches us that the point of becoming louder, that scream piercing the atmosphere, is so she, another sister, who comes after, will not be left wondering how, also where, she lost her voice in history. Perhaps, I too, as a feminist killjoy, became a poet, hearing her voice in your words, hearing what we could lose, who we could lose, how much we need to say.

We need you to know we said no.
We need that no for tears to flow.

I think back to Audre Lorde's image of power as a connected wire and her fascination with 'The Listeners'. That poem is about turning up, keeping your word, by knocking on the door. Knocking matters because of how sound travels. In considering the feminist killjoy as philosopher, I noted how we are more likely to notice doors if we hit them rather than enter them. Maybe knocking is how we share what we notice. How do you tell someone you have arrived? You knock on the door. We knock on the door so that others can hear we are here, not 'Knock, knock, who is there?' but 'Knock, knock, we are here!'

Can you hear we are here? To become a feminist killjoy poet can be about what we hear, who we hear, how we hear. I first wrote about Lorde's fascination with 'The Listeners' in my book *Complaint!* The first time I read Lorde's description of the poem out loud was when I gave a lecture I called 'Knocking on the Door'. And as I read her words, I knocked on the table, my wooden desk, making a sound, knock, knock, so my audience could hear it. And then I heard it. In *Living a Feminist Life*, I wrote about some of my experiences of growing up with a violent father. I cut one paragraph out because it was too close to the bone. It is a door story. One time when my father was hitting me, I managed to get away. I ran down the hallway and locked myself in the bathroom. I crouched in the shower, which had a glass door, which I pulled shut.

My father kicked the door of the bathroom down. The sound was so loud. He then pulled the glass door open. I was so scared it would shatter. It didn't shatter but something did. Maybe that is why, so many years later, I was attuned to the sound of shattering. My father kicked the door down and then he kicked me, over and over. Even now, so many years later, when someone knocks loudly on a door, any door, I feel panic. In other words, a knock on the door is, for me, a trigger.

It was only when I made the knocking sound so my audience could hear it that I was taken back. Sometimes we can only hear something about ourselves when we share our work with someone else. And so, I also learn, killjoy poetry might be how we get in touch, stay in touch, with the most difficult parts of ourselves and of our histories. Maybe I needed *not* to hear the knock, that sound, that trigger, to keep my ear to the door, so I could keep listening, stay connected, collect more killjoy stories. We might sometimes need to close the door to our own pasts so we can create an opening. But then, when we share what we hear, another door opens, and with it, a space between us. Maybe that is what the feminist killjoy as poet is doing, opening a space between us.

6/ The Feminist Killjoy as Activist

When I hear the word *feminism*, I hear activism. I think of marching, protesting, demonstrating, what it feels like, how energizing it is, to take to the streets, to claim that space, to push back, becoming part of a many, carrying snappy slogans, 'My Body, My Choice', 'Again We Rise', 'No Means No', 'I am Not Free While Any Woman is Unfree' (Audre Lorde), raising our voices. We are louder when we are heard together. I think of all the different feminist movements over time and across the world, how we can be united by what we oppose: sexual violence, gender-based violence, racial harassment, police violence, austerity, violence against the poor, immigrants, the undocumented. The feminist killjoy as activist is right there, marching for our lives. But we don't start there. In this chapter I explore the feminist killjoy as an activist to describe the process of getting there, of becoming part of a movement that both recognizes how violence is reproduced by social and political institutions and commits to what needs to be done to bring an end to that violence. So much of this activist work is not recognized or even visible to those who are not doing it, because it takes place where so much violence takes place, behind closed doors.

From feminism we learn that activism is not restricted to one domain; it can be what we do at home, at work, on the streets. We can share our stories of becoming feminist activists, *wherever* we do our work. I am inspired by the Feminist Freedom Warriors project, a digital archive 'documenting cross-generational conversations about justice, politics and hope with feminist scholar-activists'.[1] Scholar activists Chandra Talpade Mohanty and Linda Carty describe archiving these stories as a political project about challenging mainstream narratives of feminism, of communism and 'the left', which 'separate intellectual work from activist or movement work'.[2] If in chapter 4 I explored how activism generates knowledge, in this chapter I explore the process from the other side. The journey towards philosophizing for ourselves is the same journey we call politicization.[3] I am reminded of Marx's famous critique of how philosophers have 'interpreted the world' when 'the point is to change it'. If trying to change the system is how we learn how it works, the point is still to change it.

We can't always see the point. I suggested earlier in the handbook that being feminist killjoys leads us to be suspicious of scale: to be warned that noticing something, let alone protesting it, makes it bigger is how we are told to make it smaller, to make ourselves smaller, too. Killjoy activism can include actions that might seem small because their significance cannot be seen. I think of *no*, that small word with a lot of work to do. It is killjoy activism to say *no* to someone who has claimed authority over you, by dictating what you do with your body, yourself, whether you are at work or at home.

Our sense of scale can change from saying *no*. Many complaints about abuses of power within institutions end up as complaints against institutions for enabling the abuse, which means that a *no* directed to a person ends up being redirected to the institution. When the object widens, our lens widens, and so does our activism. We begin to understand how institutions themselves are effects of a wider system we might call, following bell hooks, 'white supremacist capitalist patriarchy'.[4] In bell hooks, we find so much killjoy inspiration: she names it, nails it, every time! I dedicate these thoughts on the feminist killjoy as activist to bell hooks.

It might seem right now, in pandemic times, when inequalities are so stark, painfully so, when so many people are struggling to make do or to get by, that the feminist killjoy is a luxury we can ill afford. But at times like these, we need the feminist killjoy even more. Fighting to change the system is how we acquire an ever-deepening knowledge of the *function of inequality*: who does the work, who cleans, who cares; how wealth depends upon the extraction of resources from land and from people and how inequalities are reproduced by that very extraction, the exhaustion of people's capacities. There are so many ways that power and violence work through exhaustion: the exhaustion of people's capacities to resist; the exhaustion of people's will to live their lives on their own terms; the exhaustion of having to navigate systems, including welfare systems, designed to make it harder for people to get what they need. When we are weary, because we are weary, we need to be in alliance. So many of us are under attack, our claims to personhood dismissed as 'identity politics', our protests as 'cancel culture', our intellectual contributions as 'vandalism'. The feminist killjoy, that history condensed into a figure, helps us to recognize these attacks for what they are: defences of an old order. I begin this chapter with a reflection on why negativity has been so important to our activism (the feminist killjoy gives us another angle on an old and queer history), before turning to what we can learn from the effort to address the problem of sexual harassment as an institutional problem, and then finally to how protests and demonstrations take the feminist killjoy out into the public realm. I will make use of my survival tips because thinking about killjoy activism is another way of thinking about the project of feminist survival.

Let us go back to our starting point, our first and core **killjoy truth** and **killjoy commitment**.

KILLJOY TRUTH:
TO EXPOSE A PROBLEM IS TO POSE A PROBLEM

KILLJOY COMMITMENT:
I AM WILLING TO CAUSE UNHAPPINESS

Our commitments derive from our truths. We are willing to cause unhappiness because of what we learnt from our experience of causing unhappiness. We know that we will have to keep exposing a problem because being treated as posing it is how it is not dealt with. So much activist work is the work of exposure: we expose the violence that is hidden by shiny happy diversity: the violence of the elevation of the family as a social norm, the couple form, reproductivity as the basis of a good life.

Following Audre Lorde, we also expose the happiness myth of neoliberalism, how making individuals responsible for their happiness leads both to the cruelty of the judgement that unhappiness is deserved and to the cruelty of abandonment. Lorde teaches how the principle that we are responsible for our own happiness can lead to moral indifference to the unhappiness of others. Consider Ursula Le Guin's dystopian short story 'The Ones Who Walk Away from Omelas'. The people of Omelas live happy lives in a meaningful sense: 'They were not naïve and happy children – though their children were in fact happy. They were mature, intelligent, passionate adults whose lives were not wretched.'[5] Their happiness has a secret. It depends on the misery of a child kept in the basement: 'The child used to scream for help at night, and cry a good deal, but now it only makes a kind of whining, "eh-haa, eh-haa" . . . They all know it is there, all the people of Omelas.'[6] The happiness of a people is premised on indifference to the child's unhappiness. The story is about the injustice of the happiness of many resting on the misery of one. This short story from the past about the future reads as if it was a description of the present. We recognize too much in Omelas: the willingness to let others suffer, to contain suffering, to hide it away by turning away, so that 'we' can hold onto the good life.

KILLJOY COMMITMENT: I AM NOT WILLING TO MAKE HAPPINESS MY CAUSE

Knowing the unhappiness caused by happiness does not make it any easier to cause unhappiness. I think of *killjoy activism* as *how* we take up the cause of not making happiness our cause. In introducing the figure of the feminist killjoy, I suggested that to reclaim her is also to inherit a long activist tradition of reclaiming insults such as *queer* that have been hurled at those who live our lives and love outside the narrow scripts of heterosexuality. In thinking of the feminist killjoy as an activist, I am giving her a queer history.

Other critics have picked up on the queerness of the killjoy. Take, for example, the work of Toronto-based lesbian artists Deirdre Logue and Allyson Mitchell and their 2013 exhibition, 'The Killjoy Kastle: A Lesbian Feminist Haunted House', in which the feminist killjoy evokes a lesbian feminist history, haunting the house of our history with a rebellious potency.[7] Lesbian feminism might be assumed to be dated, belonging to a time that is over, the lesbian feminist as a bit drab, a bit dull, possibly rather depressing (rather like the stereotype of the feminist killjoy, then). If the lesbian feminist is a figure that is drab and depressing, maybe she, too, is a warning. I think of an old statement by RADICALESBIANS about how the word *dyke* was used 'to frighten women into a less militant stand'.[8] The documentary film *Rebel Dykes* (dir. Harri Shanahan and Siân A. Williams, 2021) about the lesbian scene in post-Punk

London, reminds us of the queerness of some lesbian history, dykes who took exiting from the straight world as an opening to live more freely, to experiment sexually, to make something else of themselves and for themselves. There can be militancy and power in refusing to become *his relatives*, to allow ourselves to be given away, symbolically or not, from one man to another. Perhaps today we are invited to become shiny happy lesbians, polishing ourselves off by removing traces of dykes and other more frightening lesbian tendencies. We have to keep refusing the invitation because it keeps being made; becoming killjoys even more, all the more (*Killjoy Survival Tip 2: Become more of a feminist killjoy*).

There can be something *queer* about lesbian feminism. The word *queer* can mean odd, curious, weird and strange. These meanings of *queer* are, of course, why that word was repurposed as an insult directed towards gay people, and they are retained in its use as an insult. Queer is a killjoy term, potent, charged with negation. Indeed, queer when used as a verb can also mean to spoil. Literary theorist Eve Kosofsky Sedgwick describes queer as a 'politically potent term' because it cleaves to 'childhood scenes of shame'.[9] Rather than cutting ourselves off from a shameful history, we stick closely to it. We refuse to make light of that history, using words that gloss over it, because it is that history which gives our politics its edge. When we come out to our families, our friends, we might be told, 'Shame on you.' You are being told you should be ashamed. We become affect aliens when we are not ashamed.

KILLJOY EQUATION: QUEER PRIDE = NOT SHAMED BY ANOTHER'S SHAME

It can take a political movement to enable that refusal to be shamed. *By killjoy activism, I am thinking of that movement.* We have many movements behind us, the killjoys, affect aliens, trouble-makers, misfits, those who fuck with the national imaginary. Sarah Schulman, in her monumental history of ACT UP in New York, *Let the Record Show*, offers a detailed history of how a political movement was created by gay people with HIV and AIDS, people who had been abandoned by the state, by their families, who had to push and to press to get what they needed: 'With the lack of treatment and services also came abandonment by family – if they hadn't thrown you out or driven you away for being queer.'[10]

The history of queer activism in response to AIDS reminds us how taking up the task of looking after people who have been abandoned is a political action. Direct action – from marching, to kiss-ins, to die-ins, is not only a way of making what is going on visible, it turns our bodies into instruments. I will return to what we can do with our bodies in due course. Sometimes you have to be willing to make a spectacle of yourself. There is so much else we need to make visible, as Schulman's history reminds us: the illness and the suffering compounded not only by abandonment by family and community but by state homophobia, the organizing assumption that disease and death were punishment for deviance. So many did not survive. And so many losses were not admitted as losses; some lives were, to use Judith Butler's term, 'ungrievable'.[11] Queer scholar of colour José Esteban Muñoz wrote eloquently of how, as queers 'we take our dead with us in the various battles we must wage in their names'.[12]

We take our dead with us. This history is with us. We say *yes* to queer because of what we refuse – we don't aim to be like those who reject or repudiate us or to be more likeable to them. Refusing to aspire to be normal, to be straight, to be cis, whiter or lighter, to get as close as we can to what we are not, to pass even, is what gives us more room to be something else. It is a way of living and loving as well as a style of politics. We recognize that it is not always up to us; we can killjoy because of who we are perceived to be (*Killjoy Survival Tip 6: Know it is not always up to you*). To *claim* our affective alienation is not to try to manage that perception by modifying ourselves. We don't *tone it down*, straighten ourselves out, try to be more like you so we can get through to you. We spill over onto the streets, fierce and fabulous, our protests, parties.

We spill over, we spill out. To make happiness our political horizon, our ambition, would be to contain ourselves. Happiness too often translates into a desire for inclusion into the institutions that have promised it, such as marriage. Of course, homophobia uses the equation: gay marriage = the destruction of marriage. But this equation is too optimistic; queers need to do more than marry each other to destroy the institution of marriage. We might instead refuse to aspire to be happy or refuse to be aspirational. Or we might do something else with happiness by refusing to make it our end. The word *happiness* comes from the English word *hap*, meaning chance. The word *happiness* shares its *hap* with the words *perhaps*, *happenstance* and *haphazard*. But *happiness* seems to have lost its *hap*, becoming not what happens to you but what you have to earn. We put the *hap* back into happiness, taking a chance on it. We can be happy to be queer without turning happiness into a project of becoming worthy or deserving of it.

Being happy *to be* queer does not mean we are always happy *as* queers. Trans scholars have also questioned the expectation of happiness. Hil Malatino stresses that 'transition won't deliver you into some promised land of gendered bliss'. He expands, 'Transitioning doesn't have to be wholly curative or even minimally happy-making, in order to be imperative.'[13] Malatino is following Andrea Long Chu, who stresses not only that her new vagina won't make her happy, but that it *shouldn't* be expected to.[14] We might need to claim the freedom to be unhappy in a world that assumes happiness as evidence of being good, or at least the freedom to remain profoundly ambivalent and unsure. Life is complex, fragile and messy; and so are we.

If we need to shatter the illusion that to come out is to become happy, we need to keep shattering the illusion of happiness as inclusion. Organizations, cities, nations that brand themselves 'gay friendly', a technique sometimes called 'pink washing', remain hostile environments for many LGBTQI+ people. Last year, I was riding my bike with my girlfriend in London. We stopped for a drink of water. We were relaxed, enjoying ourselves. A man came running towards us. I thought he seemed alarmed and I looked up in concern. But then he spat at me and said with disgust, 'What a waste.' When I told somebody about it, they said, 'I didn't think that kind of thing happened any more'. It did happen. It does happen.

It still happens. In the current moment in the UK, transphobia operates in a way that is eerily similar to earlier homophobia, which tells us that homophobia is not past but present. I think of one time I was discussing a trans-phobic leaflet that had been distributed at a Reclaim the Night march. The leaflet depicted trans women as sexual predators. When I expressed my outrage, a trans-exclusionary feminist said to me, 'Are you saying it is as bad as the Holocaust?' The implication was that violence against trans people is 'relatively' minor, a footnote in a much more horrifying history of human hatred. This same critic regularly uses the expression 'the trans lobby' and 'trans Taliban'. The feminist killjoy has taught us how the minimization of harm and the inflation of power go together. Stranger danger works to locate danger in those deemed outsiders. Stranger danger also creates the figure of the endangered, most often a child, sometimes also women. Contemporary transphobia works to suggest that trans people are endangering children. One headline reads, *'Are you transphobic? Me neither, we're just worried about our children.'*[15]

This 'worried about our children' is not just an eerie echo of past worries. With that worry has come a recycling of homophobic terms for gay men and lesbians such as 'groomers' and 'predators'. These words create associations that stick. LGBTQI+ people are figured as recruiting children into our lifestyles, as child abusers, no less. Let us be clear here: we are witnessing in real time the same moral panic that legitimated the Thatcher government's Section 28 in 1988, a series of laws banning the 'promotion of homosexuality' by local authorities, including 'the publishing of materials with the intention of promoting homosexuality' or 'that teach the acceptability of homosexuality as a pretended family relationship'[16] (happy books about queer families, basically). One Tory MP recently sent letters to all the schools in his constituency expressing concern that 'books which make this ideology acceptable to embrace and such media in all its forms that glamorize this transgender lifestyle are I'm afraid reaffirming something that is nothing more than a phase'. Helpfully reminding us that concern about 'trans ideology' is premised on anti-feminism, he added, 'Boys are boys and girls are girls'.[17] We can find in such statements about what girls and boys *are* a conviction about who they *will be*. I call this conviction *gender fatalism*, and it is most often given as a command (you *will be* a girl, you *will be* a boy) to those who express a will or intent not to do or be as they are told.

KILLJOY MAXIM: STAY UNHAPPY WITH THIS WORLD!

The *anti-trans* movement is an *anti-feminist* movement. This is why so many attacks on feminism are now expressed as attacks on 'gender', which has become increasingly, in different parts of the world, a *killjoy term*. Judith Butler describes the 'anti-gender movement' as a global phenomenon that uses a range of rhetorical strategies 'to maximize the fear of infiltration and destruction that comes from a diverse set of economic and social forces. It does not strive for consistency, for its incoherence is part of its power.'[18] Butler shows how fields of academic inquiry including gender studies, queer theory and critical race theory, come to be represented as 'destructive forces' that threaten the breakdown of social institutions – marriage, the family, the nation, civilization, 'even man himself'. Sex is defended by being placed outside history. By *sex*, we would mean not only the idea of two discrete biological sexes, but corresponding ideas: that marriage is a heterosexual union, that all children should be brought up in traditional families based on such a union and that society must *shore up* the discreteness of sex by the policing of social spaces and institutions. This defence of sex is also, as Butler shows, a resistance to 'the critical questioning of norms of all kinds'.

The critical task of questioning 'norms of all kinds' has thus become all the more urgent. As the figure of the feminist killjoy has taught us, taking up that task requires being willing to be positioned as dangerous as well as deadly to human happiness. To think of the feminist killjoy as activist is to reflect on *how* we take up that task. To take up the task is to agree to be less appealing. We don't smile or try to be more appealing *to* those with power. I think of killjoy activism, and I take inspiration from Black feminists such as Stella Nyanzi, who launched a naked protest after she was locked out of her university office. She later spoke out against the President of Uganda, borrowing the tactic of 'radical rudeness' from earlier anti-colonial activists who broke the rules of British colonial culture, imposed *as* manners and politeness.[19] From Nyanzi and feminist freedom warriors, I learn how we can use our bodies and language to disrupt the system by revealing its violence. I think also of feminists of colour such as Mona Eltahawy, who says fuck off to patriarchy and keeps saying it.[20] She explains, 'I refuse to be polite or civil with anyone who does not acknowledge my full humanity. Profanity for me is political, not just personal.' From Eltahawy, I learn how feminists sometimes have to be rude, uncivil or impolite in making our demands.

When negativity is style, it is also substance: we express ourselves the way we do because of what we want for ourselves and for others. We might articulate our aims and aspirations firstly, inappropriately enough, in the negative; we do *not* want to be included in institutions that reproduce violence; we are *not* going to soften our appearance or words to make you feel more comfortable; we are *not* going to smile to create the illusion of family happiness or happy diversity; we are not going to smile to fulfil our job description, smile as servicing others. In claiming *not smiling* as a political action, we draw on a long feminist history. Shulamith Firestone's 'dream action' for the women's liberation movement was a smile boycott: 'all women would instantly abandon their "pleasing smiles", henceforth smiling only when something pleased them'. She suggests smiling becomes obligatory for oppressed groups, who 'must also appear to *like* their oppression, smiling and simpering though they feel like hell inside'.[21] Maybe if we instantly stopped smiling at the same time, we would be striking. A smile strike would get what is inside us *out*, that hell.

I think of how a *smile strike* might relate to feminist scholar Verónica Gago's cogent analysis of the women's strike in Argentina and her call for a feminist strike against *everything*. She writes:

> There is a temporality of the strike that effectively puts into practice a refusal: a way of saying 'enough!' to the violence and the way in which our time slips through our fingers, a refusal of the physical and psychic exhaustion that sustains extenuating precarity. It is saying 'no' to the fact that the multiplicity of tasks we carry out is not translated into economic autonomy, but rather is reinforced as compulsory and free labour.[22]

Gago, drawing on a conversation with scholar-activist Sylvia Federici, suggests that a feminist strike would be about 'stopping the activities that contribute to our oppression', and thus would 'free up time and energy'.[23] I will return to how killjoy activism can be about *filling up what we free up* in due course.

It can take time to get *no* out, time slipping through our fingers. In my chapter on the feminist killjoy as philosopher, I described how a student took time to get to the point where she could say *no* to a professor. She did end up saying *no*. And she said *no* because she 'wanted to prevent other students from having to go through such practice'. She understood that unless someone said *no*, he would continue to act in the same

231

way, making that course, that programme, inaccessible to other students who were unable or unwilling to comply. And what happened? When she told the convenor of the MA programme that she was intending to complain, she was warned, 'Be careful, he is an important man.' A warning is a judgement about who is important as well as a direction. She went ahead with the complaint. And, in her terms, she 'sacrificed the references'. That was when she said to me, 'That door is closed.'

The one who said *no* ends up with nowhere to go. When those who say *no* disappear, a *no* disappears with them. To say *no* to those with institutional power is to come up against the institution that gives them power. This is why saying *no* to a person who has been given power can be so politicizing – you realize who the system is working for. The consequences of saying *no* are thus *material* – you lose access to the resources you need to get through or to get by. You become extremely vulnerable to retaliation. It is hard to evidence retaliation because, so often, it is about what you do not receive, opportunities that do not come your way, doors that are not opened. The people that 'hold the door' to institutions are the same people that close the door on those who try to stop them abusing their power.

It takes a political movement to open these doors. MeToo was one such movement that went viral in 2017, but as a political campaign began much earlier in 2006, organized by Black feminist activist Tarana Burke as a 'space for supporting and amplifying the voices of survivors of sexual abuse, assault and exploitation'.[24] The voices that need to be amplified are voices that we do not hear. It is not that survivors

232

do not complain – many that can, do – but that we don't get to hear about them, sometimes because of the use of non-disclosure agreements as well as other techniques for enforcing or incentivizing silence, sometimes because those who complain often leave the institutions in which they complained, because *no* is a door.

To become a feminist killjoy activist is to hear silence as an achievement. Silence does not mean people did not say *no*. Silence can mean we have been stopped from hearing them. I spoke to a woman professor about a 'canopy of complaints' about sexual harassment and bullying by a number of men in a department at her university. She talked about how those complaints were framed: 'The feminists come along and you just spoil the fun. They were all right until you made them think about it . . . they were quite happy until you stirred it all up.' Killjoy activism can be how we 'stir it all up'. The illusion that 'they were quite happy' could only be upheld by stopping complaints from being made or, if they were made, stopping them from getting out.

Complaints are stopped or suppressed to create that illusion of happiness. Maybe the complaints end up in the basement or a filing cabinet. I spoke to another professor who supported students who made a complaint about sexual misconduct and sexual harassment by a lecturer at her university. She describes the process:

'A student, a young student, came and said to me that this guy had seduced her, basically. And then in conversation with another woman she found out he had done the same to her. And then it snowballed, and then we found out there were ten women. He was just going through one woman after another after another after another.' One student says *no*. She has conversations; she hears about others. I think of snowballing, how complaints can bring more complaints about, *watch us roll*, acquiring a momentum. *Watch us roll* was the last sentence from my book *Living a Feminist Life*. I hope you can hear what I was trying to pick up by that expression.

This is not to say that gaining momentum will be enough to change things. In my introduction, I noted that the power of the killjoy is often inflated. That inflation of the power of those who challenge power is how power is retained. The professor defended his own conduct thus, 'He came up to me and said, "It's a perk of the job." I could not believe it. He actually said it to me. It was not hearsay; this is a perk of the job. I can't remember my response, but I was flabbergasted.' The implication is that having sex with your students is like having a company car; what you are entitled to because of what you do. She added, 'The women: they were set up as a witch-hunt, hysterical, you can hear it, can't you, and as if they were out to get this guy.' When you describe an entitlement as harassment you are understood as depriving somebody of what is theirs; the complainer-as-killjoy could characterize this deprivation. As soon as you try to stop someone who has power from abusing that power, you will be identified as motivated by a desire for power. In this case, the complaint was not upheld and the lecturer returned to his post with minor adjustments to supervisory arrangements.

It is not just those who abuse power who represent complaints as contradictions of an entitlement. I think of another student who also worked as a part of a collective to put in a complaint about the convenor of their MA course for harassment and bullying. She described how they were identified as killjoys by their peers, who said they 'needed to be in "solidarity" with those whose education was now being disrupted, not the other way around.' By complaining, you are treated as acting as an individual who is causing a disruption. Killjoys are often treated as individualistic, even when we work as collectives. When you are unwilling to participate in a shared culture, you are judged as putting yourself first. You are put under more pressure to accept a situation when more people benefit from it.

KILLJOY TRUTH: POWER WORKS BY MAKING IT HARD TO CHALLENGE HOW POWER WORKS

Those who challenge power learn how it works. Let me share with you some of what I learnt from being involved in such a campaign. I began working to support students who had submitted a collective complaint about sexual harassment in 2013. As soon as I began talking to the students, I heard about other complaints, earlier complaints, earlier inquiries. It became clear that the problem was not just an individual, it was the culture of the institution. It was the institution that kept treating the problem as an individual one. 'Stranger danger' does more than tell us that violence originates with outsiders. The function of stranger danger is also to *obscure* the violence 'at home', and 'at home' can refer to domestic violence, institutional violence or state violence.

Institutional loyalty can sometimes require *being willing to obscure the problem*. The more you make the institution the problem, the more you become the problem. To manage complaints is to contain where people can express them. After three years, we could not even get a public acknowledgement that the inquiries had happened, let alone an acknowledgement of why they had happened. It was like they had not happened, which is, I rather imagine, the effect they were looking for. A whole campaign can be blanked. I shared my reasons for resigning on my feminist killjoy blog because there is no point in resigning in silence when you are protesting silence. And, very quickly, I became a feminist killjoy all over again, or an *institutional killjoy*. The university quickly launched a public relations campaign that included the following statement: 'We take sexual harassment very seriously and take action against those found to be acting in ways incompatible with our strong values relating to equality, diversity and inclusion.' Diversity (as well as equality and inclusion) can be used to *counter* the evidence of complaint, diversity as a repair job, an effort to repair the damage to reputation, papering over problems.

If I expected that reaction from the university, I did not expect that some of my feminist colleagues would also describe my action as damaging. I was reprimanded for my action by a colleague, who said I had been 'rash' and said that my action

236

was 'against the interest of many long-standing feminist colleagues who have worked to ensure a happy and stimulating environment'. If I had publicly identified as a feminist killjoy, I was here identified by another feminist as killing feminist joy. We need to learn from that fact that it is possible that a disclosure about sexual harassment could be framed as compromising not just the happiness of the university but feminist happiness ('a happy and stimulating environment'). I think of the students who were harassed. Was the university a happy and stimulating environment for them? I recall an event we organized on sexism. Some of the students spoke about the work they had been doing on sexual harassment. This was the first time they spoke in public, although there was still so much that had to be left unsaid. Afterwards some colleagues expressed concern in private that to go public about the problem would lead to people overlooking the feminist work that had been done at the college.

There is a cautionary tale here. If we are silent about sexual harassment to protect the feminist reputation of an institution, we are not working for a feminist institution. Working for a feminist institution is a project because we are not there yet. When feminism is resourced by an institution, feminists end up defending it to protect their resources. Audre Lorde told us this might happen. She suggested that it is *only* those who are resourced by the master's house who will find those who try to dismantle that house, or those who expose what goes on in there, 'threatening'.[25] When some feminists are resourced by institutions, they end up loyal to them.

KILLJOY TRUTH: SILENCE ABOUT VIOLENCE IS VIOLENCE

It is too easy to be critical of sexism or racism, of power or harassment, in general. A postgraduate student described how being critical was self-definitional for her department as long as critique pointed elsewhere: 'We are a very critical department but if those things are happening here, we can't talk about it: if they are happening elsewhere, burn the system down.' She added, 'The closer to home it is the less likely they are to take action.' To be a killjoy activist is to learn what happens when you try to address problems 'closer to home'. Sometimes action is not taken because there is a refusal to *hear* about problems *here*. In my introduction to the killjoy, I noted that we need to snap a bond when it is damaging or diminishing. We might need to snap a bond to institutions to prevent other people from being damaged by them.

KILLJOY COMMITMENT: I AM WILLING TO SNAP A BOND THAT IS DAMAGING TO OTHERS

The feminist killjoy as cultural critic lends a hand here: from her, we learnt how to read happiness. Institutions offer their own promises of happiness. You are promised happiness in return for loyalty – happiness might be offered in the form of that pay rise or that promotion or that time freed from less valued, more exhausting work. A promise is also a warning. I spoke to a student who was considering

238

making a complaint about sexual harassment. She said, 'I was repeatedly told that "rocking the boat" or "making waves" would affect my career in the future and that I "would ruin the department for everyone else".' Complaints are framed not only as damaging yourself, but as damaging a department or institution. Perhaps you are being told your own happiness is dependent on the extent to which you are willing to protect the happiness of an institution.

KILLJOY TRUTH: WHAT YOU ARE TOLD YOU NEED TO DO TO PROGRESS FURTHER OR FASTER IN A SYSTEM REPRODUCES THE SYSTEM

This is why feminist killjoys have so much to teach everyone. We learn the reproductive mechanisms, that those who have power in institutions are *those who are willing to reproduce them*. We also learn that those who are more likely to transform institutions are less likely to progress within them. If you say *yes*, you are more likely to progress. We don't stop being told what you need to do to progress. I think back to that letter inviting me to put myself forward to become a Fellow of an elite body. Once you are elected, you will be involved in determining who else is elected. To be recognized, to be rewarded, is not only to be made subject to a hierarchy, but to be required to reproduce it.

KILLJOY EQUATION:
REWARD = A REPRODUCTIVE TECHNOLOGY

It is not only that silence is compliance. You are rewarded for it. In my introduction to this handbook, I suggested that all feminists are killjoys by virtue of being feminists. Some feminists might try to maximize the distance between themselves and the very figure of the feminist killjoy; we might call these feminists *liberal or neoliberal*. To distance yourself from the feminist killjoy is to distance yourself from other feminists who are not respectable enough, those who threaten the project of upward mobility.

We need to remember here that the figure of the feminist killjoy is *sticky*, some of us become killjoys because of what we bring with us, or just by entering the room. If some women are promoted by keeping their distance from feminist killjoys, from the wrong kind of feminism, they are promoted for keeping their distance from certain people, those who seem to pose a problem wherever they go. I would call this feminism *white liberal feminism*. A woman of colour who experienced racism, sexism and harassment in her department talked to me about how she was not supported by a senior white feminist professor who was head of another department. She says, 'It's easy to be radical on paper, but in reality, it's quite different. Her politics were to do with advancing her career and nothing to do with changing the landscape for women.' Killjoy activists know all about *paper feminists* – those who are feminist on paper but not in practice.

If we can be feminists on paper, we can also be *paper feminist killjoys*, feminist killjoys in name but not in practice, feminist killjoys in public, loudly proclaiming what we are against, but not behind closed doors, when we are called upon to give our support to someone making a complaint about harassment. It is too easy to adopt the killjoy, to claim her, to have her on a T-shirt, to write through her or as her without changing what we do. I write this as a note to self. I am saying this to myself. There is more to being a feminist killjoy than saying you are one. The risk of using her *more*, is that she does *less*, becoming easier to adopt. This is a risk we take in repurposing any difficult term. Any term that comes out of struggle, which began as an insult or stereotype, can lose energy on its travels.

The problem is not only that terms can lose energy on their travels but that they can be used as covers. A woman of colour academic wrote to me: 'There's another man on my campus who has been the subject of complaint from women who has a "feminist killjoy" sign on his door. When one of the women he had harmed told him that seeing the sign on his door after everything he had done made her uncomfortable, he filed a civility complaint against her to the chair. I don't know how any of this is possible.'

I don't know how it is possible. But we need to know that it is possible. The feminist killjoy can end up as a sign on the same door shut on a woman who complained. Our terms becoming screens, assertions of their right to occupy time and space. If we say, you are doing this, appropriating the feminist killjoy for your own ends, he might look over his shoulder, assuming you are talking about someone else, or if he does see himself, defend himself, so that we become uncivil, the problem for pointing out the problem, all over again.

Appropriation is a technique for neutralizing the work, not just removing the negative energy, but redirecting it along the very path we are trying to refuse. All of our terms, from intersectionality, to decolonizing, to abolitionism, to the feminist killjoy herself, can be used to cover violence, enabling people to claim an oppositional stance without changing how they act, or even as justifications of how they act. We need to say *no* to that and perhaps, channelling the energy of Mona Eltahawy and Stella Nyanzi and others, be willing to be impolite, uncivil, shouting loudly, *Take the feminist killjoy sign off your fucking door!* If they take it down, they can, of course, put it back up again, or take it out in public, turning it into a placard to be proudly displayed in a march against the violence they enact behind closed doors. When our work is not over, nor is the risk of appropriation. These are hard lessons but they are our lessons.

Appropriation is not our only problem. A woman of colour student wrote to me about her supervisor who was a star professor, and also a woman of colour. This student admired her supervisor; she wanted to work with her, to learn from her: 'Her readings, critiques, analyses of power structures, interlocking systems of oppression, race and gender, whether aimed at literature, popular culture or injustice, in America and internationally, were elegant, bristling, derisive, biting in their precision, unflinching and loud.' Within the seminar room, her office, the woman of colour professor seemed to speak differently: 'Her abuse took the form of attacks on my still-forming or imperfectly articulated thoughts, analyses and ideas in class when other students were encouraged and helped along.' What you critique you can still enact. The woman of colour professor does not open the door for her student, another woman of colour, but shuts it on her, belittling her, criticizing her, making her feel smaller. In contrast, she praises and elevates two white students in the class: 'They were the stars and darlings of the department, well-awarded, published and conferenced, and didn't share my experiences at all, and they more or less minimized her behaviour.'

Yes, those who benefit from relationships with abusive people often minimize the abuse to keep the benefits. Perhaps some of us become professors, even star professors, singled out, by identifying with the master, becoming like him, loving whom he would love, targeting whom he would target. When diversity is an open door, that door becomes a deal. The door is opened for some of us on condition that we *shut that door* right behind us, shut the door on others like us.

KILLJOY EQUATION: DIVERSITY = THE MASTER'S TOOL

Consider again the Sewell Report discussed in chapter 3, which concluded that institutional racism does not exist in the UK. The report was authored primarily by Black and brown people. The feminist killjoy gives us the tools to offer a structural explanation of this authorship. You are more likely not to be stopped by institutional racism if you deny it exists. You might even be promoted. And then your promotion can be used as evidence racism does not exist. *Shut that door* can mean not only doing what you can to stop others from getting in but stopping even thinking of yourself as one of the others. To accept the door deal would be to distance yourself not only from the others, but from yourself, from your truths, your **killjoy truths**, the doors that are still shut because of what you bring with you. This is why the figure of the killjoy can be so profoundly threatening: she holds not only our own but other people's truths, holding up another kind of mirror, reflecting back what has been denied.

To sustain a commitment to the feminist killjoy, which is one way of thinking about *killjoy activism*, we need to hold that mirror up, to see what it reflects back to us, including about ourselves, what we do, where we do it. We need to prepare to be undone by what we might see or what we might hear or what we might have to do.

KILLJOY COMMITMENT:
I AM WILLING TO BE INCONVENIENCED

We become *institutional killjoys* when we take the sign off the door; the diversity sign, or the feminist killjoy sign, it can be any fucking sign. To take the sign off requires getting the truth out, the **killjoy truth**. We have to let it in to get it *out*, not just out of ourselves, but into the world. It is the resistance to that *outing* that makes killjoy activism so challenging. It is not so much that killjoys threaten other people's investments in persons, institutions or projects. We become killjoys because we threaten other people's investments in persons, institutions or projects. And 'other people' can include other feminists. And 'other people' can include ourselves. Killjoy activism can also be the work we have to do in order to be able to hear another person's story. We need to be prepared for our own joy to be killed, our progression slowed, if that is what it takes.

Remember our *Killjoy Survival Tip 4: Listen to the feminist killjoy as if she is another person*. We also listen to the feminist killjoy *because* she is another person. I think of this 'because' as necessary for solidarity. We learn about solidarity when we don't receive it. Killjoy activism can also be the work we have to do to make it possible to get nos out when some people can't afford to say no. Killjoy activism is about giving support to those who speak out in public about their experiences of being harassed despite the costs. Sometimes we have to find ways to get complaints out without making it possible for them to be traced to a source. We might need to use guerrilla tactics, and we have feminist and queer histories to draw upon: you can write names of harassers on books; graffiti on toilet doors and walls. I noted in my chapter on the feminist killjoy as cultural critic how so much of our work is treated as vandalism. Vandalism has queer uses. Killjoy activism might require vandalism, writing ourselves and our stories on materials that were not intended for that purpose.

Let me return to my experience of supporting students who had risked so much by complaining about harassment. I understand my resignation from my university professorship as an expression of solidarity with those students. It was also a kind of snap; my bond to the institution broke. I realized from working with the students that what we needed to provide was what they would be giving up – mentorship, supervision, references. This practical task can also be understood as an activist principle: if becoming a killjoy can stop people from progressing, *we need to find ways to stop people from being stopped*. Killjoy activism is about *sharing the costs* of killing joy, trying to protect those who are more precarious from paying too much. Killjoy activism matters as a way of dealing with the consequences of precarity. Some people cannot afford to speak out. If so, we have to find ways to get their stories out. If the costs of killing joy are material, support needs to be material.

I too received support, not from the institution but from the students I worked with. My bond with the students kept me going. The students had already begun working as a collective before I started to work with them. Their collective became *our* collective. I think of that *our* as the promise of feminism, ours not as a possession but as an invitation to combine forces.

Sometimes, we form collectives quickly, urgently, because of what is happening, what is going on. We meet up at those tables, trying to work out together what to do. If the task of trying to transform institutions leads us to become philosophers, thinking on our feet, taking up the task is how we find other killjoys, how we find our people (***Killjoy Survival***

246

Tip 3: Find other killjoys). I am grateful that the students I worked with became my complaint collective and that they, Leila Whitley, Tiffany Page, Alice Corble, with support from Heidi Hasbrouck, Chryssa Sdrolia and others, wrote about the work they began as students, how they 'moved something', in one of the conclusions of my book *Complaint!*[26] To move something can be to move so much. And it can take so much.

I noted earlier that when I shared my reasons for resigning in public, my action was treated by the institution and some of my former feminist colleagues as damaging. That was not the most important consequence. My resignation was widely reported in the national media. I was moved and inspired by how many people got in touch with me to express their solidarity, rage and care. I received messages from many different people telling me about what happened when they complained. I heard from other people who had left their posts and professions as a result of a complaint. One story coming out can lead to more stories coming out.

KILLJOY EQUATION: LEAK = A FEMINIST LEAD

By becoming a leak, I became easier to find; people came to me with their stories, including many of the killjoy stories I have shared in this handbook. What we let out is what leads others to us. A killjoy poet *lets loose*. From the project of feminist survival, we **let the feminist killjoy go** (*Killjoy Survival Tip 5*), she becomes a loose cannon; the more

247

she is detached, the more damage she causes. And from the feminist killjoy as activist, we learn that letting loose is not simply about expressing ourselves, although expression matters, but about *loosening the machinery*, the nuts and the bolts of institutions. Just create a small opening, and so much will come out.

A *no* can be that opening. To get your *no* out, to make it public, is how you release information that would otherwise be kept secret. It is also how you let people know you are there. I think of a conversation I had with an Indigenous student based in Canada. She had made an informal complaint about white supremacy in her classroom: using that term for what you encounter in institutions that understand themselves to be progressive and diverse can get you in serious trouble; she knew that but she was still willing to do it. She became in her terms 'a monster', and had to complete her PhD off campus. She said that 'an unexpected little gift', was how other students could come to her: 'They know you are out there and they can reach out to you.' It might seem that when our complaints don't get anywhere they disappear without a trace. In saying *no*, we keep a history alive; we do not let go. Sometimes you hold on by passing a *no* on.

This is why I think of killjoy activism as telling us another story about time, how we can communicate with each other even if we are not working at the same time or in the same place. Sometimes by saying *no* in the present, we can bring back past *no*s. I talked to a disabled student about how hard it was to get anywhere when she made a complaint about the failure of the university to make reasonable accommodations. It was she who described how she had to be 'grovellingly grateful' in even asking for accommodations. She told me about one very difficult meeting. A meeting can be when you feel the wall coming down. But then a file suddenly appeared, 'a load of documents turned up on the students' union fax machine, and we don't know where they came from; they were historical documents about students who had to leave.' The documents included a handwritten letter to a human rights charity by a former student who had cancer, and who was trying to get the university to let her finish her degree part-time. The student speculates that a secretary was doing 'their own little bit of direct action', releasing those documents as a way of giving support to her complaint that she was not, as a secretary, supposed to give. It is not surprising that a secretary can become a saboteur; the word *secretary* derives from secrets, the secretary is a keeper of secrets. She knows *that* there are secret files, *where* they are, *how* to release them. If the student hadn't made her complaint, that file would have stayed put, dusty and buried.

In saying *no*, we can release past *nos*, a momentum can be what is behind us. The student's own activism gathered momentum. She became what she said she was perceived to be, 'a complete pain in the ass'. She became an *institutional killjoy*. Once you are a killjoy in one institution, you can take the skills you acquire to another. She began working with a group of disabled activists to use compliance with the law as a method for putting organizations under pressure to be as accessible as they often claim to be. They also worked to provide support for disabled people to make complaints about the failure to make reasonable accommodations. She took her work onto the streets, writing letters to owners of shops that were not accessible to her as a wheelchair user. She was represented in her local media as a killjoy, trying to ruin small businesses.

KILLJOY COMMITMENT: I AM WILLING TO TAKE FEMINIST KILLJOYS WITH ME, WHEREVER I GO

We can follow her lead, and take the work of the killjoy out from institutions and onto the streets. When we come up against the walls of silence, or when our complaints are filed away, binned or buried, we need to become our complaints, *getting them out by getting ourselves out*. This is why to **become a feminist killjoy (***Killjoy Survival Tip 1***)** is an outward-facing action: we take her in to get her out. The demonstration is how we gather, becoming a killjoy assembly. The word *demonstrate* derives from *monstrum*, 'monster, monstrosity, omen, portent, sign'. To demonstrate is to be involved in the creation of ominous signs, how we carry *no*. Together, bodies become monstrous. Sometimes the point is to become an obstacle. Political histories of demonstrating are histories of those willing to put our bodies in the way, to turn our bodies into blockage points that stop the flow of human traffic, as well as the wider flow of an economy.

We stop the cars. I think of Audre Lorde stopping the car to write a poem about power, how she took *in* the violence of the police, the violence of white supremacy, to get the poem *out*. Killjoy activism can be what we have to do to stop the car. By stopping the car, I mean stopping the system. We have to stop the system from working. We have to throw wrenches in the works, or to borrow from Sarah Franklin, become 'wenches in the works'.[27] We put everything into an action, we get as many as we can behind it.

KILLJOY TRUTH: THE MORE WE COME UP AGAINST, THE MORE WE NEED MORE

We can only counter a momentum by becoming a counter-momentum. For killjoy activism, it is not the more, the merrier. It is the more, the heavier. We carry the *no* between us, so we can pass it like electricity, wired, connected.

If being part of that counter-momentum gives us killjoy joy, even that joy sometimes need to be killed. To share what we oppose is not necessarily to fight for the same things.

KILLJOY MAXIM: ENACT WHAT WE AIM FOR, NOTHING LESS WILL DO!

Behind us are long histories of failed enactments, of how critiques of the abuses of power within social movements are dismissed as distractions from a shared struggle. Part of the difficulty is not only who is judged as the obstacle, but who takes charge, who leads the way, defining what is most important, what is to be done. If those who are in front 'front' our political movements, what happens? Some of us, those assumed to come after, take up our old positions, becoming the arms that carry, the helping hands, the ones who make the tea, who clean, do the leg work, to free up the time for the heads. Perhaps that's how we end up with our signs on their door. We might be told to be patient, to wait until it is our turn.

KILLJOY EQUATION: IMPATIENCE = A FEMINIST VIRTUE

We will not wait. From feminist killjoys we learn that even if we assemble, even if we clear the ground for our own action, becoming monstrous, carrying ominous signs, we do not always or only come together. Consider Black feminist Kirsten West Savali's critique of how white women occupied the Women's March that took place in Washington after the election of President Trump. Following Lorde, Savali points to the radical uses of anger. Savali refers to how whiteness was 'most clearly evident in the self-congratulatory photos of attendees with police officers rocking pink pussy hats and the triumphant reports that there were no arrests made. There were no tanks, no clubs and no water hoses. Jovial police officers came out in full force to protect white womanhood, positioning the march as a propaganda tool for the state'.[28]

It is not simply that you are called divisive for pointing out these divisions, although that *killjoy point* does matter. In my introduction to the feminist killjoy, I used the word *occupied* to describe white feminism. What Savali shows is how that occupation happens in the space of the protest or march. In a protest, we are meant to occupy space. But consider how that occupation is turned into a celebration, a happy occasion, how the kind of triumphant reports of 'no arrests' converted a relation to the police into a recording device. Savali reminds us that a positive relation to the police as protectors is only possible for white women. For so many other women, the police are who we need to be protected from.

This is why killjoy activism turns to prison abolitionism as a necessary horizon for its political aims and aspirations. Angela Davis, Gina Dent, Erica Meiners and Beth Richie call for an 'abolition feminism' now, as being urgent, necessary. We have to fight to make what is necessary possible. I love how in their book *Abolition. Feminism. Now*, they do not just write about abolitionist feminism but from it, creating a living feminist archive of a movement that is happening now, urgent, necessary, now. Here is just one of their descriptions of abolitionist feminism:

> We recognize the relationality of state and individual violence and thus frame our resistance accordingly: supporting survivors and holding perpetrators accountable, working locally and internationally, building communities while responding to immediate needs. We work alongside people who are incarcerated while we demand their release. We mobilize in outrage against the rape of another woman and reject increased policing as the response. We support and build sustainable and long-term cultural and political shifts to end ableism and transphobia, while proliferating different 'in the moment' responses when harm does happen.[29]

What I find so powerful about this description is how resistance is framed as a response to the relationality of state and individual violence. We have to find ways of responding that do not involve the expansion of reliance on institutions that cause harm, such as the police or prisons. This does not mean abandoning accountability, but *demanding it, being inventive, creating our own resources to try and bring an end to violence.*

Killjoy activism is also about how we create and share resources, how we identify violence, including institutional violence, the violence of how institutions respond to violence. To turn to the police as the solution for the problem of gender-based violence would be to turn to an institution that targets many of us, those who are Black, brown, poor or undocumented. It would be to turn to violence as a remedy for violence. Killjoy activism would include the work we do to make the violence of the police more visible. Our activism thus includes feminist vigils. A vigil can mean to stay awake with a person who is dying; to mark or to mourn, to make a protest, to pray; to count our losses, to count her as loss, or, to borrow the name of a recent campaign in response to police violence against Black women, to *say her name.*[30]

So much violence is not seen as violence; it too becomes usual; business as usual. Killjoy activism includes the work we have to do to make that violence appear. Sometimes, we create a spectacle. To evoke an action by feminist direct action group Sisters Uncut, to protest about cuts to domestic violence services justified by austerity, we put red ink in the water so that the centre of a city seems flooded by blood.

'They cut, we bleed.' It is a snappy slogan.[31] Of course, feminist activism is not just about the creation of spectacle; there is so much work that is being done that is not seen. To value each other is also to value that work, behind the scenes, behind the doors, administrative work, housework, care work. We don't just create a spectacle. We take up more space; we take it back. In 2017 Sisters Uncut occupied Holloway Prison in north London 'to demand that the empty space be used to support local domestic violence survivors'.[32] If you have to occupy a building in order to survive, in order to have somewhere to go to escape from violence that usually happens at home, domestic violence, that occupation is a political project. We counter the violence of the system by revealing it.

Occupying buildings can also be about trying to fill those spaces in a different way. As Erika Doucette and Marty Huber note, 'The range of uses for squatted buildings is often much wider than simply providing a place to live. These projects link ideals with material realities and utopias, as a crucial point for many queer-feminist living projects is finding ways to combine affordable and politically responsible forms of living/housing.'[33] When buildings are occupied as part of a protest, space is opened up, also time, to experiment with doing things, to live together, to learn together, to find ways of sustaining each other. In the film *Rebel Dykes* mentioned earlier, one of the women interviewed described squatting a vacant building, as 'open[ing] them up and giv[ing] them some life'. We open up the question of what space is for, releasing ourselves from the obligation to fill the rooms in a certain way. We free time as well as space, time to teach, to write, to listen and to learn, to share our experience of violence; our knowledge, our **killjoy truths**.

Killjoy activism can be *how we fill up what we free up*. We start from a simple premise: we have different needs. Dismantling as a project might seem, on the surface, negative and destructive. But if, as we learnt from the feminist killjoy as poet, possibility is built out of the system, we need to destroy what is built to make some lives possible, to make it possible for some people to get what they need. In other words, dismantling is a building project. Doors matter because they are how borders can be controlled, the narrower the entry point, the more people you can stop from entering. Killjoy activism is about widening, we *widen* the doors, *widen* the routes into professions, *widen* the range of texts and stories published and read, *widen* our scripts for living, for who we are, and who we can be.

We widen, we loosen; we are building something. Our experiences of not being accommodated, not having our needs met, teach us what we need to do to build a more accommodating world. We listen to others, we ask how to address them, ask what they need, knowing that we need to be open at any moment in time for what we are creating to be reshaped when it does not allow somebody else in. We breathe life into arrangements when we know they can be changed and by trying to change them. And there can be joy in that, happiness even; we feel everything (*Killjoy Survival Tip 8: Feel everything including killjoy joy*).

Killing joy as a world-making project: we are inventing more than ourselves. We are creating room for invention.

Yes, the negation is a starting point, the shattering. But from there, so much else follows. From our many killjoy projects, our cultural criticism, our philosophy, our poetry, our activism, we are making other worlds possible. Sometimes, it does feel like a lot of work not to get very far. I think of snap, the pressure we put on something. Snapping does not only refer to the moment when we can't take it any more or to how we recover a history of those who would not take it any more. Snapping can be what we are trying to achieve. We keep making the same points to put pressure upon something, an argument, or a justification, until it snaps, until it no longer holds, no longer works. Maybe something will only snap later, after we are done, after we have gone. If so, then, we are part of a snap, of how something stops working.

I think again of the *press* in expression. The more we express ourselves, the more pressure we are applying. If we are saying it because they are doing it, we need to *say it more*. When saying it more is saying too much, **remember there is only so much you can do (Killjoy Survival Tip 7)**. What you say, what you do, is a contribution to a shared project. If we need to *say it more*, we also need *more to say it*. Yes, the need to repeat ourselves can be tiring, frustrating. But making the same points is how we share the labour.

Consider all the killjoy letters referenced in this handbook. There have been so many. In my chapter on surviving as a feminist killjoy, I shared quotes from letters by readers who addressed themselves as well as me as feminist killjoys. By killing joy, addressing a problem, *we are addressing each other.*

257

We can return to Audre Lorde's letter to Mary Daly. Lorde, in sharing the letter with her readers, turns a private correspondence into a public address. Lorde wrote that she shared her letter because she had not received a reply. Much later, Alexis de Veaux, when researching Lorde for a biography, found a reply from Daly in Lorde's archives.[34] We cannot ask Lorde about the reply, what she made of it. But we learn that the point of Lorde's letter might not have been the reply. The point of the letter might be how it was shared. Even when letters are addressed to someone, they are not always about the initiation of a dialogue. Perhaps if the letter is for Lorde's readers, the letter is addressed to them, to us, readers whom Lorde mostly did not meet. What Lorde wrote, 'has a life of its own', to use her words for her work. Killjoy letters, too, have lives of their own. Killjoy letters, sometimes written, sometimes spoken, can be an opening of an address. Killjoy activism can be what we have to do to get our letters *out*, of ourselves as well as institutions, so that we can get them *to* whoever might need them.

I think also of what it means to resign in protest. We can't all do it but some of us do. To resign is to withdraw your labour as well as yourself. In the moment of withdrawal, you can express your *no* more forcefully; they can no longer threaten they will take something from you if you have given it up. One lecturer shared with me her experience of writing a resignation letter:

'I found it was powerful to write the final resignation complaint addressed to no one (that is, without any "To" or "Dear") and refer to everyone by their name (rather than "you"). I think it alarmed my manager that the letter could land anywhere. Also, how cathartic that final letter is! Whenever I have doubts, I can read it over and remind myself what happened and why I left.'

The letter didn't use *you* to conceal *who*. It did not narrow its audience by addressing someone. In not being addressed to someone, the letter could be received by anyone.

That letter 'could land anywhere'. It is received as a threat.

That letter 'could land anywhere'. For feminist killjoys, a threat is a promise.

Our letters can take many forms: complaints, resignations, refusals, protests, demands, different ways of expressing our *nos*, what we are not willing to smile about, laugh off, agree to or with. We don't know where our letters will land. Or where we will. We don't always meet in person. We meet in the points we make. To embrace the feminist killjoy is how we connect what we are doing now to those who came before. And what we do now, the points we keep having to make, however sore, the letters we keep sending out, however pointed, can be picked up by those who are to come. This is why our words, our deeds, are not over, not yet done. Only so much can matter so much. Only so much can be more than you know.

Killjoy Truths, Killjoy Maxims, Killjoy Commitments and Killjoy Equations

Killjoy truths are the insights we have about the nature of social reality from our experience of killing joy, that world-making project. We learn about the world from what comes back at us because of what we say or do. Once you have become a feminist killjoy, and more of a feminist killjoy (in accordance with our first two killjoy survival tips), a **killjoy truth** is clear and striking, even obvious. The obvious is often obscured by happiness. We become killjoy critics by showing the obvious.

A **killjoy truth**, even when it seems obvious, takes time to reach. It can sometimes be hard to reach because of how it gets in the way of our own happiness. A **killjoy truth** can also be hard to reach because to admit some things can mean not being able to contain them. So, for example, you might have to work to open the door to violence, even when it is directed at you, because letting it in means letting it get everywhere. We become killjoy philosophers because of what we let in. We have to let it in to get it out. Getting **the killjoy truths** out is what killjoy poetry and killjoy activism are about.

Killjoy truths are thus hard-worn wisdoms. When we express **killjoy truths**, we feel less alone.

To expose a problem is to pose a problem.

If you have to shout to be heard, you are heard as shouting.

We have to keep saying it because they keep doing it.

Things are fluid if you are going the way things are flowing.

There is only so much you can take on as there is only so much you can take in.

When you have to fight for existence, fighting can become an existence.

You can't always choose battles; battles can choose you.

There can be nothing more unconvincing than the effort to be convinced.

If happiness requires turning away from violence, happiness is violence.

The unconventional daughter of the migrant family is a conventional form of social hope.

The less we see ourselves reflected the more we see in a reflection.

Discomfort is revealing of worlds.

To be given room is to be given room for error.

For some, to be is to be in question.

Those who are not 'at home' in categories tend to know more about them.

To become conscious of possibility can involve mourning for its loss.

You notice worlds when they are not built for you.

Just because they welcome you, it does not mean they expect you to turn up.

The more we challenge structures, the more we come up against them.

We learn about institutions from trying to transform them.

What is hardest for some does not exist for others.

When Black and brown people become poets, we are fighting against history.

Those who don't fit the old forms need to create their own forms.

Some have to insist on what is given to others.

What we create is fragile because we need it to survive.

Silence about violence is violence.

What you are told you need to do to progress further or faster in a system reproduces the system.

Power works by making it hard to challenge how power works.

The more we come up against, the more we need more.

Killjoy maxims are rules for action; the dos and don'ts of being a feminist killjoy. They lay out paths we can follow in living a feminist life. **Killjoy maxims** derive from our truths, those hard-worn wisdoms; what we learn about existence from our effort to transform it. If **killjoy maxims** generalize from an experience, they are not universal. As a feminist killjoy, write your own rules.

When it is not funny, do not laugh!

Become a feminist infection!

Be maladjusted, don't adjust to an injustice!

Get a *no* out so that others can follow!

Stop the world from making sense!

If you are charged with wilfulness, accept and mobilize the charge!

Become monstrous!

Let loose!

Stay unhappy with this world!

Enact what we aim for, nothing less will do!

Killjoy commitments are how we express our hopes for the future. All of our killjoy truths can be turned into commitments. Commitments are key to killjoy activism because the point of our work is to change the world.

Killing joy is a future-orientated practice insofar as we oppose what exists. We aim for something to counter what exists. **Killjoy commitments** can be thought of as the wills and won'ts of being a feminist killjoy. Being a feminist killjoy is not only about what we hope to bring about, it is what we are prepared to do in order to bring it about.

I am willing to cause unhappiness.

I am willing to get in the way of feminist happiness.

If being a feminist killjoy is a phase, I am willing to remain in that phase.

I am not willing to get over what is not over.

When critique causes damage, I am willing to cause damage.

I am willing to be inconvenient.

I am not willing to make happiness my cause.

I am willing to snap a bond that is damaging to others.

I am willing to be inconvenienced.

I am willing to take feminist killjoys with me, wherever I go.

Killjoy equations are another way of expressing kill-joy truths (what we learn from the experience of killing joy) with an emphasis on what is revealing and sometimes humorous about that knowledge. As some of these equations might seem rather obscure without the context in which I came up with them, I have provided you with some context!

Rolling eyes = feminist pedagogy

This is my oldest equation, which I used to call a feminist equation but I am now repurposing as a killjoy equation. When I share this equation in lectures, people laugh. When we are known as feminists, people tend to roll their eyes at us before we even say anything, expressing their exasperation. We learn about the world from the bother feminism causes. What is directed at us can be how we get each other. We roll our eyes at each other, recognizing what each other recognizes about the world.

Over-sensitive = sensitive to what is not over

We are often judged to be over-sensitive or too sensitive when we refuse to laugh at an offensive joke or to make light of something. This equation plays with the significance of 'over'. It suggests that over-sensitive is a judgement made against anyone who refuses to accept the fantasy that we are 'over' racism or other unfinished histories of oppression (I sometimes call this fantasy 'overing'.)

Affect alien = alienated by how you are affected

I have a T-shirt with the words 'affect alien'. I call it a worn argument. An affect alien is the person who is alienated because they are not affected in the same way as other people or in the right way. A killjoy might be the one who is not made happy by the right things or made happy by the wrong ones. You can also be an affect alien when you are not sad at the right time or when you do not express your sadness in an appropriate way. You might be told, for instance, that it is the wrong time to be critical of the monarchy when others are mourning the death of a monarch.

Feminism = a history of unnatural women

Many oppressions are justified with reference to nature. And many of us are told our desires are unnatural and that we have deviated from the path of nature (and happiness too). This equation helps us to explain why feminism came out of the willingness to be unnatural if that is what it takes. It might also point to how feminism requires better artifices.

White feminism = blanking

To be blanked is how some are not acknowledged or recorded as being there. The word *blank* derives from white. This equation suggests that feminism becomes white not because Black women and women of colour were not there, but because we were not acknowledged or recorded as being there.

Noticing = the feminist killjoy's hammer

So much oppression works by becoming ordinary, so that we don't even notice it. We hammer away at the world by noticing how it is made. We bring what has receded into the background to the front, in order to confront it.

Privilege = an energy-saving device

Having privilege is about what you don't have even to think about or do. If it saves you energy, it gives you more time, which allows you to do more valued things. Not having privilege can be about the additional time it takes to do things – from opening a door, to getting a promotion.

Survival of the fittest = survival of those who fit

This equation is a reworking of an old formula (usually attributed to Darwin, but first used by Herbert Spencer) to account for institutional power. When *fit* is used to explain how organisms are adjusted to their environment, the word *fittest* confused this idea with optimal, physical and mental performance. Some progress not because they are fitter but because they fit, because the world is built to enable their progression.

Opinionated = when some of us express our opinions

Opinionated is a judgement that falls unequally. If you are not supposed to have opinions of your own, any opinion means you are likely to be heard as opinionated. They might also call you opinionated because they don't like your opinions or because you refuse the request to give your opinions up.

269

Wilful = having a will of our own

Wilful too is a judgement that falls unequally. If you are not supposed to have a will of your own, any will is a wilful will. Wilful can also mean you are not willing to do what someone wills you to do.

Raised eyebrows = lesbian feminist pedagogy

Raised eyebrows are an expression of disbelief. My experiences of raised eyebrows mostly come from travelling while lesbian. People are like, really, you want a double bed? Raised eyebrows teach us about social expectations. We learn from being unexpected.

Queer pride = not shamed by another's shame

Queer pride can be a protest or a party, but it can also be a refusal of the expectation that you should be ashamed because others are ashamed of you. The refusal usually requires a political movement. We are that movement.

Reward = a reproductive technology

The word *reward* has the same root as *warden*. To be rewarded can mean to be under guard. Institutions are reproduced by rewarding people who are willing to reproduce them – to be silent, to be compliant. This also means that those who are more willing to challenge institutions are less likely to progress within them.

Diversity = the master's tool

Diversity can mean being willing to smile for their brochures, or to help create the illusion that organizations are more diverse than they are. But diversity can also mean how the door is opened to some of us on condition we identify with the master, denying racism, and by shutting the door on others like us; shutting the door by not even thinking of ourselves as one of the others.

Leak = a feminist lead

We are asked to express our institutional loyalty by keeping a lid on it, staying silent about institutional violence. When we share our story, leaking information, we are often described as being institutionally disloyal. When you leak information, other people are led to you. The more we leak, the easier we are to find.

Impatience = a feminist virtue

Many virtues, including patience, can be understood as idealizing the act of submission to authority. Feminism makes virtues out of the refusal of submission. We will not be patient. We will not wait. We demand change now!

Recommended Reading for Feminist Killjoys

I have created this list of some of the books I have found helpful in my intellectual and life journey as a feminist killjoy and have included commentaries on why. Throughout the handbook, I have cited many feminist books. Citation is feminist memory. The feminist killjoy herself could be understood as memory, a way of recalling past struggles. In a way, then, *The Feminist Killjoy Handbook* is itself a recommended reading list for feminist killjoys.

The books shared here combine strong critiques of the world as it is with imaginative and daring refusals to comply with that world. Many of them experiment with language and form to convey something about the difficulty of feminist survival given that we have to live with, and work under, the very systems we oppose. Some are well-worn books that I have read over and over again. I call them *companion texts*. Others are fairly new and have held my imagination and attention. When an individual author has written multiple books that have given me killjoy inspiration, I have listed just two of my favourites.

Please note: I am only referring to non-fiction books in this list. If I was also including fiction, I would add Ama Ata

Aidoo's *Our Sister Killjoy* and Toni Morrison's *The Bluest Eye*, discussed in this handbook, and Virginia Woolf's *Mrs Dalloway* and George Eliot's *Mill on the Floss*, discussed in my earlier book *Living a Feminist Life*. If I was to include poetry, I would add Suhaiymah Manzoor-Khan's *Postcolonial Banter*, Adrienne Rich's *Diving into the Wreck*, Jasmin Kaur's *When You Ask Me Where I'm Going*, Joan Anim Addo's *Haunted by History* and Dionne Brand's *Inventory*. I carry their work with me and have been glad to share some of their words with you. Also note: the writers I include in my recommended reading list do not use the term *killjoy* to describe themselves or their work. In addressing them as my killjoy inspirations, I acknowledge that they are more, do more, say much more, than that.

Gloria Anzaldúa, *Borderlands / La Frontera: The New Mestiza* (San Francisco: Aunt Lune Books, 2nd edn, 1999)
This is a dizzying, wilful and daring text by a queer Chicana writer. This book changed my idea of what theory is and what it can do. We write by keeping close to the skin. The borders that Anzaldúa crosses are physical borders (specifically the US/Mexico border), but they are also cultural and psychological. When lines are used to tell us where to go and who to be, we need to cross them, to create our own pathways, imaginative and real. Anzaldúa shows how domination can be a demand for access to our being, but also how we can resist that demand through asserting ourselves or making ourselves anew. 'What I write,' she says, 'feels like I'm carving a bone.' She adds, 'It is always a path/state to something else.'

Lauren Berlant, *The Queen of America Goes to Washington City* **(Durham: Duke University Press, 1997) and** *Cruel Optimism* **(Durham: Duke University Press, 2011)**

I have been learning from Lauren Berlant for what seems like a lifetime. Berlant was a cultural critic who paid attention to the political or public nature of feelings and offered endless inspiration to killjoys (I think they knew their queer potential well). In *Queen*, which is my favourite of Berlant's books, they show how structural problems are made 'a problem of will and ingenuity'. In *Cruel Optimism* they offer a powerful critique of how objects can hold us in place because of what they promise – happiness or the good life. I have never encountered anyone else so able to explain the difficulty we have giving up attachments, and yet so alive to the potential for rearranging things, turning slips and slippages into starting points for another story.

Judith Butler, *Gender Trouble: Feminism and the Subversion of Identity* **(New York: Routledge, 1990) and** *Precarious Life: The Powers of Mourning and Violence* **(London: Verso, 2004)**

I first read Judith Butler as an undergraduate student. Their work blew my mind open and taught me that as a feminist academic you can take on anything and anyone! Consider this sentence from the first page of *Gender Trouble*:

> *To make trouble was, within the reigning discourse of my childhood, something one should never do, precisely because that would get one in trouble. The rebellion and its reprimand*

275

seemed to be caught up in the same terms, a phenomenon that
gave rise to my first critical insight into the subtle ruse of power:
the prevailing law threatened one with trouble, even put one in
trouble, all to keep one out of trouble.

Trouble can be what we are threatened with; trouble can be what we are we willing to be *in*. In *Precarious Life*, Butler offers a sustained reflection on the politics of grief, what they call 'grievability': whose lives and loves are grievable (and whose are not). Given that feminist killjoys are affect aliens, it can be through our grief that we express something not only about ourselves but our relation to the world. We might *not* grieve when we are supposed to, or we might grieve for what or whom we are *not* supposed to. Butler takes negativity seriously as a starting point for crafting alternative, more bearable worlds.

Angela Y. Davis, *Freedom is a Constant Struggle* (Chicago: Haymarket Books, 2016) and *Abolition. Feminism. Now.*, with Gina Dent, Erica R. Meiners and Beth E. Richie (Chicago: Haymarket Books, 2021)

When I am feeling politically defeated, I listen to online lectures by, or conversations with, Angela Davis. I offer this as another killjoy survival tip! Davis models for me what killjoy activism is about: critiquing systems of violence, including racial capitalism and the prison-industrial complex, whilst refusing to give up on the collective project of struggling for alternatives. We learn what freedom means by fighting for it. Davis in many of her works provides strong critiques of the reformist impulse – the attempt to improve institutions that are themselves violent. As Davis and her co-authors describe in *Abolition. Feminism. Now.*: 'As new formulations surface, others fade; networks and groups proudly identify as feminist, queer, crip, Black, and/or abolitionist. Rattled by their demands and sometimes simply their formation, dominant institutions struggle to contain and manage these movements.' I rather imagine a killjoy movement as what it takes to become unmanageable.

Reni Eddo-Lodge, *Why I'm No Longer Talking to White People about Race* (London: Bloomsbury, 2017)

This book has now sold over a million copies – a fact that brings me such killjoy joy! And what a killjoy title! The irony is that Eddo-Lodge has ended up talking about race to white people in talking about not talking about it. This is a killjoy irony, one of which Eddo-Lodge is well aware, teaching us that to challenge how much space a problem takes up requires giving that problem more space. That is what it takes to do the work of trying to change the conversation on race. Eddo-Lodge offers bundles of insight into histories of race relations in the UK and how those histories shape conversations that do and do not happen about race. As she puts it, 'Freedom of speech does not mean the right to say what you want without rebuttal, and racist speech and ideas need to be challenged in the public sphere. White fear tries to stop this conversation from happening.'

Mona Eltahawy, *Seven Necessary Sins for Women and Girls* (Dublin: Tramp Press, 2021)

I am such an admirer of Mona Eltahawy's rude and uncivil feminist stance – she gives us so much feminist killjoy inspiration! In this book Eltahawy shows how what is considered a vice might be what girls and women need to refuse to submit to patriarchy authority. Here is just one quote from the book:

> We must teach girls that their anger is a valuable weapon in defying, disobeying, and disrupting patriarchy, which pummels and kills the anger out of girls. It socialises them to acquiesce and be compliant, because obedient girls grow up to be the foot-soldiers of the patriarchy. They grow up to internalise its rules, which are used to police other women who disobey. Well-behaved, quiet, acquiescent, and calm: no more.

Yes to no more!

Marilyn Frye, *The Politics of Reality: Essays in Feminist Theory* (Trumansburg: The Crossing Press, 1993)

I have drawn on this book over many years in my reflections on the politics of anger and in my early discussions of the feminist killjoy. One of the best analyses of sexism as a philosophical as well as political problem. Frye demonstrates how power and oppression shape us from the outside in (one of the few writers to consider the 'press' in 'oppression'). She teaches us how some of us become 'difficult' because we do not agree to or with something. As she puts it, 'Anything but the sunniest countenance exposes us to being perceived as mean, bitter, angry or dangerous.' Frye evokes the feminist killjoy without using her name!

Roxane Gay, *The Bad Feminist* (London: Corsair, 2014)

I am a mega-fan of Roxane Gay not only for her written work, fiction and non-fiction, but also for her public role in creating space for minority and marginal artists and writers, and her lively and fierce contributions to feminism through her social media presence. I think of the feminist killjoy and the bad feminist as close kin! In this book Gay shows how being a feminist is not always about having a clear position. It can be painful and difficult. From this ambivalence, she offers sharp and astute readings of popular culture. I love how Gay ends this text by making explicit her *commitments*: 'I am committed to fighting fiercely for equality as I am committed to disrupting the notion that there is an essential feminism.'

Alexis Pauline Gumbs, *Undrowned: Black Feminist Lessons from Marine Mammals* (Chico, CA: AKA Press, 2020)

That a book which teaches us how to breathe by learning from marine mammals gives us so much killjoy inspiration is telling us something very precious! As Gumbs describes, 'And since I can't help but notice how marine animals are queer, fierce, protective of each other, complex, shaped by conflict and struggling to survive the extractive and militarized context our species has imposed on the ocean, this world is accountable to the movements that are boldly seeking to transform the meaning of life on the planet right now.' An extraordinary and visionary text that shows how dominant systems work to contain and to hold and how a project of survival is about creating room and pockets of air.

Ruby Hamad, *White Tears, Brown Scars: How White Feminism Betrays Women of Color* (New York: Orion, 2020)
Hamad's critique of how white women use tears and expression of hurt is such a powerful testimony of the difficulty many Black and brown women experience in feminist spaces as well as the wider world. When we try and talk about racism, and white women become upset, the attention shifts from our critiques to its effects on them. It is such a recognizable problem and such a relief to read a rigorous unpacking of it. Hamad ends her book with a memorable invitation: 'White women can dry their tears and join us, or they can continue on the path of the damsel, a path that leads not toward the light of liberation, but only into the dead end of the colonial past.'

Saidiya Hartman, *Wayward Lives, Beautiful Experiments: Intimate Histories of Social Upheaval* (London: Serpent's Tail, 2009)
Hartman's work is a model of a method for searching for signs of life in the margins, in the blank spaces, the doorways, and finding in them so much activity, beauty and potential. In her work she has shown how we need new methods to bring out the violence and brutality of slavery and

how we need to keep accounting for what she has called its 'after-lives'. In this book Hartman shows how Black women historically experimented to create room for themselves and each other: I appreciate her attention to *waywardness*. I rather imagine Hartman as modelling for us what a *killjoy historiography* might involve: how we have to look beyond 'the sociological picture' to what might be assumed to be blank spaces, and the speculative work we need to do to find traces in places of killjoys (note: those traces might involve trauma, be opaque and they might also be lively and joyful).

bell hooks, *Feminist Theory: From Margin to Center* (London: Pluto Press, 2000) and *Talking Back: Thinking Feminism, Thinking Black* (Boston: South End Press, 1989) This handbook is dedicated to bell hooks (along with my friend Nila and my Auntie, Gulzar) and I could list all of her work as my killjoy inspiration, but that would be a very long list! hooks wrote. How she wrote! From hooks, I have learnt that we need to name the system we oppose: white supremacist capitalist patriarchy. *We have to name it to nail it.* She also taught me to think about how to resist that system by naming or writing ourselves into existence. And she taught me to teach. From hooks, I have been inspired to consider how the feminist killjoy has been my teacher. We learn from the reactions that other people have to the work we do about why we need to do it. hooks also taught me that to be part of a struggle for an alternative can be an expression of love.

Audre Lorde, *Sister Outsider: Essays and Speeches* **(Tru-mansburg: The Crossing Press, 1984) and** *A Burst of Light: Essays* **(Ithaca: Firebrand Books, 1988)**

The first book I wrote that tried to give the feminist kill-joy a voice was dedicated to Audre Lorde 'for teaching me so much about everything'. In truth, everything I do is indebted to Audre Lorde for teaching me just that. In *Sister Outsider*, Audre Lorde taught me to turn towards what is painful, to learn from it, to listen to anger, to have our vision sharpened by it. She taught me that feminism is about our commitment to enact our principles, to give form to feeling. She helped me to learn to stop and let the full weight of history come down to make better sense of it. In *A Burst of Light,* a book written as Lorde was going through treatment for cancer, she taught me to listen to bodies, and that taking care of each other is a necessary part of building better futures for all.

Aileen Moreton-Robinson, *Talkin' Up to the White Woman: Indigenous Women and Feminism* **(Brisbane: University of Queensland Press, 2020) and** *The White Possessive: Property, Power and Indigenous Sovereignty* **(Minneapolis: University of Minnesota Press, 2015)**

I heard Aileen Moreton-Robinson speak in 1999 at the university of Adelaide. It was like hearing a series of epiphanies! It was such a relief to hear an Indigenous feminist speak *in* as well as speak back *to* the institutions of whiteness. Moreton-Robinson's critique of whiteness in Australian feminism is full of insight into how power works. From her more recent book, *The White Possessive*, I learnt also how whiteness can be about property in multiple senses; how whiteness can be about the ownership of land, of people; how the nation can become a white possession, and feminism, too. Moreton-Robinson's account of becoming the 'angry Black woman' is so brilliant – she really captures how pointing out racism and colonialism in feminism is to be judged as destroying something precious. All feminists in Australia and beyond need to make Indigenous sovereignty a first principle, which means for those of us who are settlers (and to be a settler of colour is still to be a settler) to hear what her work is teaching us is to change how we relate to history and to land.

Mikki Kendall, *Hood Feminism: Notes from the Women White Feminism Forgot* (London: Bloomsbury, 2020)
There have been many recent critiques of white feminism, but this is one of my favourites. I love how Kendall shares her journey with us in a way that is careful and nuanced, showing us how she learnt; things she got quickly and those it took her time to get. I appreciated the attention to economic conditions – to poverty - and the intersection of class and race. I also thought her book included one of the most astute descriptions of the political function of anger:

> Demands that the oppressed be calm and polite and that forgiveness come before all else are fundamentally dehumanising. If your child is killed by the police, if the water in your community is poisoned, if a mockery is made of your grief, how do

you feel? Do you want to be calm and quiet? Do you want to for-
give in order to make everyone else feel comfortable? Or do you
want to scream, to yell, to demand justice for the wrongs done?

Some questions are razor sharp, cutting through the noise.

Lola Olufemi, *Feminism, Interrupted: Disrupting Power* (London: Pluto Press, 2020)

This book is a brilliant call to feminist arms. I love how Olufemi opens this text with a discussion of how she was politicized and with her recognition that to share our stories of becoming activists is to reach out to others with an open hand. Olufemi asks us to consider what we need to do for feminism to live up to its radical potential, how we need to recover past histories especially of Black feminist struggle (that we might not know about because of how radical histories are withheld) and to look forward to new possibilities opened up by imagining what does not yet exist. Olufemi calls for a feminism that is expansive, that builds from relations of care and that recognizes that feminist work is justice work. She writes: 'Feminism seeks to give us back the ability to care and relate to one another in ways we have yet to imagine.'

Claudia Rankine, *Citizen: An American Lyric* (Minneapolis: Greywood Press, 2014) and *Just Us: An American Conversation* (London: Allen Lane, 2020)

Rankine is one of the writers who has really captured how whiteness can be experienced viscerally by Black people and people of colour in everyday encounters, in what is said, how you are seen or not seen. In *Citizen* she writes: 'Hold up, did you just say, did you just see, did you just do that?' And then, 'the voice in your head silently tells you to take your foot off your throat because just getting along shouldn't be an ambition.' Killjoy moments can be the gap between what we hear and what we say not so much to ourselves as to others. In *Just Us*, Rankine reflects on a conversation she had on a flight with a white man who talked about diversity in his company and then said, 'I don't see color.' Rankine describes, 'The phrase "I don't see color" pulled an emergency brake in my brain. Why would you be bringing up diversity if you don't see color.' That metaphor of pulling an emergency brake in our brain is a good way of capturing the internal drama of being a killjoy.

Prisca Dorcas Mojica Rodriguez, *For Brown Girls with Sharp Edges and Tender Hearts: A Love Letter to Women of Color* (New York: Seal Press, 2021)
I am a little in love with the subtitle of this book! I also wonder if this handbook is its own kind of love letter to Black, brown and Indigenous feminist killjoys. Rodriguez opens her love letter with a sharp critique of gate-keeping in the academic world, and then generously spills her knowledge to us, her brown feminist readers. She writes about how to enact decolonial commitments: 'Decoloniality is a form of resisting, and decoloniality is lived and experienced daily. Decoloniality requires that we fight, and I have a reservoir of fight left in me. But it also requires us to rest and be gentle with ourselves.' This is a fierce and loving call for a brown feminism.

285

Chelsea Watego, *Another Day in the Colony* (Brisbane, University of Queensland, 2021)

There is so much I admire in this book particularly the clarity of its address to the Black community. Watego tells her story and stands her ground. I deeply admire how she renders her story-telling an act of resistance. As she writes 'This is a book of stories, stories that are mine. I tell these not to center myself or to universalise my experience. I tell this story of the colony through my experience of it, as a means of adhering to an ethics of practice grounded in Indigenous terms of reference in which knowledge is embodied and relational.' This is a deeply impactful book about surviving the colony, and the structure of white supremacy that Watego encounters every day in another way. There is so much truth in this book.

Rafia Zakaria, *Against White Feminism* (London: Hamish Hamilton, 2021)

I admire the title of this book– how it makes being against what it is about – as well as the book itself. I was especially persuaded by Zakaria's critique of white feminism as 'relatability', how 'the language of personal preference [is] used to legitimize the narrowness of white empathy'. From Zakaria I learn that to challenge white feminists (and we have to keep challenging them because of what they keep doing) is to offer our own more radical feminism. Zakaria concludes with a powerful critique of how feminism has become a project of liberal inclusion and self-empowerment. She writes, 'No movement that is unable to do justice among its own adherents is likely to accomplish any wider goals towards justice.'

A Final Word

You might have noticed how many of these texts are written by Black feminists, feminists of colour and Indigenous feminists who offer critiques of white liberal feminism or discuss the difficulty of having conversations about whiteness or racism in private or public spaces. It is telling us something about what we are up against that we find so much killjoy inspiration in these critiques. And there will be more critiques of how whiteness and racism function to stop conversations from happening, because what is critiqued still goes on.

Still, we go on. I could have chosen many more books by many more authors. My choices of books are a product of my own intellectual journey as a queer woman of colour. As a feminist killjoy, you will have your own journey and find your own texts. Share your companion texts with your killjoy companions! In sharing resources, we become each other's resources. I wish you killjoy joy in that becoming!

Feminist Killjoy Reading Group: Discussion Questions

One of my survival tips for feminist killjoys is to find other feminist killjoys. I referred to a 'Feminist Killjoy Reading Group' set up by Rajni Shah in Sydney, Australia as an example of how you can do this. We find out so much about ourselves and each other by sharing our experiences of killing joy as well as our readings of feminist texts, old and new. For those of you who are interested in setting up a Feminist Killjoy Reading Group, I offer these questions to guide your discussion of the handbook. As a group, you may also be interested in discussing any (or all!) of the books on my recommended killjoy reading list. Or you might find it helpful to write about your own experiences of being a feminist killjoy and to share your writing with others.

In this handbook, I describe experiences of being a feminist killjoy as a resource. Have you had any such experiences? What have you learned from them?

Why is being a feminist killjoy sometimes experienced as 'a crisis'?

One of my suggestions for living a feminist life is to assemble a feminist killjoy survival kit. What would you put in yours? Try assembling one and seeing what happens!

Why is it important to listen to a killjoy as if, or because, she is another person?

Can you think of examples of films or novels in which the feminist killjoy (or another kind of killjoy) has turned up. What role does the killjoy have in that story?

Why have feminists been critical of the imperative to be happy? Is there such a thing as feminist happiness or queer happiness?

How do some histories get 'polished away' by being told in happy terms? How are happy histories used to create a sense of national belonging?

How does the figure of the feminist killjoy relate to the figure of the angry Black woman, unhappy queer or melancholic migrant?

Why do I suggest that *not* being at home in a world teaches us more about it? Do you agree? Why? Why not?

In the handbook I emphasize the creativity of feminist killjoys (despite or even because of the shattering and difficult nature of killjoy experience). Why? What kind of creative outputs could you imagine that draw from this figure? Feel free to make them as well as imagine them!

How or why might feminist killjoys form a political movement? Relatedly, why do killjoys need more killjoys?

The tagline for my blog www.feministkilljoys.com is 'killing joy as a world-making project'. What do you think I mean by this? Now you have read the handbook, do you understand what I mean any differently?

Write your own **killjoy truths**, **killjoy maxims**, **killjoy commitments** and **killjoy equations**.

If you would like to share any of your answers (or stories or outputs or truths or maxims or commitments or equations!), please feel free to email me at *thefeministkilljoyhandbook@gmail.com* or tag me on twitter @SaraNAhmed.

In killjoy solidarity,
Sara xxx

Notes

1. Introducing the Feminist Killjoy

1 *OED*. https://www.oed.com/

2 Lowther, A. 'The Kill-Joys', *The English Review* (1929), London, p. 607.

3 Lowther. 'The Kill-Joys', p. 608.

4 Lowther. 'The Kill-Joys', p. 612.

5 Bergler, E. 'Psychology of the Killjoy', *Medical Record*, 162 (1949), pp. 11–12; 'The Type: "Mr Stuffed Shirt"', *American Imago*, 17: 4 (1960), pp. 407–12.

6 Bergler. 'The Type', p. 408.

7 Bergler. 'The Type', p. 407.

8 Bergler. 'The Type', p. 409.

9 https://www.chroniclelive.co.uk/news/north-east-news/crackers-1604191.

10 https://www.thesun.co.uk/news/6534923/pc-killjoys-
    including-tesco-and-bradford-council-have-banned-
    offensive-st-george-flags/.

11 Snowdon, C. *Killjoys: A Critique of Paternalism.* London:
    IEA (2017).

12 https://www.dailymail.co.uk/news/article-1257445/
    Gloucester-cheese-rolling-event-Coopers-Hill-cancelled-
    200-years.html.

13 Cole, J. 'Who Cancelled Christmas?', https://www.york
    press.co.uk/news/1073118.who-cancelled-christmas/.

14 https://www.theguardian.com/lifeandstyle/2021/dec/23/
    winterval-man-who-created-christmas-is-cancelled-myth.

15 https://www.dailymail.co.uk/home/article-2058830/
    Clarifications-corrections.html?ito=feeds-newsxml.

16 Johnes, M. *Christmas and the British: A Modern History.*
    London: Bloomsbury (2016), p. 176.

17 https://www.dailymail.co.uk/news/article-10264835/
    No-snogging-mistletoe-says-cabinet-minister-Boriss-
    team-branded-Christmas-killjoys.html.

18 https://www.dailymail.co.uk/news/article-10249975/
    Ministers-warned-using-word-Christmas-jab-drive-
    offend-minorities.html.

19 https://www.rt.com/op-ed/500663-shrunken-heads-
    oxford-museum/. No longer accessible at time of writing.

20 Cady, S. 'Garden Echoes with Eighteen Rah Rah Rahs for Tradition', *The New York Times* (18 February 1972), p. 29.

21 Dewsbury, R. 'You Want to Ban Men from Wolf Whistling? That's a Cute Idea Sweetheart', https://www.dailymail.co.uk/debate/article-2112142/International-Womens-Day-Plans-ban-wolf-whistling-men-saying-darling.html, np.

22 Franklin, S. 'Nostalgic Nationalism: How a Discourse of Sacrificial Reproduction Helped Fuel Brexit Britain', *Cultural Anthropology* , 34: 1 (2019), pp. 41–52.

23 This comment was made by Jacob Rees-Mogg on 20 January 2021. See https://www.standard.co.uk/news/politics/fish-better-rees-mogg-brexit-british-b899228.html.

24 https://www.standard.co.uk/comment/comment/miss-ms-or-mrs-i-don-t-care-what-you-call-me-7496731.html.

25 Bolotin, S. 'Voices from the Post-Feminist Generation', *The New York Times* (17 October 1982).

26 Weldon, F. *What Makes Women Happy.* London: Fourth Estate (2006), p. 52.

27 Berlant, L. 'Desire', in C. R. Stimpson and G. Herdt (eds). *Critical Terms for the Study of Gender.* Chicago: University of Chicago Press (2014), p. 66.

28 See my book, *Complaint!* (Durham: Duke University Press (2020)) for a systematic presentation of the findings from this research. In this study, I collected forty oral testimonials and eighteen written testimonials and spoke informally

to hundreds of academics, administrators and students about their experience of making formal complaints at universities. I return to these stories in *The Complainer's Handbook*, which I am currently writing as a follow-up text to this one. In this handbook, I will focus on what we learn (and how we learn) about institutions when we make formal complaints within them. I will also consider how complaints are made against those who are trying to challenge abuses of power as well as how some complainers acquire the capacity to be heard via their proximity to power (yes, I will be dealing with *Karen*).

29 Rankine, C. *Just Us: An American Conversation*. London: Allen Lane (2002), p. 155.

30 Aidoo, A. A. *Our Sister Killjoy: Or, Reflections from a Black-Eyed Squint.* Harlow: Longman (1977), p. 10.

31 Cusk, R. *Arlington Park*. London: Faber and Faber (2016), pp. 15–17.

32 Daly, M. *Gyn/Ecology: The Metaethics of Radical Feminism*. Beacon Press: Boston (1978), p. 15.

33 Schlosser, E. 'I'm a Liberal Professor and My Liberal Students Terrify Me', https://www.vox.com/2015/6/3/8706323/college-professor-afraid.

34 The term 'incitement to discourse' is from Foucault, M. *A History of Sexuality*. Vol. 1, Part 2, Ch. 1. Translated by R. Hurley. Harmondsworth: Penguin Books (1990).

35 This statement was made by Ricky Gervais at the end of his show, 'Superpower', Netflix (2022). For a good discussion of

comedy and cancellation see Laws, C. and Morgan, L. 'Cancel Culture Isn't Cancelling Comedy, It's Improving It', https://www.glamourmagazine.co.uk/article/cancel-culture-comedy.

36 This is why even using words like *racism* or *transphobia* is treated as censorship, as the effort to curtail free speech. Although most feminists recognize this problem, some feminists have also positioned trans and trans-inclusive feminist activists as censoring them using the exact same tactics often used against feminists. In 2015 a letter was published in the *Guardian* by some feminists that claimed 'no-platforming' was being 'used to prevent the expression of feminist arguments critical of the sex industry and of some demands made by trans activists'. Since then, there have been many such letters. Almost all the examples referred to in this letter were not instances of no-platforming. When trans and trans-inclusive feminists objected to the letter, myself included, our objections were not treated as expressions of free speech, but as the effort to curtail it. For further discussion, see my post: https://feministkilljoys.com/2015/02/15/you-are-oppressing-us/.

37 Levy, A. *Fruit of the Lemon*. London: Headline Book Publishing (1999), pp. 150–51.

38 Levy. *Fruit of the Lemon*, p. 156.

39 Levy. *Fruit of the Lemon*, p. 158.

40 Thobani, S. 'War Frenzy and Nation Building: A Lesson in the Politics of "Truth-Making"', *International Journal of*

Qualitative Studies in Education, 16: 3, pp. 399–414, 2003; hooks, b. *Feminist Theory: From Margin to Center*. London: Pluto Press (2000); Lorde, A. *Sister Outsider: Essays and Speeches*, Trumansburg: The Crossing Press (1984); Moreton-Robinson, A. *Talkin' Up to the White Woman*. Brisbane: University of Queensland Press (2020).

41 Lorde. *Sister Outsider*, p. 131.

42 Lorde, 'An Open Letter to Mary Daly', *Sister Outsider*, pp. 70–71

43 Eddo-Lodge, R. *Why I'm No Longer Talking to White People About Race*. London: Bloomsbury Publishing (2017); Hamad, R. *White Tears, Brown Scars*. New York: Orion (2020); Zakaria, R. *Against White Feminism*. London: Penguin (2022).

44 Moreton-Robinson. *Talkin' Up*, p. ix.

45 Thanks to Hermione Thomson for the term 'killjoy-to-be'.

2. Surviving as a Feminist Killjoy

1 This is from Lorde's poem 'A Litany for Survival', *Black Unicorn*. New York: W. W. Norton (1978), p. 31.

2 Gumbs, A. P. 'The Shape of my Impact', https://thefeministwire.com/2012/10/the-shape-of-my-impact.

3 Lorde, A. *A Burst of Light: Essays*. Ithaca, New York: Firebrand Books (1988), p. 131.

4   Lorde. *A Burst of Light*, p. 121.

5   Kim, J. M. and Schalk, S. 'Reclaiming the Radical Politics of Self-Care: A Crip-Of-Colour Critique', *South Atlantic Quarterly*. 120: 2 (2021).

6   Kafer, A. *Feminist, Queer, Crip*. Bloomington: Indiana University Press (2013), p. 15.

7   Kim and Schalk, 'Reclaiming the Radical Politics of Self-Care', p. 339.

8   Hajjar, C. 'Eye-Rolling, Disrupting and Worldbuilding', https://christinahajjar.com/writing/embodying-the-feminist-killjoy/.

9   Kinouani, G. *Living While Black: The Essential Guide to Overcoming Racial Trauma*. London: Penguin Books (2021), p. 144.

10 Shah's introduction is available online here: https://autumnbling.blogspot.com/2019/07/too-many-notes-on-armouring-smiling.html. Further information about the Feminist Killjoy Reading Group is available here: https://feministkilljoysrg.tumblr.com/.

11 Brah, A. 'Journey to Nairobi', in *Charting the Journey: Writings by Black and Third World Women*, ed. S. Grewal, J. Kay, L. Landor, G. Lewis and P. Parmar. London: Sheba Feminist Press (1988), p. 75.

12 Mirza, H. 'Introduction', in *Black British Feminism*, ed. H. Mirza. London: Routledge (1997), p. 6.

13 Lorde, A. 'Interview: Frontiers', in *Charting the Journey*, p. 130.

14 Lorde. 'Interview: Frontiers', p.127.

15 Hamad. *White Tears, Brown Scars*, p. ix.

16 Brah. 'Journey to Nairobi', p. 85.

17 Ahmed, S. *Strange Encounters: Embodied Others in Post-Coloniality.* London: Routledge (2000).

18 hooks, b. *Feminist Theory: From Margin to Center.* London: Pluto Press (2000), p. 56.

19 Cited in Zackodnik, T. *Press, Platform, Pulpit: Black Feminist Publics in the Era of Reform.* Knoxville: University of Tennessee Press (2011), p. 99.

20 Davis, A. *Women, Race and Class.* New York: Vintage (1981), p. 61.

21 This lecture was published in Wittig, M. *The Straight Mind and Other Essays.* Boston: Beacon Press (1982).

22 Lorde, A. 'The Master's Tools will Never Dismantle the Master's House', in *Sister Outsider*, p. 112

23 Oakley, A. *Sex, Gender and Society.* Isleworth: Maurice Temple Smith (1972), p. 16.

24 Oakley, A. 'A Brief History of Gender', in A. Oakley and J. Mitchell (eds). *Who's Afraid of Feminism?*, London: Hamish Hamilton (1987), p. 30.

25 Delphy, C. 'Rethinking Sex and Gender', *Women's Studies International Forum*, 16: 1 (2010), p. 3.

26 Dworkin, A. *Woman Hating*. New York: E. P. Dutton (1972), pp. 175–6.

27 Lorde, A. 'Learning from the 60s', in *Sister Outsider*, p. 140.

28 Lorde, A. 'The Uses of Anger: Women Responding to Racism', in *Sister Outsider*, p. 125.

29 Watego, C. *Another Day in the Colony*. Brisbane: University of Queensland Press (2021), p. 198.

30 Ralph, N. https://disabilityarts.online/magazine/news/nila_gupta_memorial/.

31 Goldman, E. *Living My Life*, Vol.1. New York: Cosimo Publications (2008), p. 56.

32 https://www.etymonline.com/word/silly#etymonline_v_23518.

33 Ahmed, S. *The Cultural Politics of Emotion*. Edinburgh: Edinburgh University Press (2004), p. 189.

3. The Feminist Killjoy as Cultural Critic

1 Mayne, J. 'The Woman at the Keyhole: Women's Cinema and Feminist Criticism', *New German Critique*, Spring–Summer, 23 (1991), pp. 40–41.

2   Gay, R. *Bad Feminist: Essays.* London: Corsair (2014), p. xi.

3   Cited in Shulman, M. 'How Meryl Streep Battled Dustin Hoffman, Retooled Her Role, and Won Her First Oscar', *Vanity Fair* (2016), np. https://www.vanityfair.com/hollywood/2016/03/meryl-streep-kramer-vs-kramer-oscar.

4   Cited in Shulman, 'How Meryl Streep Battled'.

5   Manne, K. *Down Girl: The Logic of Misogyny.* Oxford: Oxford University Press (2017).

6   Frey, B. S. and Stutzer, A. *Happiness and Economics: How the Economy and Institutions Affect Human Well-Being.* New Jersey: Princeton University Press (2002), p. vii.

7   Aristotle, *Nicomachean Ethics*, ed. William Kaufman. New York: Dover Publications (1998), p. 1. Aristotle is not defining happiness as a feeling (although feeling does play a role in his ethics) but as virtue. The Greek word *eudaemonia* is sometimes translated as *flourishing*. The association of happiness with feeling is a modern one from the eighteenth century onwards. Happiness has become a heavier word given it has acquired both moral and emotional meaning.

8   Aristotle, *Nicomachean Ethics*, p. 8.

9   Wollstonecraft, M. *A Vindication of the Rights of Woman.* New York: W. W. Norton (1975), p. 5.

10 Rousseau, J.-J. *Émile*, trans. Barbara Foxley. London: Everyman (1983), p. 431.

11   Rousseau. *Émile*, pp. 439–40.

12   Rousseau. *Émile*, p. 441.

13   'Parochial Schools Bill', *Commons and Lords Hansard*, vol. 9 (13 June 1807), pp. 788–806, http://hansard.millbanksys tems.com/commons/1807/jun/13/parochial-schools-bill.

14   Whilst there have been a number of recent critiques of happiness, they do not acknowledge or reference this long feminist history. See, for example, W. Davies. *The Happiness Industry*. London: Verso (2015).

15   Beauvoir, de S. *The Second Sex*. New York: Vintage Books, 2nd edn (2011), p. 16.

16   Oakley, A. *Sex, Gender and Society*. London: Routledge, 2nd edn (2016), p. 139.

17   Beauvoir. *Second Sex*, p. 474.

18   Beauvoir. *Second Sex*, pp. 471–2.

19   Beauvoir. *Second Sex*, p. 474.

20   Hochschild, A. *The Managed Heart: Commercialization of Human Feeling*. Berkeley: University of California Press, 2nd edn (2003), pp. 59–60.

21   Garden, N. *Annie on My Mind*. New York: Farrar, Straus & Giroux (1982), p. 191.

22   Schroeder, M. and Shidlo, A. 'Ethical Issues in Sexual Orientation Conversion Therapies: An Empirical Study of

Consumers', in A. Shidlo, M. Schroeder, J. Drescher (eds). *Sexual Conversion Therapy: Ethical, Clinical, and Research Perspectives*. Philadelphia: Haworth Press (2002), pp. 134–5.

23 At the time of writing, the position of the UK government is that they will ban the use of conversion therapy but with exemptions and without banning the use of conversion therapy against trans people.

24 Serano, J. 'Alice Dreger's disingenuous campaign against transgender activism' (2015), http://juliaserano.blogspot.com/2015/04/alice-dreger-and-making-evidence-fit.html

25 Not all arguments for conversion therapy rest on care for happiness. Recently a 'gender critical' feminist claimed that we should try to 'reduce' the number of people who transition, because everyone who transitions is 'damaged' and 'a huge problem' for the sane world, 'whether they are happily transitioned, unhappily transitioned or de-transitioned'. This moral indifference to the happiness of trans people is more than just cruel. It teaches us the violence of the assumption that sex is destiny – the speaker presented trans people as a problem because they are 'disassociated' from 'the truth of sex'. One way to eliminate a group of people is by making it hard to preserve their identity or to exist on their own terms.

26 The story was based on the real-life experiences of Jamie Campbell, in County Durham. Jamie reflects on how his story became a West End musical here: https://www.bbc.co.uk/bbcthree/article/e3ebeab8-a351-4289-8b44-7be088b365d4.

27 Lorde, A. *The Cancer Journals.* Aunt Lute Books: San Francisco (1997), p.76.

28 Lorde, A. *Zami: A New Spelling of My Name.* London: Sheba Feminist Publishers (1984), pp. 17–18.

29 McClintock, A. *Imperial Leather: Race, Gender and Sexuality in the Colonial Context.* London: Routledge (1995), p. 75.

30 Rankine. *Just Us*, p. 151.

31 Lewis, G. 'Birthing Racial Difference: Conversations with My Mother and Others', *Studies in the Maternal*, 1: 1, https://doi.org/10.16995/sim.112, p. 13.

32 Morrison, T. *The Bluest Eye.* London: Picador (1979). pp. 13–14.

33 Aidoo. *Our Sister Killjoy*, p. 12.

34 Aidoo. *Our Sister Killjoy*, p. 12.

35 Fanon, F. *Black Skin, White Masks.* Pluto Press: London [1952] (1986), p. 84.

36 Aidoo. *Our Sister Killjoy*, p. 12.

37 Aidoo. *Our Sister Killjoy*, p. 129.

38 Friedan, B. *The Feminine Mystique.* Harmondsworth: Penguin (1965).

39 Naipaul, V. S. 'Our Universal Civilization', *The New York Times*; http://www.nytimes.com/books/98/06/07/specials/naipaul-universal.html (5 November 1990).

40 Commission on Race and Ethnic Disparities Report, https://assets.publishing.service.gov.uk/government/ uploads/system/uploads/attachment_data/file/974507/ 20210331_-_CRED_Report_-_FINAL_-_Web_Accessible. pdf (2021).

41 McClintock. *Imperial Leather*, p. 137.

42 Mill, J. 'Bruce's Report on the East India Negotiation. *The Monthly Review* (1813), p. 30. A number of utilitarian philosophers, including James Mill, John Stuart Mill and Thomas Babington Macaulay, had administrative roles in empire (specifically for the East India Company). We still have more to learn from this connection between moral philosophy and colonial administration. For further discussion, see *Utilitarianism and Empire*, ed. B. Schultz and Varouxakis, G. Maryland: Lexington Books (2005), and my book, *What's the Use? On the Uses of Use.* Durham: Duke University Press (2019).

43 Home Office, *Life in the United Kingdom: A Journey to Citizenship.* Stationary Office Books (TSO): Norwich (2005), p. 32.

44 https://www.sbs.com.au/nitv/article/celeste-liddle-changing-the-date-wont-fix-australia-day/ioxhtoc2i.

45 Petre, J. 'They Kant be Serious!', *Mail on Sunday*, https://www.dailymail.co.uk/news/article-4098332/ They-Kant-PC-students-demand-white-philosophers-including-Plato-Descartes-dropped-university-syllabus. html.

46 The quote is by Jim Rickards, as cited in this newspaper article by Harriet Alexander: https://www.dailymail.co.uk/news/article-9263735/Woke-teachers-cut-Shakespeare-work-white-supremacy-colonisation.html.

47 Skinner, J. *Anglo-American Cultural Studies*, Germany: Utb Gmbh (2016), p. 351.

48 Definition is from https://www.etymonline.com/word/vandal#etymonline_v_4628.

49 Bacon, G. 'What is Wokeism and How Can It be Defeated', *Common Sense Thinking for a Post-Liberal Age* (2021), p. 22.

50 Rishi Sunak made this statement during his campaign to be leader of the Conservative party on 11 August 2022.

4. The Feminist Killjoy as Philosopher

1 Crenshaw, K. 'Demarginalizing the Intersection of Race and Sex: A Black Feminist Politics of Antidiscrimination Doctrine, Feminist Theory and Anti-Racist Politics', *University of Chicago Legal Forum*, 139–67 (1989), p. 139.

2 Davis, A. *Freedom is a Constant Struggle*. Chicago: Haymarket Books (2016), p. 19.

3 Russell, B. *The Problems of Philosophy*. Oxford: Oxford University Press (2001), p. 1.

4 Russell, *The Problems*, p. 6.

5   Banfield, A. *The Phantom Table: Woolf, Fry, Russell, and the Epistemology of Modernism.* New York: Cambridge University Press (2000), p. 66.

6   Morrison, T. *Playing in the Dark: Whiteness and the Literary Imagination.* London: Picador (1992), p. 4.

7   Morrison. *Playing in the Dark*, p. 17.

8   Butler, J. 'Performative Acts and Gendered Constitution: An Essay in Phenomenology and Feminist Theory', *Theatre Journal*, 40: 4 (1988), p. 522.

9   Aidoo. *Our Sister Killjoy*, pp. 12–13.

10   Douglas, M. *Purity and Danger: An Analysis of the Concepts of Pollution and Taboo.* London: Routledge [1966] (1994), p. 35.

11   Mirza, H. '"One in a Million": A Journey of a Post-Colonial Woman of Colour in the White Academy', in D. Gabriel and S. A. Tate (eds). *Inside the Ivory Tower: Narratives of Women of Colour Surviving and Thriving in British Academia.* London: UCL Press (2017), p. 43.

12   Bettcher, T. M. 'When Tables Speak: On the Existence of Trans Philosophy', https://dailynous.com/2018/05/30/tables-speak-existence-trans-philosophy-guest-talia-mae-bettcher/.

13   Ahmed, S. *Queer Phenomenology: Orientations, Objects, Others.* Durham: Duke University (2006), p. 22.

14   Berlant, L. 'Can't Take a Joke', interview with C. Markbreiter, *The New Inquiry* (2019), https://thenewinquiry.com/cant-take-a-joke/

15 Young, I. M. 'Throwing Like a Girl: A Phenomenology of Feminine Comportment, Motility and Spatiality', *Human Studies* (1980), pp. 144–5.

16 Bartky, S. *Femininity and Domination: Studies in the Phenomenology of Oppression.* London: Routledge (1990), pp. 11–12.

17 Ahmed, S. 'Interview with Judith Butler', *Sexualities*, 9: 4 (2016), pp. 486–7.

18 Titchkosky, T. *The Question of Access: Disability, Space, Meaning.* Toronto: University of Toronto Press (2011), p. 61.

19 Hamraie, A. *Building Access: Universal Design and the Politics of Disability.* Minneapolis: University of Minnesota Press (2017), p. 19.

20 Garland-Thomson, R. 'The Story of My Work: How I Became Disabled', *Disability Studies Quarterly* 34: 2 (2014), http://dx.doi.org/10.18061/dsq.v34i2.4254.

21 Garland-Thomson, R. 'Misfits: A Feminist Materialist Disability Concept', *Hypatia: A Journal of Feminist Philosophy* 26: 3 (2011), pp. 592–3.

22 Frye, M. *The Politics of Reality: Essays in Feminist Theory.* Freedom, California: The Crossing Press (1993), p. 2.

23 Ahmed. *What's the Use?*, p. 84. The example of the building without a design is from Darwin, C. *The Variations of Animals and Plants.* London: John Murray (1868), pp. 248–9.

5. The Feminist Killjoy as Poet

1 Definition is from Online Etymology Dictionary, https://www.etymonline.com/word/express#etymonline_v_14105.

2 Rankine. *Just Us*, p. 110.

3 Rankine. *Just Us*, p. 117.

4 Morrison. *The Bluest Eye*, p. 5.

5 Interview with Ama Ata Aidoo, http://panafricannews.blogspot.com/2012/11/know-your-author-ama-ata-aidoo.html.

6 Aidoo. *Our Sister Killjoy*, p. 112.

7 Aidoo. *Our Sister Killjoy*, p. 112.

8 Walker, A. *In Search of Our Mothers' Gardens*. San Diego: Harcourt Brace (1983), p. xi.

9 hooks, b. *Talking Back: Thinking Feminism, Thinking Black*. Boston: South End Press (1989), p. 6.

10 Anzaldúa, G. *Borderlands / La Frontera: The New Mestiza*. San Francisco: Aunt Lute Books (1999), p. 88.

11 Anzaldúa. *Borderlands*, p. 75.

12 Anzaldúa. *Borderlands*, p. 76.

13 Peña, L. G. *Community as Rebellion: A Syllabus for Surviving Academia as a Woman of Color*. Chicago: Haymarket Books (2022), p. xi.

14 Frye. M. *Willful Virgin: Essays in Feminism, 1976–1972*. Freedom, California: Crossing Press (1982). p. 9.

15 Moraga, C. 'Catching Fire': Preface to the 4th edn. *This Bridge Called My Back: Writings by Radical Women of Color*. New York: Suny Press (2015), pp. xxii.

16 Cliff, M. *If I Could Write This in Fire*. Minneapolis: University of Minnesota Press (2008), p. x.

17 Lorde, *A Burst of Light*, pp. 75–6.

18 Moraga, C. 'The Welder', in *This Bridge Called My Back*, p. 219.

19 Quote is from this archive site: https://archive.mith.umd.edu/womensstudies/ReferenceRoom/Publications/about-sheba-press.html

20 O'Sullivan, S. (ed.). *Turning the Table: Recipes and Reflections from Women*. London: Sheba Feminist Press (1987).

21 O'Sullivan, S. 'The Cookbook with a Difference and How to Use It', *Turning the Table*, p. 1.

22 Smith, B. 'A Press of Our Own: Kitchen Table Women of Colour Press'. *Frontiers: A Journal of Women Studies* 10: 3 (1989), p. 11.

23 Smith. 'A Press of Our Own', p. 12.

24 Young, I. M. *On Female Body Experience*, Oxford: Oxford University Press (2005), p. 159.

25 Rich, A. *Of Woman Born*. London: Virago (1991), p. 23.

26 Lorde, A. 'Age, Race, Class and Sex: Women Redefining Difference', in *Sister Outsider*, p. 116.

27 Rich, A. 'Notes Toward a Politics of Location', in *Blood, Bread, and Poetry: Selected Prose 1979–1985*. New York: W. W. Norton & Company (1986), p. 213.

28 Rich. 'Notes Toward a Politics of Location', p. 213.

29 Rich, A. *The Fact of a Doorframe: Poems 1950–2001*. New York: Norton, new edn (2002), p. xv.

30 Marx, K. *Capital:* Volume 1. Translated by B. Fowkes. London: Penguin Classics [1867] 1990, p. 163.

31 Rich. *The Fact of a Doorframe*, p. xv.

32 Rich, A. 'The Phenomenology of Anger', in *Driving in the Wreck: 1971–72*. New York: W. W. Norton (1973), p. 29.

33 Audre Lorde says these words in an interview shared in the film *A Litany for Survival* (2005), the documentary about her life by African-American film-makers Ada Gay Griffin and Michelle Parkerson.

34 Lorde, A. 'Poetry is not a Luxury', in *Sister Outsider*, p. 36.

35 Lorde. 'Poetry is not a Luxury', p. 36.

36 Lorde. 'Poetry is not a Luxury', p. 38.

37 Lorde. 'Poetry is not a Luxury', p. 38.

38 Lorde. 'Poetry is not a Luxury', p. 38.

39   Lorde, A. 'Eye to Eye: Black Women, Hatred and Anger', in *Sister Outsider*, p. 152.

40   Lorde, A. 'Interview with Adriene Rich', *Signs*, 6: 4 (1981), p. 734.

41   Lorde, A. 'Power', in *The Black Unicorn*. New York: Norton (1978), pp. 108–9.

42   Lorde. 'Interview with Adrienne Rich', p. 715.

43   Lorde, A. 'A Litany for Survival', in *The Black Unicorn*, p. 31.

44   Hartman, S., *Wayward Lives, Beautiful Experiments: Intimate Histories of Social Upheaval*. London: Serpent's Tail (2009), p. 31.

45   Brand, D. *The Map to the Door of No Return*. Toronto: Vintage Canada (2001), p. 19.

46   Brand. *The Map*, p. 19.

47   Brand. *The Map*, p. 25.

48   Anim-Addo, J. 'Another Doorway: Black Women Writing the Museum Experience', *Journal of Museum Ethnography*, 10 (1998), p. 93.

49   Anim-Addo. 'Another Doorway', p. 94.

50   Anim-Addo. 'Another Doorway', p. 104.

51   Lorde, A. 'The Transformation of Silence into Language and Action', in *Sister Outsider*, p. 41.

52 Manzoor-Khan, S. 'The Muslim Woman's Burden', in L. Olufemi, O. Younge, W. Sebatindira and S. Manzoor-Khan (eds). *A Fly Girl's Guide to University*. Birmingham: Verve (2019), p. 146.

53 Manzoor-Khan. 'The Muslim Woman's Burden', p. 147.

54 Manzoor-Khan. 'The Muslim Woman's Burden', p. 146.

55 Butler, J. *Undoing Gender*. New York: Routledge (2004), p. 237.

56 Stryker, S. 'My Words to Victor Frankenstein above the Village of Chamounix: Performing Transgender Rage', *GLQ* 1: 3 (1994), p. 247.

57 Stryker. 'My Words to Victor Frankenstein', p. 249. In this article, Stryker points out that she is not the first 'to link Frankenstein's monster and the transsexual body'. She describes how Mary Daly had already 'made that connection explicit' in her description of transition as the violation of boundaries and the invasion of female space. Stryker's article could thus be read as another letter to Mary Daly, a companion letter to Audre Lorde's, addressing the problem of transphobia in Daly's feminism. Thanks to Emma Bigé for thoughtful feedback on this issue.

58 Gumbs, A. P. *Spill: Scenes of Black Feminist Fugitivity*. Durham, NC: Duke University Press (2016), p. xi.

59 Gumbs, A. P. *Undrowned: Black Feminist Lessons from Marine Animals*. Chicago: AK Press (2021), p. 109.

60 Butler, J. *Precarious Life: The Powers of Mourning and Violence.* London: Verso (2004), p. 31.

61 Lorde. 'Poetry is not a Luxury', p. 38.

62 You can find information about The Pansy Project here, https://thepansyproject.com/.

63 Kaur, J. *When You Ask Me Where I am Going.* New York: Harper Collins (2020), p. 40.

6. The Feminist Killjoy as Activist

1 http://feministfreedomwarriors.org/.

2 Mohanty, C. T. and Carty, L. 'Introduction'. *Feminist Freedom Warriors: Genealogies, Justice, Politics and Hope.* Chicago: Haymarket Press (2018), p. 3.

3 Gago, V. *Feminist International: How to Change Everything.* London: Verso (2020).

4 hooks, b. *Outlaw Culture: Resisting Representations.* New York: Routledge (1994). hooks makes use of the term 'white supremacist capitalist patriarchy' an impressive eighteen times in this book.

5 Le Guin, U. 'The Ones Who Walk Away from Omelas', in *The Wind's Twelve Quarters.* New York: Perennial (1987), p. 278.

6   Le Guin. 'The Ones Who Walk Away from Omelas', p. 281.

7   Mitchell, A. and McKinney, C. *Inside Killjoy's Kastle: Dykey Ghosts, Feminist Monsters, and Other Lesbian Hauntings.* Vancouver: UBC Press (2019).

8   RADICALESBIANS, 'The Woman Identified Woman', https://library.duke.edu/digitalcollections/wlmpc_wlmms 01011/ (1970), np.

9   Sedgwick, E. K. *Touching Feeling: Affect, Pedagogy, Performativity.* Durham, NC: Duke University Press (1993), p. 4.

10 Schulman, S. *Let the Record Show: A Political History of* ACT UP, 1987–1993. New York: Farrar, Strauss and Giroux (2021), p. 7.

11 Butler, J. *Precarious Life: The Powers of Mourning and Violence.* New York: Verso (2004).

12 Munoz, J. *Disidentification: Queers of Color and the Performance of Politics.* Minneapolis: University of Minnesota Press (1999), p. 74.

13 Malatino, H. *Side Affects: On Being Trans and Feeling Bad.* Minneapolis: University of Minnesota Press (2022), p. 3.

14 Chu, A. L. 'My New Vagina Won't Make Me Happy: And it Shouldn't Have To', https://www.nytimes.com/2018/11/24/opinion/sunday/vaginoplasty-transgender-medicine.html.

15 Liddle, R. *The Times* (2017). https://www.thetimes.co.uk/
    article/are-you-transphobic-no-me-neither-were-just-
    worried-about-our-children-kfp6csn0z.

16 The original legislation can be seen here: https://www.
    legislation.gov.uk/ukpga/1988/9/section/28/enacted.

17 These letters were sent by Conservative MP Nick Fletcher
    in June 2022. https://news.sky.com/story/trans-children-
    going-through-nothing-more-than-a-phase-conservative-
    mp-says-12635863.

18 Butler, J. 'Why is the Idea of "Gender" Provoking Back-
    lash the World Over?', https://www.theguardian.com/
    us-news/commentisfree/2021/oct/23/judith-butler-gender-
    ideology-backlash.

19 Nothias, T. and Kagumire, R. 'Digital Radical Rudeness:
    The Story of Stella Nyanzi', https://www.asc.upenn.edu/
    research/centers/center-on-digital-culture-and-society/
    the-digital-radical/digital-radical-rudeness naked protest.

20 Eltahawy, M. 'Why I Say Fuck', https://www.feministgiant.
    com/p/essay-why-i-say-fuck.

21 Firestone, S. *The Dialectic of Sex: The Case for Feminist Rev-
    olution*. New York. Bantam Books (1970), p. 90.

22 Gago, V. *Feminist International: How to Change Everything*.
    London: Verso (2020), p. 24.

23 Gago. *Feminist International*, p. 25.

24 Quote is from Giribet, A. G. 'Tarana Burke: The Woman behind Me Too', *Amnesty International* (2018).

25 Lorde. 'A Master's Tools', p. 112.

26 Whitley, L., Page, T., Corble, A., Hasbrouck, H. and Sdrolia, C. 'Collective Conclusions', in Ahmed, S. *Complaint!* Durham: Duke University (2021), p. 273.

27 Franklin, S. 'Sexism as a Means of Reproduction', *New Formations* 86 (2015), p. 22.

28 Savali, K. W. 'The Radical Uses of Anger: All White Women Aren't the Enemy, but White Supremacy Always Is', https://www.theroot.com/the-radical-uses-of-anger-all-white-women-are-not-the-1791727529.

29 Davis, A. Y., Dent, G., Meiners, E. and Richie, B. *Abolition. Feminism. Now.* Chicago: Haymarket Books (2021), p. 3.

30 Crenshaw, K. W., Ritchie, A. J., Anspach, R., Gilmer, R. and Harris, L. *Say Her Name: Resisting Police Brutality Against Black Women.* Available at: https://scholarship.law.colum bia.edu/faculty_scholarship/3226.

31 For a song and video entitled, 'They Cut, We Bleed', by Gaptooth (feat. Sisters Uncut), see https://www.youtube.com/watch?v=oykTtUldOLE.

32 For details, see https://www.sistersuncut.org/2017/05/27/press-release-feminists-occupy-holloway-prison-to-demand-more-domestic-violence-services/.

33 Doucette, E. and Marty, H. 'Queer-Feminist Occupa-
   tions'. *eipcp* 6 (2008), http://eipcp.net/transversal/0508/
   doucettehuber/en/print.

34 Veaux, A. de. *Warrior Poet: A Biography of Audre Lorde.*
   W. W. Norton: New York (2006).

Acknowledgements

Even though being a feminist killjoy can sometimes lead us to become estranged from family and friends, it can be how we find our people. Being a feminist killjoy is how I found my people. My appreciation to all those who got in touch with me to share their feminist killjoy stories and especially to readers who kindly gave me permission to quote from their letters. I am also grateful to Joan Anim-Addo, Jasmin Kaur, Suhaiymah Manzoor-Khan, Christina Hajjar, Nim Ralph and Rajni Shah for permission to quote from their wonderful posts and poems. Thanks again to the many people who shared testimonies about their experience of making complaints. Your words, your wisdom and your work have made this handbook possible as they will the next. Thanks as ever to my complaint collective, Leila Whitley, Tiffany Page, Alice Corble, Heidi Hasbrouck and Chryssa Sdrolia, and others I cannot name. I am still learning from our experience of complaining together.

So many doors are open because of who came before. To Ama Ata Aidoo, thanks for the gift that is *Our Sister Killjoy*. It is a joyous killjoy debt that I have to you. My appreciation to Audre Lorde, bell hooks, Angela Davis, Adrienne Rich, Claudia Rankine, Toni Morrison, Lauren Berlant and

Judith Butler for the many lifelines you have thrown to us through your work. Thanks to Gail Lewis, Avtar Brah and Heidi Mirza for opening up so much more space for Black and brown feminist scholars in the UK.

This is my first trade book and it has felt a bit like leaping into another world. Thanks to my incredible agent Nicola Chang, for reaching out, for guidance, and for keeping this project close. Thanks to David Evans for steady hands in the last stages of this project. And to my editors, Maria Bedford and Kyle Gipson, thanks for your clarity and purpose in helping bring this work to the world. With thanks to Claire Peligry for the meticulous care she gave to this text. My appreciation to my killjoy co-travellers on social media for encouragement in taking this path.

To be a feminist killjoy is to live in such good company. To my fierce feminist partner Sarah Franklin: your killjoy spirit makes so much in my life possible. I love the life we have built together. To my beautiful companions Poppy and Bluebell, thank you for you, and for my survival. Thanks to friends and killjoy comrades who I know are always there even if I don't always get to see you, especially Sirma Bilge, Rumana Begum, Jonathan Keane, Campbell X, Ulrika Dahl, Heidi Mirza, Aileen Moreton-Robinson, Fiona Nicoll, Sandra Peel, Fiona Probyn-Rapsey and Elaine Swan. Thanks to Jonathan Keane and Sarah Franklin for helpful feedback on earlier versions of this handbook and for encouraging me to write it and to find my own path. To the many outspoken women in my family including my mother, aunties, sisters, nieces and cousins, I am grateful for learning with you how we can remake families to give each of us more room to be. And to my wider feminist and queer communities: being part of a shared struggle means everything.

ALLEN LANE
an imprint of
PENGUIN BOOKS

Also Published

Naomi Klein, Doppelganger: A Trip Into the Mirror World

Ludovic Slimak, The Naked Neanderthal

Camilla Nord, The Balanced Brain: The Science of Mental Health

John Gray, The New Leviathans: Thoughts After Liberalism

Michèle Lamont, Seeing Others: How to Redefine Worth in a Divided
World

Henry Farrell and Abraham Newman, Underground Empire: How
America Weaponized the World Economy

Yascha Mounk, The Identity Trap: A Story of Ideas and Power in Our Time

Kehinde Andrews, The Psychosis of Whiteness: Surviving the Insanity of
a Racist World

Ian Johnson, Sparks: China's Underground Historians and Their Battle
for the Future

Diarmuid Hester , Nothing Ever Just Disappears: Seven Hidden Histories

David Sumpter, Four Ways of Thinking: Statistical, Interactive, Chaotic
and Complex

Philip Gold, Breaking Through Depression: New Treatments and Discoveries for Healing

Wolfram Eilenberger, The Visionaries: Arendt, Beauvoir, Rand, Weil and the Salvation of Philosophy

Giorgio Parisi, In a Flight of Starlings: The Wonder of Complex Systems

Klaus-Michael Bogdal, Europe and the Roma: A History of Fascination and Fear

Robin Lane Fox, Homer and His Iliad

Jessica Rawson, Life and Afterlife in Ancient China

Julian Jackson, France on Trial: The Case of Marshal Pétain

Wesley Lowery, American Whitelash: The Resurgence of Racial Violence in Our Time

Rachel Chrastil, Bismarck's War: The Franco-Prussian War and the Making of Modern Europe

Lucy Jones, Matrescence: On the Metamorphosis of Pregnancy, Childbirth and Motherhood

Peter Turchin, End Times: Elites, Counter-Elites and the Path of Political Disintegration

Paul McCartney, 1964: Eyes of the Storm

Theresa MacPhail, Allergic: How Our Immune System Reacts to a Changing World

John Romer, A History of Ancient Egypt, Volume 3: From the Shepherd Kings to the End of the Theban Monarchy

John Rapley and Peter Heather, Why Empires Fall: Rome, America and the Future of the West

Scott Shapiro, Fancy Bear Goes Phishing: The Dark History of the Information Age, in Five Extraordinary Hacks

Elizabeth-Jane Burnett, Twelve Words for Moss

Serhii Plokhy, The Russo-Ukranian War

Martin Daunton, The Economic Government of the World: 1933-2023

Martyn Rady, The Middle Kingdoms: A New History of Central Europe

Michio Kaku, Quantum Supremacy: How Quantum Computers will
    Unlock the Mysteries of Science – And Address Humanity's Biggest
    Challenges

Andy Clark, The Experience Machine: How Our Minds Predict and
    Shape Reality

Monica Potts, The Forgotten Girls: An American Story

Christopher Clark, Revolutionary Spring: Fighting for a New World
    1848-1849

Daniel Chandler, Free and Equal: What Would a Fair Society Look Like?

Jonathan Rosen, Best Minds: A Story of Friendship, Madness, and the
    Tragedy of Good Intentions

Nigel Townson, The Penguin History of Modern Spain: 1898 to the
    Present

Katja Hoyer, Beyond the Wall: East Germany, 1949-1990

Quinn Slobodian, Crack-Up Capitalism: Market Radicals and the
    Dream of a World Without Democracy

Clare Carlisle, The Marriage Question: George Eliot's Double Life

Matthew Desmond, Poverty, by America

Sara Ahmed, The Feminist Killjoy Handbook

Bernard Wasserstein, A Small Town in Ukraine: The place we came
    from, the place we went back to

Mariana Mazzucato and Rosie Collington, The Big Con: How the
    Consultancy Industry Weakens our Businesses, Infantilizes our
    Governments and Warps our Economies

Carlo Rovelli, Anaximander: And the Nature of Science

Bernie Sanders, It's OK To Be Angry About Capitalism

Martin Wolf, The Crisis of Democractic Capitalism

David Graeber, Pirate Enlightenment, or the Real Libertalia

Leonard Susskind and Andre Cabannes, General Relativity: The
    Theoretical Minimum

Dacher Keltner, Awe: The Transformative Power of Everyday Wonder

William D. Cohan, Power Failure: The Rise and Fall of General Electric

John Barton, The Word: On the Translation of the Bible

Ryan Gingeras, The Last Days of the Ottoman Empire

Greta Thunberg, The Climate Book

Peter Heather, Christendom: The Triumph of a Religion

Christopher de Hamel, The Posthumous Papers of the Manuscripts Club

Ha-Joon Chang, Edible Economics: A Hungry Economist Explains the
    World

Anand Giridharadas, The Persuaders: Winning Hearts and Minds in a
    Divided Age

Nicola Rollock, The Racial Code: Tales of Resistance and Survival

Peter H. Wilson, Iron and Blood: A Military History of German-speaking
    Peoples since 1500

Ian Kershaw, Personality and Power: Builders and Destroyers of Modern
    Europe

Alison Bashford, An Intimate History of Evolution: The Story of the
    Huxley Family

Lawrence Freedman, Command: The Politics of Military Operations from
    Korea to Ukraine